Weeds of the
United States
and Their Control

WEEDS OF THE UNITED STATES AND THEIR CONTROL

Harri J. Lorenzi

Copersucar Technology Center
Piracicaba
São Paulo, Brazil

Larry S. Jeffery

Department of Agronomy and Horticulture
Brigham Young University
Provo, Utah

An **avi** Book
Published by Van Nostrand Reinhold Company
New York

On the cover: Flower of *Carduus nutans* L. (Musk thistle)

An AVI Book
(AVI is an imprint of Van Nostrand Reinhold Company Inc.)
Copyright © 1987 by Van Nostrand Reinhold Company Inc.

Library of Congress Catalog Card Number 87-2062

ISBN 0-442-25884-4

Printed in the United States of America

Van Nostrand Reinhold Company Inc.
115 Fifth Avenue
New York, New York 10003

Van Nostrand Reinhold Company Limited
Molly Millars Lane
Wokingham, Berkshire RG11 2PY, England

Van Nostrand Reinhold
480 La Trobe Street
Melbourne, Victoria 3000, Australia

Macmillan of Canada
Division of Canada Publishing Corporation
164 Commander Boulevard
Agincourt, Ontario M1S 3C7, Canada

16   15   14   13   12   11   10   9   8   7   6   5   4   3   2   1

Library of Congress Cataloging-in-Publication Data

Lorenzi, Harri, 1949–
    Weeds of the United States and their control.

    "An AVI book."
    Bibliography: p.
    Includes indexes.
    1. Weeds—United States—Identification.   2. Weeds—
Control—United States.   3. Herbicides.   I. Jeffery, Larry S.
II. Title.
SB612.A2L67   1987   632'.58'0973   87-2062
ISBN 0-442-25884-4

CONTENTS

1
INTRODUCTION

A weed is an unwanted plant. In general, weeds interfere with man's use of land and compete with his crops for water, nutrients, light, carbon dioxide, and space. Weeds reduce the yield and quality of crop and forage species. They restrict movement of water, reduce the efficiency of irrigation systems, cause navigation problems, reduce fish availability, and contribute to poor quality water unsuited for culinary and industrial uses. They obstruct the vision of motorists and become fire hazards around buildings. Weeds spread pollens that cause allergies, resulting in misery and loss of work time and efficiency.

In some cases a plant is a weed just because it does not have proper aesthetic value in the eyes of the beholder. Many plants are unsightly when they occur along roadsides and rights-of-way or in lawns and landscape plantings. Some plants are also considered weeds because they are poisonous to man or livestock. Some weeds secrete toxic substances (allelopathic effects) into the soil that inhibit the growth of other plants, especially crop plants. Weeds also have indirect effects, such as harboring insects, which can attack crops, animals, or man; providing shelter to harmful rodents; or acting as reservoirs of inoculum for plant diseases.

Most weeds have some redeeming attributes in that they can reduce soil erosion on unprotected land, add organic matter to the soil, provide food and cover for wildlife, yield useful drugs or delicacies, serve as forages for farm animals, and beautify the landscape.

Agricultural losses due to weeds are much larger than generally recognized. In the United States and other developed temperate areas where efficient weed control methods are being used, losses due to weeds range from 10 to 15% of the total value of agricultural and forest products. Losses due to weeds exceed the losses caused by any other class of agricultural pest. While losses due to insects or diseases may be more dramatic because of their occasional severity, losses due to weeds are fairly constant, year after year. A gardener, home owner, farmer, or rancher need not question the fact that he will have weeds every year.

Weeds are enemies to man. Before an enemy can be controlled and destroyed, it must be identified. The objectives of this text are to provide the homeowner, the farmer, the agricultural consultant, and anyone else interested in agriculture with an easy method of weed identification and to provide some possible methods of control.

Weed Identification

A number of weed identification texts are available that provide drawings, sketches, and technical descriptions. Notwithstanding, it is difficult for many who desire to identify a weed to correlate the descriptions with the drawings.

For many people a well-defined photograph provides a sense of security in identification. The relative size, location, position, angle, and color of flowers, leaves, and other plant parts are more exact. The photographic plates of this text have been prepared to provide even the lay person, who has no formal training in plant identification, with a means to identify a weed.

Photographic plates in this book were prepared from fresh samples collected in most cases in the eastern United States, using a portable copy stand, black felt as a background, and a 35 mm Cannon F-1 camera with a 50 mm macro lens. Kodak Kodachrome 64 ASA film was used.

Weed identification and descriptions were obtained from plant identification texts listed in the Bibliography. The identification of each plant was verified by comparison with material on file in the herbarium located in the Department of Botany at the University of Tennessee. Because of size of the distribution maps, it is not intended that exact locations be given but only a general indication as to where a specific weed may be identified.

Each weed has one scientific or Latin name. Each may also have a number of common names depending on where it was collected and the person who identified it. The Weed Science Society of America has prepared a list of standardized common names. These names have been used throughout this book.

Weed Control Methods

Once a weed is properly identified, possible methods of control can be suggested. The weed control methods presented in this book have been selected from agricultural extension service publications, herbicide labels, technical publications, weed control texts, and personal experience.

Preventive Weed Control

The old saying "an ounce of prevention is worth a pound of cure" is especially applicable to weed control. Initially, many of our most important weeds were introduced unintentionally into their present habitats by man and his activities. As the farmer has moved from one area to another he has been accompanied by his hated weeds as contaminants in his crop seeds and animal feeds. If this accidental introduction could have been prevented, many weed control programs would not be needed. Therefore, a basic rule to any weed control program is to prevent the introduction of new species of weeds into the country, state, farm, or garden and to prevent the reproduction and proliferation of existing weeds. The reproductive portions of weeds (seeds, bulbs, tubers, nutlets, roots, rhizomes, stolons etc.) may be moved from place to place by wind, water, animals, birds, or man. If we thoroughly understand these methods of dispersal, we can devise methods to prevent further introduction and increase of existing propagules.

Many weed seeds are equipped with mechanisms for air travel. They may have tufts of hairs or fibers attached to one end. Some are encased in a papery envelope, while others may be attached to a wing or propeller. It is difficult to prevent the movement of weed seeds once they become airborne; therefore, preventative measures must be initiated at the source of supply. This is done by control measures that prevent seed production in areas adjacent to the noninfested area.

Many weed seeds and vegetative parts are bouyant in water because of corky layers, oily surfaces, or trapped air. Introduction by this method is prevented by land leveling, construction of dikes, and otherwise preventing the movement of water onto the land. In irrigated areas, screens and filters can be installed to catch incoming seeds. However, seed production should be prevented along the water course, thus preventing seed from contaminating the water supply in the first place.

Introduction by animals and birds can be prevented by controlling their movement into a given area. If new animals are brought to the farm, they should be held in an enclosure for at least 48 hours to allow passage of seeds in the intestinal tract. The manure should be collected and allowed to ferment before use. Also, animals should be cleaned to remove all seeds adhering to the skin, fur, or hair. Feeds and feedstuffs should be checked for foreign weeds. Introduction of weeds by birds is difficult to prevent; therefore, periodic inspection of fence rows, wind breaks, weedy areas, etc., for newly established foreign weeds and subsequent control is encouraged.

Tools, machinery, and supplies all are potential transporters of weeds. All equipment, whether it be hand tools, planting equipment, cultivating equipment or harvesting equipment, should be thoroughly cleaned and inspected as it is moved from field to field or even allowed on the farm. Seed for planting should be cleaned and certified to be weed free. Transplants and nursey stock should be free of weed seeds and vegetative parts of perennial weeds. Bedding and mulching material should come from a weed-free source or should be sterilized with heat or gas-type fumigant. Manure and plant composts periodically should be thoroughly mixed, moistened, and fermented to destroy viable seeds. Dirt, gravel, and rock for filling holes, maintaining grounds, roads, etc., should come from a weed-free source. In final analysis, it is the responsibility of the land owner or manager to enforce the preventive methods of weed control.

Mechanical Weed Control

Mechanical weed control is the physical removal of the weed from the soil or the manipulation or stirring of soil to destroy weed growth. A number of weed control methods fall into this category.

Hand Pulling   This is probably the oldest weed-control method. As man started to raise plants for food, he probably learned that they grew better if nonfood-providing plants were not growing closely around them. He would have used his hands to remove them. Hand pulling is still highly selective and should be practiced by the home gardener in flower and shrub beds. This method is highly effective for control of annual and biennial weeds but has little effect on established perennial weeds.

Hand Hoeing or Hand Cultivation   This method of weed control is probably used by more people worldwide than any other method. It is highly effective in controlling annual and biennial weeds but is only effective on perennial weeds if the perennial is never allowed to grow undisturbed for more than about two weeks. The objective is to force constant regrowth without sufficient time to replenish the underground food reserves; thus, starvation occurs. When using a hand hoe the following points should be kept in mind. (1) A sharp hoe cuts easier and cleaner than a dull hoe. (2) To be effective the hoe need only to cut the seedlings or plants off slightly below the soil surface; deep hoeing brings new seeds to the soil surface where new germination will occur. (3) Whenever possible the hoe should be used in long even strokes instead of sharp deep jabs, as this will provide more uniform coverage with less human energy expended.

Deep Plowing   With the invention of the moldboard plow and disk plow, it is possible to completely invert the soil, thereby destroying annual and biennial weeds and inflicting some damage to the root systems of perennial weeds. Deep plowing brings rootstocks of perennial weeds to the surface where they may be destroyed by desiccation or freezing. Chisel plows can be used for breaking the soil, allowing deeper freezing and pulling rootstalks to the surface without inversion of the soil. It leaves much of the old crop residue on the soil surface, which aids in erosion control.

Mechanical Cultivation   This is performed with a variety of implements such as harrows, cultivators, rotary hoes, rod weeders, etc. Cultivation is very effective for the control of small annual and biennial weeds. If the implement is operated properly it will not cause excessive damage to the crop. Cultivators should be set to till no more than the top 1 to 2 inches of the soil surface, so as not to bring new seeds to the soil surface and to minimize root pruning of the crop.

Clipping or Mowing   This method of weed control is effective in reducing the spread and increase of some weed species in pastures, along rights-of-way, and in waste areas. It is most effective if performed before the weeds flower and after each rotation of rotational grazing. Mowing prevents seed production of many weeds. In general, it does not kill weeds but slows their growth and makes them more susceptible to competition. If mowing is coupled with rotational grazing, correct stocking rates, and good fertilizer management, desirable species will have an advantage and many weeds will be controlled. Mowing leaves residues on the soil surface, thus reducing soil erosion, but it does not control perennial weeds.

Burning   Fire is effective for control of young annual weeds and to destroy the aerial portions of dry mature weeds. However, it will only slow the growth of perennial weeds. Special equipment is required before fire can be used to selectively control weeds in standing crops. Only a slight amount of soil on top of weed seeds protects them from fire. Fire will also destroy insects and pests and can be used to clean up unsightly areas, but should be used with great care to prevent expensive losses of fences, buildings, and crops. In addition, it is prohibited in some areas because it is a source of air pollution.

Mulches   A mulch can be defined as any type of covering applied to the soil surface to protect the area covered. In general, mulches are applied to prevent soil erosion or to conserve soil moisture. Mulches, if applied properly, can be very effective weed-control agents. Table 1.1 lists the various materials that can be used for mulching. With the exception of black plastic, mulch materials must be applied in a layer 2 to 5 inches deep for adequate weed control to be achieved. The mulch should be less deep around the stem of the crop so that moisture does not collect and contribute to disease occurrence. If materials such as wood chips, fresh sawdust, or shredded bark are used, extra amounts of nitrogen should be added to prevent nutrient deficiencies in the crop.* Mulches are effective by preventing seed germination and thus aid in the control of annual weeds. They are not very effective, however, in controlling new perennials arising from vegetative propagules.

Cultural Weed Control

Various cultural practices common to farm management can be used effectively for controlling weeds. Practices such as use of weed-free seed and clean equipment fall under the category of preventive weed control, as discussed earlier. Other practices such as the use of cover crops, smother crops, and crop rotation can be worked into farm management programs in such a way as to reduce many weed problems.

Cover Crop　A cover crop generally is planted during a period when land is not being used for a cash crop, to help prevent soil erosion, to prevent the loss of nutrients from the soil, and to improve the tilth and organic matter of the soil. Simple cover of the soil surface will prevent the germination or establishment of many weed species. The cover crop is generally not harvested, but is destroyed before the succeeding crop is planted. In the past, this destruction has been by plowing or disking prior to seed bed preparation. With the advent of contact herbicides and no-tillage farming, however, it is possible to plant the cash crop directly into the herbicide-killed cover crop with minimum soil manipulation. This leaves a mulch on the soil surface, which aids in weed control. Recent research has shown that some plant residues contain substances that are toxic to other plants. These substances, found in some varieties of cover crops as well as other plants, are either secreted or leached into the environment. Some crop varieties contain more of these substances than do others. This biochemical interaction between plants is called allelopathy. The use of specific cover crop varieties to provide allelopathic weed control may become an important tool of the future, but presently a variety that is competitive and provides a good mulch is suggested.

Smother Crop　Smother crops are well-adapted crop species that are highly competitive with the weed species of a given area. Smother crops include barley, rye, alfalfa, sweet clover, sudangrass, and buckwheat. These and others are competitive with weeds for moisture, nutrients, space, and light. They can be used at strategic points during crop rotation to reduce a heavy population of weeds and still provide farm income.

Crop Rotation　This is a system whereby different kinds of crops are grown in recurrent succession on the same land. Crop rotations become part of farm management systems to maintain or increase soil fertility, to control soil erosion, to provide good soil tilth, to control crop insect and disease pests, and to better manage and control weed populations. In many cases, certain weeds will become a problem in a specific crop. For example, wild garlic populations will increase in

*See footnote to Table 1.1.

Table 1.1. Common Mulches That Can Be Used in Home Gardens, Landscaped Areas, and in Some High Value Crops

Type of mulch	Comments
Tree bark	Decomposes slowly, can be worked into landscaping around trees and shrubs, and can be used as walkway material in some areas.
Compost	Mulch from well-decomposed compost spread to a uniform depth will do much to control weeds. Compost that has been inadequately prepared may contain viable weed seeds; therefore, compost should be well mixed and fermented before use. The fermentation process will kill most weed seeds.
Grass clippings[a]	Clippings can be used on a limited scale. They should not be used if a herbicide has been applied recently, but can be added to the compost pit, where herbicide residues will be decomposed. Fresh clippings to be used as a mulch should be stirred periodically.
Grass hay or straw[a]	These materials are dry and coarse and may not give adequate weed control depending on depth. A uniform covering approximately 10 inches deep will control most annual weeds but will not control many of the perennial weeds. Also, new weed seeds may be introduced with these materials.
Leaves[a]	Leaves are inexpensive but often are difficult to use because they are light and fluffy when dry but tend to mat and seal the soil when wet. They provide good control of most annual weeds.
Manure	In most cases, manure is best used as a fertilizer; however, if manure contains large portions of strawlike materials it can be used effectively in the same way as straw or hay. Because it contains many weed seeds, it must be fermented before use.
Sawdust[a]	Sawdust can be either an excellent mulch or a potential hazard. Its limitations must be understood. It is best to use aged, well-rotted sawdust, which has been mixed periodically to encourage aerobic decomposition and to allow pungent smelling organic acids to decompose. Sour smelling sawdust should not be used as a mulch as it may cause crop injury.
Cardboard	This material is generally available in the form of discarded boxes, packaging, etc. It can be cut to fit between rows or placed on the soil surface under coarser mulching materials around shrubs or similar landscape plantings. If used alone wind displacement can be prevented by placing rocks or branches on the surface or anchoring the edges to the soil with nails or spikes. After thorough soaking by rain or irrigation the noncardboard materials may be removed.
Newsprint[a]	A readily available inexpensive source of mulching materials for areas where appearance is not very important. It can be spread as sheets or shredded. It will be necessary to weight

Table 1.1. (*Continued*)

Type of mulch	Comments
	it down with some type of solid objects until after water stabilizes it.
Black plastic	Polyethylene film or black plastic is a very popular mulch material. Clear or white plastic cannot be substituted as it allows light to reach the soil surface. Black plastic can be held in place by burying the edges in a shallow trench. Young transplants can be set by planting through narrow slits made in the plastic. If the area covered with plastic is more than 3 feet wide, small holes should be punched to allow water to enter the soil.

[a] When certain organic materials are used for mulch, the soil microflora initiate natural degradation processes to convert the mulch to soil humus. As this occurs the soil microflora increase and competition with crop plants for soil nutrients such as nitrogen can occur. When grass clippings, hay, straw, leaves, sawdust or newsprint are used for mulch, some additional fertilizer, especially nitrogen, should be used to prevent nutrient deficiencies in the crop.

wheat but can be controlled by mechanical cultivation in soybeans. Cockleburs may become a problem in cotton or soybeans but can be controlled easily by some of the herbicides used in corn. Therefore, crop rotation coupled with available weed control methods for each specific crop in the rotation can do much to reduce weed population on any given area.

Biological Control

The use of natural enemies to control certain weeds is known as biological weed control. In most cases, considerable research must be done before an effective control can be found, because usually the weed to be controlled is not a native species but has been introduced. When it was introduced it was essentially freed of its natural predators. To initiate control, the area of origin must be visited and natural enemies or predators must be found. These natural enemies must be specific in their eating habits so as not to cause injury to economical crops growing in the same area. These biological control agents must be introduced free of their own natural predators and must not have any natural predators in the area in which they will be introduced. This makes it possible for the population of the biological control agent to increase to a point where it can control the weed population in the area. In most cases biological weed control is not practical for the individual homeowner, farmer, or rancher. It is generally undertaken by a federal or state agency, and, once perfected, benefits individuals over a wide area. The biological control agent or predator is not restricted by fences or other artificial boundaries; therefore its population can respond to shifts in the weed population.

After introduction, the predator population should increase sufficiently to bring the weed population under control and cause a decrease in weed population. As the weed population decreases, the predator population will decrease because of lack of food. After the predator population has dropped sufficiently, the weed population will again start to increase, which will cause the predator population to increase. These cycles continue over time, though with each cycle the population numbers will be lower and the magnitude of the cycle will be less. At some point, the weed population and the predator population will stabilize. Eradication is never possible with a biological control agent, but hopefully the population will be stabilized to a tolerable level.

Chemical Weed Control

Chemicals used to control weeds are called herbicides. Selective chemical weed control is a relatively new practice, having been introduced since 1945. The use of herbicides has caused drastic changes in weed control methods. The mechanical cultivator supplemented by hand hoeing has been replaced by chemicals, which may be supplemented by mechanical cultivation. The savings in time and human energy expended to control weeds, man's most universal agricultural enemy have been phenomenal. In many cases, herbicides have freed man from the shackles of the hoe and the drudgery of unending rows of weed-infested crops and have allowed him to produce more and better crops and even to pursue other, more pleasant, aspects of life.

Herbicides are classified according to either chemistry or method of application. The latter classification needs to be explained and defined to give the user of this book an understanding of the terms used herein. The various methods of application and comments about each are presented in Table 1.2.

Weeds and crops differ in their response to herbicides. Some herbicides are quite selective in their action, making it possible to control specific weeds in specific crops, while other herbicides are more general in their activity and control almost all weeds, although the crop is tolerant. Extensive research has been conducted by commercial companies and state and federal agencies to determine which herbicides can be used to control specific weeds in specific crops without adverse effects to the crop. Also, extensive research has been conducted to insure that man's food and fiber contain no harmful herbicide residues. The methods for use of each herbicide have been carefully tested. After all of the testing and data have been collected on efficacy in weed control, methods of application, crop response, and possible side effects to man, animals, and the environment, the commercial companies petition the Environmental Protection Agency (EPA) to obtain permission in the form of a label to manufacture, market, and sell the herbicide. The label presents information on correct use, active ingredient, manufacturer and address, directions for use, warnings and cautions, antidotes if needed, and an EPA number.

In Tables 1.3 to 1.8 we present herbicides labeled for specific uses in specific crops or for specific weed control situations. This information should in no way be construed to indicate that the authors recommend a specific herbicide for a specific situation; the only intent is to provide the user with a quick reference as to which herbicides are available. Each herbicide has at least three names: (1) the commercial name or names whereby it is sold in the retail trade, (2) the common name or generic name whereby it is known in scientific and technical literature, and (3) the chemical name whereby it is identified by the manufacturing and chemical industries. The common or generic names are used throughout this publication. The

Table 1.2.   Methods of Herbicide Application

Method	Comments
Preplant (Incorporated)	The herbicide is applied before the crop is planted and generally incorporated into the top 2 or 3 inches of the soil profile, using a rototiller, disk, field cultivator, or other type of incorporation tool. Because of differences in incorporation efficiency, the disk should be set to penetrate 4 to 5 inches deep, the field cultivator 3 to 4 inches, and the rototiller at the desired 2- to 3-inch depth. Two incorporation trips should be made across the land with either a disk or field cultivator, whereas a single trip is sufficient for the power driven rototiller.
Preplant (Foliar)	A contact or translocated herbicide is applied to control existing weed vegetation before the crop is planted. This method is used for control of perennial weeds where the recommended herbicide would also be toxic to the crop if applied during the cropping season. It is also used to control weeds growing in areas where reduced tillage, conservation tillage, minimum tillage, or no tillage will be practiced.
Preemergence (Surface applied)	The herbicide is applied after the crop is planted and prior to the emergence of the crop. The herbicide is generally root absorbed and will kill weeds either as they germinate or shortly thereafter. The crop is generally tolerant to the herbicide, either due to biological resistance or to physical protection because of planting depth.
Preemergence (Incorporated)	The herbicide is applied after the crop is planted and incorporated to a shallow depth—never over 1 inch—with a spike tooth harrow, rolling cultivator, rotary hoe, or similar device. Sometimes incorporation is needed to protect the herbicide from photodecomposition or to improve weed control.
Emergence	The herbicide is applied as the crop is emerging from the soil. This is also called the "cracking" stage. Since 3 to 5 days generally elapse between planting and emergence of the crop, this delay in herbicide application extends the period of control by several days for the short residual herbicides.
Postemergence (Overtop)	The herbicide is applied as a broadcast treatment after the crop has emerged. The crop is generally tolerant to the herbicide exhibiting few if any signs of injury. Weed susceptibility depends on the species and the stage of weed growth at time of herbicide application.
Postemergence (Directed)	The herbicide is applied after the crop is well-established. The herbicide is generally toxic to the crop, therefore, it must be directed toward the lower portion of the crop underneath the lower leaves. The weeds of necessity must be considerably smaller than the crop, thereby making it possible to cover their leaves with the spray without severely injuring the crop.

Table 1.3. Herbicides Labeled for Use in Agronomic Crops[a]

	Alfalfa	Barley	Beans (dry, kidney, pinto)	Bermudagrass	Birdsfoot trefoil	Clovers	Corn	Cotton	Flax	Lespedeza	Oats	Peas	Peanuts	Rice	Rye	Safflower	Sorghum (Grain)	Soybeans	Sudangrass	Sunflower	Sugarbeets	Sugarcane	Tobacco	Turfgrass	Vetch	Wheat
Acifluorfen			2										3	3				3								
Alachlor			2				4	4				2	2				2			2						
Ametryn							3																			
Atrazine							7										5									
Barban		3							3			3				3		3			3					3
Benefin	1					1							1													
Bensulide					1			2															1	4		
Bentazon							3					3	3	3				3						2		
Bromoxynil		3					3				3				3											3
Chloramben			2										2					2		2						
Chlorpropham			2		3	3						1				1		2								

Chlorsulfuron	1		3				3						3						3									3
Cyanazine			2		1		5	5																	1			
Cycloate				3		1	5	2																	1			
Dalapon	2				3	1	2	2	2	3			3									3		6	3		2	
DCPA	3	2				2	2	2																				
Diallate			1	1	1	1	1					1		1				1						1				
Dicamba		3	3			5	5						3		3			3								3		3
Dichlobenil	3																											
Diclofop		3	3												3													3
Difenzoquat		3									3																	3
Dinoseb	5	3	5	5		2	2	7		5		2	3	2	5	3		3		2								3
Diphenamid							2	3		2	2											2				2		
Diuron	3	2	3		3	5	5	3	1	1		1	5		3	3		5				3						5
DSMA						3																						
EPTC	1	1	1	1	1	4	3	3	1	1		1	1			1								1	1			
Ethalfluralin		4												4				4										
Fluazifop-butyl							3	3						3														

(continued)

11

Table 1.3. (*Continued*)

	Alfalfa	Barley	Beans (dry, kidney, pinto)	Bermudagrass	Birdsfoot trefoil	Clovers	Corn	Cotton	Flax	Lespedeza	Oats	Peas	Peanuts	Rice	Rye	Safflower	Sorghum (Grain)	Soybeans	Sudangrass	Sunflower	Sugarbeets	Sugarcane	Tobacco	Turfgrass	Vetch	Wheat
Fluchloralin								1					1					1				1				
Fluometuron								5																		
Glyphosate	8	8	8	9	8	8	8	8		8	8	8	8	8			8	8						9		8
Isopropalin																							1			
Linuron							5	3									5	5								2
MCPA		3							3		3	3														
Metolachlor			4				4					4														
Metribuzin	2	3										5					2	2			5	5				3
Molinate														4				4			3					
Monuron								5																		
MSMA								3																3		

12

Napropamide																			2				
Naptalam													2										
Oryzalin	4		2							2	2				3								
Paraquat			1							7	7			3	7	1							4	
Pebulate															1									
Pendimethalin	1		2				1	3		2	4	1		3		1								
Prometryn			5	5	5																	5		
Pronamide	5																				3	5		
Propachlor			2				2			2			2											
Propazine										4														
Pyrazon												5												
Sethoxydim	3		3		3		3			3	3	3		3										
Siduron																			5					
Simazine	2		2	9										2	2				9					
Terbacil	3												4											
Terbutryn	3																						3	
Triallate	4						4																4	

(continued)

Table 1.3. (*Continued*)

	Alfalfa	Barley	Beans (dry, kidney, pinto)	Bermudagrass	Birdsfoot trefoil	Clovers	Corn	Cotton	Flax	Lespedeza	Oats	Peas	Peanuts	Rice	Rye	Safflower	Sorghum (Grain)	Soybeans	Sudangrass	Sunflower	Sugarbeets	Sugarcane	Tobacco	Turfgrass	Vetch	Wheat
Trifluralin			1					4				1	1			1					1					1
Vernolate													4					4								
2,4-D		5					5							3	5		3				5			3		5
2,4-DB					3	3							3					3								

[a] 1. Applied preplant; 2. applied preemergence; 3. applied postemergence; 4. preplant and preemergence; 5. preemergence and postemergence; 6. preplant and postemergence; 7. preplant, preemergence, and postemergence; 8. applied preplant or postemergence as a spot treatment; 9. special conditions

Table 1.4. Herbicides Labeled for Use in Vegetable Crops[a]

	Asparagus	Beans (pole, snap)	Beans (lima)	Beets (table)	Carrots	Celery	Broccoli	Brussels sprouts	Cabbage	Cauliflower	Cucumber	Squash	Cantaloupes	Eggplant	English peas	Greens, mustard or turnip	Irish potatoes	Kale	Lentil	Lettuce	Okra	Onion	Pepper	Pumpkin	Southern peas	Spinach	Sweet corn	Sweet potatoes	Tomatoes	Watermelon
Alachlor		4	2												2												2			
Atrazine																											7			
Barban															3	3			3	3										
Benefin																				1										
Bensulide		3	3		2		2	2	2	2	1	1	1							1		1	1	1					1	1
Bentazon						3																			3					
CDAA							2	2	2	2					2		2					2								
Chloramben		2	2		2						2		2		2							2	2	2	2			2	2	2
Chlorpropham		2																											3	
Cycolate				1													✓													
Cyanazine																											5			

(continued)

15

Table 1.4. (Continued)

	Asparagus	Beans (pole, snap)	Beans (lima)	Beets (table)	Carrots	Celery	Broccoli	Brussels sprouts	Cabbage	Cauliflower	Cucumber	Squash	Cantaloupes	Eggplant	English peas	Greens, mustard or turnip	Irish potatoes	Kale	Lentil	Lettuce	Okra	Onion	Pepper	Pumpkin	Southern peas	Spinach	Sweet corn	Sweet potatoes	Tomatoes	Watermelon
Dalapon	4	4													4		5										2			
DCPA		2					2	2	2	2			3	2		2	2	2		3		2	2		2		2	2	3	
Diallate															1		1		1											
Dinoseb		2	2								2		2		4		4					3		2			4			2
Diphenamid																	2					2	2					2		2
EPTC															1		1											1		
Linuron					2	2											2									5	1			

16

																					6	
Metribuzin	2					2										2						
Napropamide																			2		2	
Naptalam					1	1	1	2	2													
Nitrofen										3		3										
Paraquat	3					2	2			3		3		3					3		3	
Pronamide											1											
Prometryn			5																			
Pyrazon		4																				
Simazine	2																					
Trifluralin	1	2			1	1	1	1	1	1		1		1		1					1	
Vernolate															4							
2,4-D	2																					4

Table 1.5. Herbicides Labeled for Use in Fruit and Nut Crops[a]

	Almond	Apple	Apricot	Blackberry	Blueberry	Boysenberry	Cherry	Cranberry	Filbert	Gooseberry	Grapefruit	Grape	Lemon	Loganberry	Macadamia nut	Orange	Peach	Pear	Pecan	Plum	Raspberry	Strawberry	Walnut (English)
Ametryn											X					X							
Atrazine															X								
Bromacil			X								X		X			X							
Dalapon		X						X			X	X				X	X	X		X			
DCPA																						X	
Dichlobenil	X	X	X	X	X		X	X	X		X	X	X			X	X		X	X	X	X	X
Dinoseb	X			X	X	X	X		X	X	X	X	X	X		X	X	X	X	X	X		X
Diphenamid		X														X	X				X	X	
Diuron		X		X	X	X				X	X	X	X	X	X	X	X	X	X		X		X

EPTC	X	X							X		X	X	X			X			X
Fluazifop-butyl	X	X	X	X	X	X	X		X	X	X	X	X	X	X	X	X	X
Glyphosate		X				X												
MSMA	X	X			X		X		X	X	X		X	X		X		X
Napropamide	X	X			X						X		X	X		X	X	
Norflurazon	X	X	X	X	X		X		X	X	X	X	X	X	X	X	X	X
Oryzalin	X	X			X			X			X		X	X		X		X
Oxyfluorfen	X		X		X			X	X				X	X	X	X		X
Paraquat	X	X	X	X	X	X	X	X	X	X	X	X	X	X	X	X	X	X
Sethoxydin	X	X	X	X	X	X	X	X	X	X	X	X	X	X	X	X	X	X
Simazine	X	X	X	X	X		X	X	X	X	X	X	X	X	X	X	X	X
Terbacil			X				X		X		X	X						
Trifluralin	X	X					X	X	X	X	X	X	X		X			X

a Refer to the labels to determine exact uses.

Table 1.6. Herbicides Labeled for Control of Weeds in Turf[a]

Herbicide		When to apply	Weeds controlled	Comments
Common name	Commercial name			
New Seedings				
Glyphosate	Roundup	Preplant Foliar	Annual and perennial grasses and Broadleaf weeds	No active soil residue; plant 7 days after application
Methyl bromide	Brom-O-Gas Meth-O-Gas Celfume	Preplant	Most weed seeds and plant parts; disease organisms, nematodes, and insects	A soil fumigant; highly toxic. Follow label carefully
Siduron	Tupersan	Preemergence	Annual grasses	May injure bermudagrass
2,4-D plus dicamba	Various	Postemergence	Annual and perennial broadleaf weeds	Do not apply near shrubs and desirable ornamental plants
Established Grass				
Benefin	Balan	Preemergence	Annual grasses	Will injure bentgrass and red fescue
Bensulide	Betasan; prefar	Preemergence	Annual grasses	Apply on established turf; do not use on dichondra
DCPA	Dacthal	Preemergence	Annual grasses	Will injure bentgrass, red fescue and newly sprigged bermudagrass and zoysiagrass
Dicamba	Banvel	Postemergence	Annual and perennial, broadleaves	Apply at labeled rate only Do not apply near desirable shrubs or ornamental plants
Diphenamid	Enide	Preemergence	Annual grasses; some broadleaf weeds	Repeat treatments at 6 month intervals
DSMA	Various	Postemergence	Many annual weeds	Will temporarily discolor turf. Cannot be used on some southern grasses. Follow the label
Mecoprop	MCPP-D4, MCPP-K4	Postemergencee	Annual broadleaves	Do not spray near desirable broadleaf plants
Pronamide	Kerb	Pre- or Post-emergence	Annual bluegrass	Use only in bermudagrass turf in Southern United States
Siduron	Tupersan	Preemergence	Annual grasses	May injure bermudagrass
2,4-D[b]	Various	Postemergence	Annual and perennial broadleaf weeds; wild garlic, onion, nutsedge	Do not apply near desirable shrubs and ornamental plants

[a] See specific label for rates and methods of control.
[b] For broader spectrum control of broadleaf weeds, mixtures of 2,4-D plus dicamba may be applied. Follow the label and do not apply near desirable shrubs or ornamental plants.

Table 1.7. Herbicides Recommended for Use in Pastures[a]

Herbicide		Comments
Common name	Commercial name	
Control of Broadleaf Weeds		
Dicamba	Banvel	Apply in spring when weeds are actively growing. Will control many annual and perennial broadleaf species. Nonselective on clover. See label for specific restrictions.
2,4-D	Various	Apply when weeds are actively growing. Will control many annual and perennial broadleaf species. Repeated applications necessary for some species. Will injure clover, but a high portion will recover. Do not graze until 7 days after application. Follow other label restrictions.
Simazine	Princep	Apply only in established bermudagrass pastures to control winter annual broadleaf weeds.
Renovation of Pastures		
Paraquat	Paraquat; Gramoxone	Use to reestablish legumes in pastures. Apply broadcast or in bands before sod seeding of legume. Follow label instructions carefully.

[a] See specific labels for rates and methods of application.

commercial and chemical names of all herbicides mentioned in this publication are listed in Table 1.9. Each herbicide has been labeled for a specific use as set forth by the manufacturer. Labels should be read, understood, and followed explicitly. If specific weed control recommendations are desired, the potential herbicide user should contact the local county agricultural agent or specialist for up-to-date recommendations for the local area.

Responsibilities of the Herbicide User

Herbicides should be used with care and caution. As a group they are not as toxic to man and animals as are most other pesticides, but if not used correctly they can either injure the applicator or destroy his crops or make them unfit for human use. Herbicides must be used with caution by responsible individuals who are willing to accept the results of their successes and mistakes. Herbicides should be used in strict accord with the written label. It is the sole responsibility of the herbicide user and applicator to read and understand the herbicide label and to follow the directions explicitly. If questions exist, the authors recommend that the herbicide user contact the local agricultural extension agent, an agricultural consultant in the geographical area, or a representative of the manufacturer for more information.

**Table 1.8. Herbicides Suggested for Control of Weeds in Fence Rows, Waste
Areas, and Industrial Sites**

Herbicide		
Common name	Commercial name	Comments

Control of Annual and Perennial Herbs, Shrubs, and Trees

2,4-D	Dacamine; Esteron; Formula 40; Weed-B-Gon; Weedar-64; Weedone; various others	Selective for broadleaves. Little injury to most grasses. Do not apply near desirable broadleaf crops, trees, or shrubs. Spray at a time of no air movement or use a drift control agent to prevent drift. Herbicide should be applied when plant is actively growing.
Dicamba	Banvel	Same as above. Gives better control of some species.
Picloram	Tordon	Same as for 2,4-D plus dicamba but has a long soil residue and restricted usage.
Glyphosate	Roundup	Do not mix with other herbicides. Controls most annual and perennial vegetation; has no soil residual action.
Paraquat	Paraquat CL; Gramoxone	Kills most annual vegetation, but only defoliates perennials; has no soil residual action.

Control of Annual and Perennial Grasses

Dalapon	Dowpon	Apply when plants are actively growing and before boot stage. See label for specific grasses. Takes 2 weeks for symptoms to appear
Glyphosate	Roundup	Do not mix with other herbicides. Takes 10 days to 2 weeks for symptoms to appear.
Paraquat	Paraquat	Kills most annual grasses, but will only topkill many perennial grasses.

Table 1.8. (*Continued*)

Herbicide		
Common name	Commercial name	Comments

Soil Sterilants—Control of All Vegetation

Common name	Commercial name	Comments
Atrazine	Various	Nonselective. Apply before weeds emerge, only where residual control is desired. Use high rates. Does not control some perennial grasses.
Bromacil	Hyvar; others	Apply before weeds emerge. Use where residual control is desired. Will control many species.
Diuron	Karmex; Dynex	Apply preemergence before weeds emerge. Use only where residual control is desired. Will control many species.
Hexazinone	Velpar	Apply just before or just after weed emergence. Will control many species, including woody vines. Use only if bare ground is desired.
Prometon	Primatol	Apply either preemergence or postemergence. Controls many species. Nonselective. Use only where bare ground is desired.
Simazine	Various	Use high rates. Does not control some perennial grasses. Adequate moisture needed to activate herbicide.
Sulfometuron	Oust	Apply preemergence or postemergence. Nonselective. Controls many species. Extreme care must be taken to prevent drift to desirable plants or agricultural land.
Tebuthiuron	Spike	Apply preemergence or postemergence. Do not apply close to desirable trees or where their roots will extend. Use only where bare ground is desired.

Table 1.9. Common and Trade Names and Manufacturers of Common Herbicides and Other Characteristics

Common name	Commercial name(s)	Manufacturer	Application rate (lb/acre, active ingredient)	Method of application[a]
Acifluorfen	Blazer	Rohm & Haas	0.25–1.0	POST
Alachlor	Lasso	Monsanto	1.5–4.0	PRE
Ametryn	Evik	Ciba-Geigy	1.5–6.0	POD
Amitrole	Amino Triazole	American Cyanamid	2.0–4.0	POST
	Amitrol	Union Carbide	2.0–4.0	POST
	Weedazol			
Atrazine	Aatrex	Ciba-Geigy	0.5–4.0	PRE
	other brands	Others	10–60	SS
Barban	Carbyne	Velsicol	0.25–0.5	POST
Benefin	Balan	Elanco	0.75–1.0	PPI
Bensulide	Betasan	Stauffer	2.0–15.0	PPI, PRE
	Prefar	Stauffer		
Bentazon	Basagran	BASF	0.3–1.0	POST
Bromoxynil	Brominal	Union Carbide	0.25–1.0	POST
Bromacil	Hyvar X	DuPont	2.0–8.0	PRE
			3.0–30.0	SS
Butachlor[b]	Lambast, Machete	Monsanto	1.5–4.0	PPI, PRE
Butylate	Sutan	Stauffer	3.0–4.0	PPI
CDAA	Randox	Monsanto	3.0–6.0	PRE
Chloramben	Amiben	Union Carbide	2.0–4.0	PRE
Chlorpropham	Chloro IPC	PPG Industries	2.0–8.0	PRE
Chlorsulfuron	Glean	DuPont	0.125–0.375	PRE, POST
Chloroxuron[b]	Tenoran	Ciba-Geigy	1.0–4.5	POST
Copper sulfate	various	Phelps-Dodge	(1–4 ppm)	POST
		Applied Biochem.	(1 ppm)	
Cyanazine	Bladex	Shell	1.2–4.0	PRE, POST, POD
Cycloate	Ro-Neet	Stauffer	3.0–4.0	PPI
Dalapon	Dowpon	Dow	0.75–20.0	PPF, POST

24

DCPA	Dacthal	SDS Biotech	6.0–10.5	PRE
Diallate	Avadex	Monsanto	1.5–3.0	PRE
Dicamba	Banvel	Velsicol	0.25–8.0	POST
Dichlobenil	Casoron	Thompson-Hayward	1.5–8.0	PRE
Dichlorprop	Weedone 2,4-DP	Union Carbide	0.5–12.0	POST
Diclofop	Hoelon	Amer. Hoechst	0.75–1.5	POST
Difenzoquat	Avenge	American Cyanamid	0.8–1.2	POST
Dinoseb	various	Vertac	1.0–9.0	PRE, POST, POD
Diphenamid	Enide	Tuco	3.0–10.0	PRE
Diquat	Diquat H/A	Cheveron	1.0–2.0	POST
Diuron	Karmex	DuPont	0.75–10.0	PRE
			5.0–50.0	SS
DSMA	various	SDS Biotech, Vertac	2.0–4.0	POST, POD
Endothall	Endothal	Pennwalt	1.5–2.0	POST
EPTC	Eptam Eradicane	Stauffer	2.0–7.5	PPI
Ethalfluralin	Genep Sonalan	PPG Industries Elanco	0.75–1.5	PPI
Fenac[b]	Fenatrol	Union Carbide	2.0–15.0	PRE
Fluazifop-butyl	Fusilade	ICI	0.125–2.0	POST
Fluchloralin[b]	Basilin	BASF	0.5–1.5	PPI
Fluometuron	Cotoran	Ciba-Geigy	1.0–2.0	PRE
Fosamine	Krenite	DuPont	6.0–12.0	POST
Glyphosate	Roundup, Kleen-up, Rodeo	Monsanto	0.5–4.0	POST
Hexazinone	Velpar	DuPont	5.0–12.0	PRE, POST
Isopropalin	Paarlan	Elanco	1.0–2.0	PPI
Linuron	Lorox	DuPont	0.5–3.0	PRE, POST
MCPA	various	Rhone-Poulenc, Union Carbide, Vertac	0.2–2.0	POST

(continued)

Table 1.9. (*Continued*)

Common name	Commercial name(s)	Manufacturer	Application rate (lb/acre, active ingredient)	Method of application[a]
Mecoprop	various	Vineland, Boots	1.0–2.0	POST
Methazole[b]	Probe	Velsicol	0.5–2.0	PRE
Methyl Bromide	Brom-O-Gas, Meth-O-Gas	Various	—	PPI[c]
Metolachlor	Dual	Ciba-Geigy	1.0–4.0	PRE
Metribuzin	Lexone, Sencor	DuPont, Mobay	0.33–1.0	PRE, POST
Molinate	Ordram	Stauffer	2.0–3.0	PPI
Monuron[b]	Telvar	DuPont	0.5–5.0	PRE
MSMA	various	SDS Biotech, Vertac	2.0–5.0	POD, POST
Napropamide	Devrinol	Stauffer	1.0–8.0	PPI, PRE
Naptalam	Alanap	Uniroyal	2.0–8.0	PRE
Nitrofen	Tok	Rohm & Haas	2.0–6.0	PRE
Norflurazon	Zorial	Sandoz-Wander	1.0–8.0	PRE
Oryzalin	Surflan	Elanco	0.75–3.0	PRE
Oxadiazon[b]	Ronstar	Rhone Poulenc	1.0–4.0	PRE
Oxifluorfen	Goal	Rohm & Haas	0.25–2.0	PRE
Paraquat	Paraquat+Plus, Gramoxone	Chevron, ICI	0.38–1.0	POST
Pebulate	Tillam	Stauffer	3.0–4.0	PPI
Pendimethalin	Prowl	American Cyanamid	1.5–2.0	PPI, PRE
Perfluidone[b]	Destun	3M Company	1.0–3.0	PRE
Picloram	Tordon	Dow	0.25–8.0	POST

Prometon	Pramitol	Ciba-Geigy	10.0–60.0	SS
Prometryn	Caparol	Ciba-Geigy	0.2–3.0	PRE, POST
Pronamide	Kerb	Rohm & Haas	0.25–2.0	PRE
Propachlor	Ramrod	Monsanto	4.0–6.0	PRE
Propazine	Milogard	Ciba-Geigy	1.0–3.2	PRE
Propanil	Stam	Rohm & Haas	3.0–6.0	POST
	Stampede	Rohm & Haas		
	Propanil 4	Vertac		
Pyrazon	Pyramin	BASF	3.0–7.0	PRE
Sethoxydim	Poast	BASF	0.2–0.4	POST
Siduron	Tupersan	DuPont	2.0–12.0	PRE
Simazine	Princep	Ciba-Geigy	0.8–6.0	PRE
			20.0–40.0	SS
Sulfometuron	Oust	DuPont	0.016–0.05	PRE
Tebuthiuron	Spike	Elanco	2.0–6.0	PRE
Terbacil	Sinbar	DuPont	0.8–12.0	PRE
Terbutryn	Igran	Ciba-Geigy	1.2–2.4	PRE
Triallate	Far-go	Monsanto	1.0–1.5	PRE
Trifluralin	Treflan	Elanco	0.5–2.0	PRE
Vernolate	Vernam	Stauffer	2.0–3.0	PPI
2,4-D amine	Various	Union Carbide	0.3–6.0	POST
or ester		Vertac, Kalo,		
		Rhone-Poulenc,		
		others		
2,4-DB	Butyrac	Union Carbide	1.0–1.5	POST
	Butoxone	Vertac		

[a] Abbreviations for methods of application: PPI = preplant incorporated; PRE = preemergence; POST = postemergence; POD = postemergence directed; SS = soil sterilant rate.

[b] Herbicides no longer distributed in the United States.

[c] See label.

2
DESCRIPTION, HABITAT, AND CONTROL OF U. S. WEEDS

The number preceding each species name and description in Chapter 2 corresponds to the number of the illustration in the color plates section. The caption beneath each photograph in the color plates section gives the Latin name of the weed followed by the common name in parentheses. The color plate number is repeated in front of each weed name and description in Chapter 2.

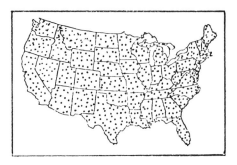

1A
Chara spp.
Musk-grass
Green algae (Characeae)

Description

A perennial aquatic alga that has 5–60 cm long, moderately slender stems. The internodes are one to three times as long as the whorled branchlets which are about 3–4 cm long. It is green and rooted to the bottom mud. The plants may be encrusted with calcareous deposits that give the stems and leaves a coarse, gritty feeling. When crushed between the fingers, this alga is ill smelling, emitting a skunk-like odor. The presence of calcareous deposits sometimes causes the plant to change color slightly. Dense weed growth causes severe problems in ponds, lakes, and canals where it may impede waterflow and interfere with fishing. It reproduces mainly by vegetative means.

Habitat

Musk-grass is generally found in the shallow water of lakes, ponds, streams, and canals, but may be found as deep as 7 m in very clear water. It is a native of North America.

Suggested Control

Aquatic—Apply copper sulfate or a copper complex to one-half to one-third of pond at a time; allow 7 to 14 days between applications or apply dichlobenil or simazine in early spring before weed initiates active growth to ponds where little or no run-off will occur after treatment.

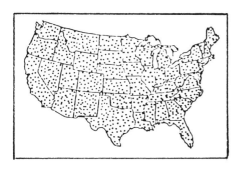

1B
Pithophora spp.
Pithophora
Green algae
(Cladophoraceae)

Description

An aquatic filamentous alga that is irregularly branched. Initial growth is usually made as an attached or rooted alga, but as soon as dense growth occurs, gases are trapped and the floating mats of algae occur. These floating mats often resembles a mass of wet wool. The individual strands are about the size of a coarse thread. Dense growth of this weed interferes with or prevents sport fishing, depletes oxygen, provides favored mosquito-breeding sites, and gives an undesirable appearance to the body of water. It reproduces by vegetative means.

Habitat

Pithophora is found in small ponds, lakes, and slow-moving streams and canals. It is a native of North America.

Suggested Control

Aquatic—Weed can be controlled by light exclusion through shading with phytoplankton (stimulated by fertilization) or by herbivorous fish, *viz.,* goldfish, common carp, or white amur at 200 fish per acre. Chemical control can be obtained with copper sulfate, dichlobenil, diquat, diuron, or simazine applied in spring or endothall applied in late spring or early summer.

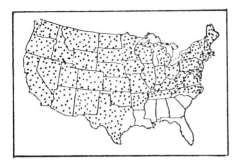

1C
Equisetum arvense L.
Field horsetail
Horsetail family
(Equisetaceae)

Description

Field horsetail is a perennial plant that grows in marshy areas. Its erect hollow, ribbed stems are 20–60 cm tall. The fertile stem, appearing in early spring, is yellow-brown with easily separable nodes, and produces a terminal head of spores. Sterile or vegetative stems are shown in this picture. These have much smaller nodes, with lateral branches in whorls around the main stem. True leaves are on the vegetative stem only, in the form of toothed sheaths at the nodes. The vegetative shoots are produced in late spring after the fertile ones. Reproduction is by spores and rhizome borne tubers.

Habitat

Field horsetail can be found growing in wet soil along stream banks, in low areas in pastures and waste places and in marshes. Field horsetail is poisonous to livestock and is a native of North America.

Suggested Control

Cropland—Drain the area and cultivate to deplete food storage in the extensive underground root system. Young seedlings can be controlled with 2,4-D or MCPA. Dichlobenil can be used to control this weed in orchards, alfalfa and clover. *Noncrop Areas and Waste Areas*—Use bromacil.

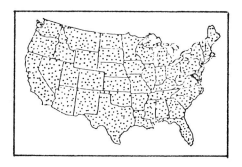

1D
Pteridium aquilinum (L.)
  Kuhn
Bracken
Ferns (Polypodiaceae)

Description

Perennial fern that arises from extensive creeping, coarse, hairy rootstocks. Leaves or fronds arise directly from the rootstock, with a 30–150 cm long petiole and are scattered, deciduous, broadly triangular with many divisions bearing numerous leathery leaflets. Spores are borne on the lower surface of each leaflet in a brown, narrow band, covered by a thin membrane. Reproduction is by spores or vegetatively by rootstocks.

Habitat

Eastern bracken is found in newly cleared or burned areas, along roadsides, in poorly managed pastures and in fallowed fields. It is poisonous to livestock, especially horses and cattle. It is a native of North America.

Suggested Control

New Cropland—Use a crop rotation that includes row crops. Cultivation will control this pest and with each successive crop, fewer ferns will be present. *Pastures*—Practice good management techniques, maintain a thick stand of the desired species, adjust pH, and fertilizer regularly. Use rotational grazing and mowing following each rotation. On thin stands sheep can be used effectively for close grazing and weakening the plants. Hogs will rout out and destroy rootstocks. Dicamba can be applied for selective control in grass pastures and should be applied before the frounds are fully expanded. *Roadsides and Waste Areas*—Treat with amitrole, dicamba, or fosamine.

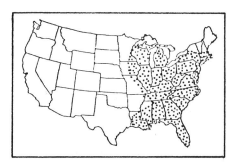

1E
Azolla caroliniana Willd.
Atlantic azolla
Salvinia family (Salviniaceae)

Description

Atlantic azolla is a free floating, aquatic perennial fern with lobed leaves. Fronds or leaves are banded together in a scalelike manner forming a continuous mat up to 50 cm in diameter. Individual plants are 5–10 mm wide, branched and widely spreading. The upper leaf lobes are much smaller than the lower lobes. The upper lobes are above or on the water surface while the lower lobes are submerged. The lower surface of the leaves bear inconspicuous rootlets. This weed reproduces by spores and by vegetative budding.

Habitat

Atlantic azolla floats along the edges of ponds and lakes and may cover the water surface. It is a native of North America.

Suggested Control

Aquatic—Physically remove with a fine mesh seine or spray with 2,4-D. Follow all herbicide label restrictions.

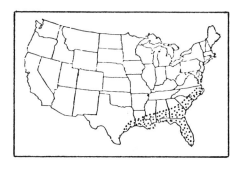

1F
Salvinia rotundifolia Willd.
Salvinia
Salvinia family (Salviniaceae)

Description

A free floating aquatic fern that has unlobed leaves. Fronds or leaves are rounded or elliptic, bright-green, thickish, 10–16 mm long, hairy on both sides and often arranged along a common stem with as many as 20 to 30 apparently two-ranked leaves. In sparse infestations the leaves may be found either isolated or in small groups. The lower surface of the leaf is commonly brownish or purplish and bears a fascicle of rootlets. The reproductive structures (sporocarps) are formed on the lower surface of the leaves. Reproduction is by spores and by vegetative budding of young leaves that break loose from the plant.

Habitat

Salvinia may be found in the shallow water of warm canals. It is a native of South America.

Suggested Control

Aquatic—Physically remove with a fine mest seine or spray with diquat or 2,4-D. Follow all herbicide label restrictions.

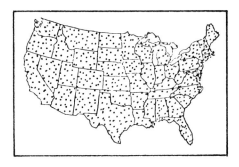

1G
Typha latifolia L.
Common cattail
Cattail family (Typhaceae)

Description

A perennial aquatic herb that arises from creeping tuberous root-stocks. The stems are without nodes and 1–3 m tall. The leaves are 1–2.5 cm wide, smooth, flat, and waxy, and blue-green in color. Inflorescenses are dense and terminal spikes have distinct male and female portions that are more or less contiguous. The female is on the lowermost portion, 10–15 cm long, and is approximately 2.5 cm thick. The male portion is uppermost and 7–12 cm long, light brown in color, thinner and less dense. The fruit is 1 mm long, nutlike and has downy hairs underneath. Common cattail reproduces by seeds and by fleshy rootstocks. Flowers are formed from May to July.

Habitat

Cattail is found growing in marshy areas around ponds and lakes and in shallow areas along ditches and rivers. It is a native of North America.

Suggested Control

Moist Pastures, Margins of Lakes and Ponds—Drainage of moist pastures followed by periodic mowing will control cattail in moist pastures. The edges of lakes and ponds can be made deeper and steeper. Cattail can be controlled with amitrole, dalapon, or glyphosate. Addition of a surfactant to the herbicide mixture may be advantageous. Diquat can be used for burn down of above water portions.

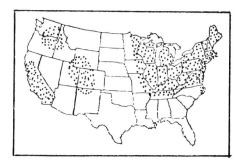

1H
Potamogeton crispus L.
Curlyleaf pondweed
Pondweed family
(Potamogetonaceae)

Description

Curlyleaf pondweed is a perennial, rooted aquatic herb. The stem is sparingly branched, flat, smooth, submerged and 30–80 cm long. Leaves are simple, alternate, all submersed, linear-oblong, rounded, or pointed at apex. The leaf margin is wavy and minutely toothed. The base is rounded or sharply narrowed, without a petiole. Leaves are 3–8 cm long and 5–12 mm wide, net-veined, and have three to five conspicuous veins. Stipules are membranaceous and about 4 mm long. The inflorescence is a 1 cm long spike, borne at the end of a 2–5 cm long stalk. The fruit is one-seeded, egg-shaped, and 3 mm long. Curlyleaf pondweed reproduces by seeds and stem sections. It flowers from May to September.

Habitat

This plant may occur in calcareous waters of ponds, lakes, and in sluggish areas of streams and canals. It is a native of Europe.

Suggested Control

Aquatic—Treat infested water area with endothall, dichlobenil, diquat, fenac, or simazine. Follow label directions in detail.

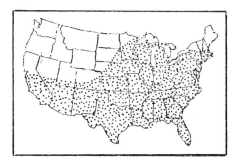

1I
Potamogeton illinoensis
 Morong
Illinois pondweed
Pondweed family
(Potamogetonaceae)

Description

Illinois pondweed is a rooted aquatic herb with a coarse underwater rhizome. Leaves are two types. Submersed leaves are elliptic, lanceolate, strongly veined, slightly arched, with wavy margins, sessile or short petioled, and 10–15 cm long. Floating leaves are elliptic to ovate, entire with a wedge-shaped based, pointed at the tip, 4–8 cm long with a petiole up to 15 cm long. (Picture shows only submersed leaves.) The stipules are linear and up to 6 cm long. The inflorescence is a cylindric spike 2–4 cm long, with an 8 cm long peduncle, borne at the tip of the stem that is emerged from the water. Illinois pondweed reproduces vegetatively and by seeds and flowers from May to September.

Habitat

This plant may occur in calcareous areas in canals, streams, ponds, and lakes. It is a native of North America.

Suggested Control

Aquatic—Treat infested water area with diquat, dichlobenil, endothall, or simazine. Follow label directions in detail.

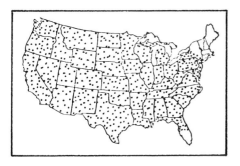

2A
Potamogeton nodosus Poir.
American pondweed
Pondweed family
(Potamogetonaceae)

Description

American pondweed is a rooted, aquatic perennial herb. The branched stem is submerged and is up to 1 m long. Leaves are both submerged and floating. The submerged leaves are pale green, thin, narrowly lanceolate or linear, pointed at the tip, conspicuously 7- to 15-veined and up to 35 cm long. The floating leaves are lance-oblong to lance-elliptic, smooth, shiny, wavy, dark green, 9- to 21-veined, 5–12 cm long and the base gradually narrows to a 5–20 cm long petiole. The stipules on the emersed leaf are similar to those on the submersed leaves, but are slightly wider and are 4–10 cm long. The inflorescence is a dense and cylindric spike, 3–5 cm long. Seeds are broadly semiovoide and are approximately 3–4 cm long. This plant reproduces by seeds and broken stem sections and flowers during August and September.

Habitat

American pondweed occurs in the shallow waters of ponds and lakes or even at greater depths in clear water. It is a native of North America.

Suggested Control

Aquatic—Treat infested water area with dichlobenil, diquat, endo-thall, or simazine. Follow label directions in detail.

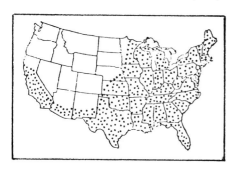

2B
Potamogeton pectinatus L.
Sago pondweed
Pondweed family
(Potamogetonaceae)

Description

Sago pondweed is a submersed rooted aquatic perennial herb, with a slender rootstock and small tubers. The stem is 0.5–1.2 m long, widely branched, and repeatedly forked toward the tip, with longer internodes on the lower portion. The leaves are bristlelike on the upper portion tapering to pointed tips, one-veined, 3–9 cm long, and 0.5–1.5 mm wide. The stipules are united to the blade, 1–3 cm long with a free tip 3–10 mm long. The inflorescence is a cylindric, 1.5–5 cm long, interrupted spike with two to six flowers, and borne on a wavy stalk. Fruits are one-seeded, egg-shaped, and approximately 4 mm long. It reproduces by seeds and rootstocks and flowers from June to September.

Habitat

Sago pondweed usually occurs in shallow water around the edges of ponds and lakes where it forms dense tangles of vegetation that choke the water. It is native of Eurasia.

Suggested Control

Aquatic—Treat infested water area with dichlobenil, diquat, endothall, or simazine. Follow label directions in detail.

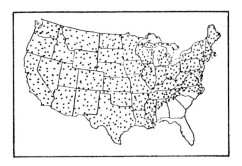

2C
Potamogeton pusillus L.
Small pondweed
Pondweed family
(Potamogetonaceae)

Description

Small pondweed is a perennial, rooted, and submerged aquatic plant. Stems are up to 40 cm long, very slender, with numerous branches toward the tip. Leaves are linear, alternate, obtuse, or sharply pointed, rather conspicuously three-veined, 0.5–3 mm wide and 1–8 cm long. Stipules are thin, delicate, membranaceous, and 4–7 mm long. It is borne on a 1–5 cm long filiform stalk located in the upper leaf axils. Fruits are 3 mm long, egg-shaped, and one-keeled. This weed reproduces by seeds and stem sections. It flowers from June to September.

Habitat

Small pondweed usually occurs in calcareous waters of ponds and lakes forming a thick mat of dark-colored vegetation on the bottom close to the shore in shallow waters.

Suggested Control

Aquatic—Treat infested water area with dichlobenil, diquat, endothall, or simazine. Follow label directions in detail.

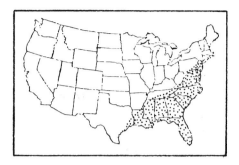

2D
Najas guadalupensis
(Spreng.) Magnus
Southern naiad
Water-nymph family
(Najadaceae)

Description

Southern naiad is an annual submerged aquatic herb. The stems are slender, firm, much branched, very leafy, and dark green to purple in color. Leaves are linear, rounded or acute, at the tips and 1–2 cm long, with the smaller ones clustered in the axils. Leaf margins have minute spines. Flowers are inconspicuous. The dull yellowish seeds are about 3 mm long with 10–20 rows of minute splotches. This plant reproduces by seeds and vegetative means. Flowers appear from August to October.

Habitat

Southern naiad occurs in fresh and brackish waters of ponds, lakes, and canals. It is native to North America.

Suggested Control

Aquatic—Mechanically control by raking with a hand rake to remove vegetative growth in areas frequently used for swimming or use diquat, endothall, or simazine. Follow label instructions explicitly.

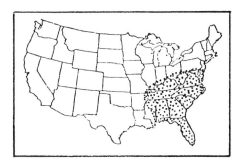

2E
Najas minor All.
Naiad
Water-nymph family
(Najadaceae)

Description

Naiad is a slender annual submerged aquatic herb. Its stems are slender, many-branched, up to 1 m long. Leaves are opposite, narrowly linear, often recurved toward the tip, very fine and 1–2.5 cm long. Leaf margins have 6–15 minute spinulose teeth. The unisexual flowers are inconspicuously located in the leaf axils. Fruits are 3–5 mm long, with one seed. Seeds are small, with 12–18 longitudinal ribs connected by a transversal areolae. It reproduces by seeds and vegetatively by broken stem sections.

Habitat

Naiad grows densely near the shore of ponds, lakes, and streams and forms a thick, dark mass from the bottom to the surface. It is native to Eurasia and Africa.

Suggested Control

Aquatic—Mechanically control somewhat by raking to remove weed from areas frequently used for swimming or use simazine. In farm ponds, edges of the pond may be deepened and winter fertilization may be practiced to promote an algae bloom, which will shade this submerged weed. Dichlobenil, diquat, endothall, or simazine can be used for chemical control, but label restrictions must be followed.

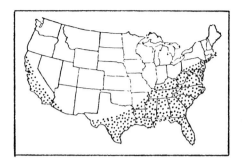

2F
Sagittaria calycina Engelm.
California arrowhead
Water-plantain family
(Alismataceae)

Description

California arrowhead is a perennial aquatic herb. Stems are erect and glabrous. The plant is rooted to the bottom mud. Leaves are simple, arrowhead-shaped, long-petioled, about 1–20 cm wide and 4–40 cm long. Flower shoots are coarse and 10–80 cm long. Flowers are borne in whorls of two to ten. The upper male flowers are on long narrow pedicels. The lower female flowers are on short, coarse pedicel. The petals are white and 7–15 mm long. The sepals are persistent and 4–12 mm long. Achenes (one-seeded fruits) are 2–3 mm long, and narrowly winged. California arrowhead reproduces mainly by seeds. Flowers appear from July to September.

Habitat

California arrowhead is found in marshes, ponds, streams, and irrigation ditches. It is native to North America.

Suggested Control

Aquatic—Deepen the edges of the pond or lake, or spray with 2,4-D, diquat, or endothall in accordance with label restrictions.

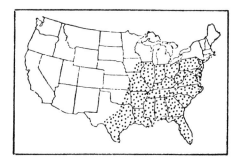

2G
Sagittaria graminea Michx.
Coastal arrowhead
Water-plantain family
(Alismataceae)

Description

Coastal arrowhead is a rooted perennial herb emerging above the water, 10–60 cm tall. Erect leaves are 4–10 cm long and arise as a rosette from the tubers on the rhizomes. The 10–50 cm long flower shoot is simple, with 2 to 12 white flowers borne in whorls. The upper flowers are usually male borne on slender and erect pedicels and the lower female flowers are on thicker and spreading pedicels. Bracts are ovate, membranaceous, 3–6 mm long. Seed pods are narrowly obovate, 1–2 mm long and have one or two slender ridges. Coastal arrowhead reproduces by seeds and rootstocks. Flowers appear from May to September.

Habitat

Coastal arrowhead usually occurs in swamps, shallow water, and along drainage ditches. It is native of North America.

Suggested Control

Aquatic—Deepen the edges of the pond or lake, or spray with 2,4-D, diquat, or endothall. Follow label restrictions.

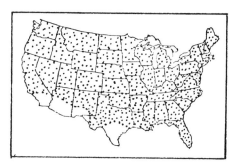

2H
Sagittaria latifolia Willd.
Common arrowhead
Water-plantain family
(Alismataceae)

Description

Common arrowhead is a perennial aquatic herb. It is an erect plant, rooted in the bottom mud of ponds and wet areas. Its leaves are arrowhead-shaped and rarely without lobes. The basal lobes are triangular-ovate to linear, 2–20 cm wide and 5–40 cm long. The flower shoot is erect, either simple or branched, and is 10–100 cm tall. Flowers are in whorls of 2 to 15. The upper male flowers are on short pedicels, and the lower usually female flowers are on longer, terete pedicels. Petals are white, broadly ovate, and 5–7 mm long. The fruit is 3–4 mm long and winged on both edges. This aquatic weed reproduces by seeds and stolons. Flowers appear from July to September.

Habitat

Common arrowhead occurs in wet places along lakes, ponds, streams, and swamps. It is native of North America.

Suggested Control

Aquatic—Deepen the edges of the pond or lake, or spray with 2,4-D, diquat, or endothall. Follow label restrictions.

2I
Egeria densa Planch.
Egeria
Frog's-bit family
(Hydrocharitaceae)

Description

Egeria is a perennial submersed aquatic herb, rooted in the bottom mud. Stems are branched, with short internodes and very leafy. Leaves are in whorls of four to six; are 1–4 cm long and up to 5 mm wide. They are lance-shaped and taper gradually toward the apex. They are dark-green. The lower leaves are further apart and they become more crowded toward the top. Flowers rise above the water surface. Male and female flowers are separated by different plants. The male flowers are white and showy, the female flowers are not known to occur in the United States. This plant reproduces only by vegetative means (broken stem sections). It flowers from June to October.

Habitat

Egeria occurs in quiet waters of ponds, lakes, and in slow-moving streams. It is a native of Argentina.

Suggested Control

Aquatic—Mechanically remove from small areas with hand rake. Control chemically with dichlobenil, diquat, or endothall. Follow label restrictions.

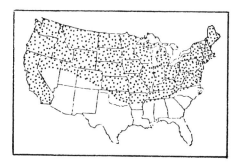

3A
Elodea canadensis Michx.
Elodea
Frog's-bit family
(Hydrocharitaceae)

Description

Elodea is a submersed aquatic perennial herb. Both female and male plants occur. Female plants have slender, branched stems, regularly forming in pairs from creeping threadlike stolons. The lower leaves are opposite, ovate and small; the upper dark-green leaves are in whorls of threes, oblong-ovate, with minutely toothed margins. Female flowers protrude above water on a 2–15 cm threadlike stalk. Male plants are rare and have thin linear leaves. Male flowers reach the water surface on a threadlike 10–20 cm stalk. Primarily reproduction is by vegetative means. Flowers appear from July to September.

Habitat

Elodea occurs in the quiet waters of quarries, lakes and ponds. It is native of North America.

Suggested Control

Aquatic—Mechanically remove from small areas with a hand rake or from larger areas with a mechanical harvester. Repeat as needed. Can be controlled chemically with either dichlobenil, diquat, or endothall.

3B
Hydrilla verticillata (L. F.)
Casp.
Hydrilla
Frog's-bit family
(Hydrocharitaceae)

Description

Hydrilla is a submersed aquatic perennial herb. It has slender, much-branched stems which form loose floating mats. It grows from water surface to as deep as 12 m. The leaves have tiny, spiny teeth. The lower leaves are opposite, small, lance-shaped, and the upper leaves are in whorls of three. They are about 2 mm wide and 11–13 mm long. Flowers are inconspicuous, arising singularly from a spathe near the growing tip, which is extended to the water surface. The flowers have three white petals. Seeds are rarely produced. The plant forms an underground pealike tuber, as well as winter buds that detach. It reproduces vegetatively. Flowers occur from August to October.

Habitat

Hydrilla occurs in drainage and irrigation canals, freshwater ponds, and streams. Native of Africa.

Suggested Control

Aquatic—Inject a mixture of copper sulfate, diquat, or endothall below the water surface. Due to the importance of this weed, if its presence is suspected, contact an aquatic weed specialist for positive identification and up-to-date recommendation for its control.

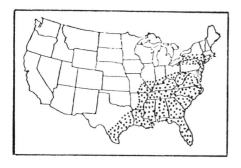

3C
Limnobium spongia (Bosc.)
   Steud.
Frogbit
Frog's-bit family
(Hydrocharitaceae)

Description

Frogbit is a perennial aquatic plant that varies in size and habit. Most often frogbit occurs as a free floating mat, but can grow up to 50 cm tall and be rooted in muddy shores. Leaves are bright green, heart-shaped, with long petioles and are often spongy on the lower surface. They are 3–7 cm long and wide, with somewhat inflated and spongy stalks. Nonshowy white flowers are borne on peduncles one-third the length of the leaves. This plant reproduces by seeds and rootstocks. Flowers occur from July to September.

Habitat

Frogbit can be found floating in still or stagnant water of ponds, lakes, and marshes or rooting in the mud as marshes dry up. It is a native of tropical America.

Suggested Control

Aquatic—The edges of the pond should be deepened and/or low spots marshy in nature should be filled. Infested area can be treated with 2,4-D or diquat. Follow label restrictions.

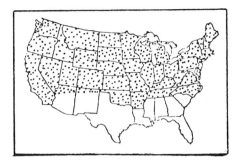

3D
Agropyron repens (L.) Beauv.
Quackgrass
Grass family (Gramineae)

Description

A perennial grass with slender, white creeping rhizomes which forms big clumps. The stems are erect, branching at the base and 30–100 cm tall. Leaves are sheathed with small earlike lobes at the base of the blades, finely ribbed, sparsely hairy on the lower sheaths, and the upper sheaths are smooth or nearly so. The inflorescence is a narrow spike, 5–25 cm long, with short-bearded florets flattened against the axis. Spikelets separate above the spikelet bracts (glumes) at maturity. Quackgrass reproduces by seeds and by extensively creeping rhizomes. It flowers from May to September.

Habitat

Quackgrass is a native of Europe but has spread to cultivated fields, pastures, lawns, and waste places across North America.

Suggested Control

Home Gardens—Quackgrass is very difficult to control. Cultural control: (1) plow or dig up all roots and burn; don't allow any green leaves to emerge; keep the land bare by cultivation every 7 to 10 days; (2) after the initial destruction of the root system, cover the area with black plastic, anchor well, and prevent new growth from occurring, or (3) spray with amitrole, dalapon, fluazifop-butyl, glyphosate and sethoxydim. Re-treat every few weeks as needed. *Cropland*—Labeled herbicides are amitrole, atrazine, dichlobenil, fluazifop-butyl, pronamide, sethoxydim simazine, and terbacil. *Industrial*—Dalapon, fluazifop-butyl, glyphosate, and sethoxydim will provide initial control, but should be followed with a soil sterilant such as atrazine, bromacil, or simazine to prevent reinfestation.

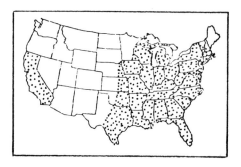

3E
Andropogon virginicus L.
Broomsedge
Grass family (Gramineae)

Description

Broomsedge is shallow-rooted, summer perennial bunchgrass. Erect stems originate from a crown and form small clumps that are reddish-brown when dry. The stems are 50–120 cm tall and well-branched at the top. Leaves are flat or folded. They are very hairy on the upper surface where they attach to the stem. The blades are up to 35 cm long. Leaf sheaths are compressed and keeled on the back. The inflorescence is a narrow panicle with pairs of fingerlike feathery 1–4 cm long racemes bearing tufts of conspicuous white hairs. Seeds are bearded, brownish in color and about 3 mm long. Broomsedge reproduces mainly by seeds which are easily dispensed by the wind. Flowers occur from September to December.

Habitat

Broomsedge is well established in pastures, open meadows, roadsides, and waste places. It is a native of North America.

Suggested Control

Pastures and Meadows—Increase the level of management. Infested areas should have soil pH adjusted to 6.5–7.0 and should be fertilized with nitrogen fertilizer or with a complete fertilizer. Encourage desirable pasture species. Graze heavily in the spring of the year when broomsedge is palatable. Mow after grazing. Do not overgraze in mid- or late season and mow occasionally to prevent seed production. If broomsedge is a predominant species, the pH should be adjusted. The soil should be fertilized and disked lightly, and a desirable competitive grass seeded. *Roadsides and Waste Areas*—Encourage more desirable species by adjusting pH and fertility coupled with periodic mowing to prevent seed production. Spot spray with dalapon or glyphosate before plants become woody. Re-seed with desirable species.

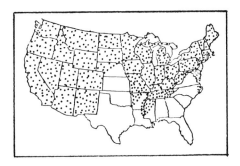

3F
Avena fatua L.
Wild oats
Grass family (Gramineae)

Description

This weed is summer annual grass, with an extensive and fibrous root system. Its stems or tillers are erect, smooth and coarse, and 0.4–1.2 m tall. Leaves are 10–20 cm long. The inflorescence is an open panicle, with slender, spreading branches, bearing plump spikelets. Wild oats are distinguished from cultivated oats by the long awns that are twisted like a corkscrew near the base and bent sharply at a right angle in the upper part (the awn is straight in cultivated oats), because of the round callus at base of the grain (absent in cultivated oats), and by slightly roughened leaves (smooth in cultivated oats). Seeds vary in color from white to yellow to tan and are usually hairy near the base. Reproduction is only by seeds. Flowering occurs from June to October.

Habitat

Wild oats are associated with the cultivation of small grains and flax, where it ripens earlier than the cereals; the seeds then shatter thus increasing its dispersion. It is a native of Europe and has spread to all the areas of the world where spring cereals are produced.

Suggested Control

Cropland—Use a crop rotation program where, if possible, cultivated row crops can be rotated with small grains and herbicides such as atrazine, bromacil, dalapon, EPTC, ethalfluralin, fluazifop-butyl, napropamide, pebulate, pronamide, and triallate can be used if crop tolerance exists. When small grains are planted, barban, diclofop, difenzoquat, or triallate should be sprayed at the correct growth stages as specified on the label.

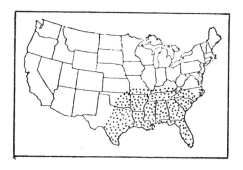

3G
Brachiaria platyphylla
(Griseb.) Nash
Broadleaf signalgrass
Grass family (Gramineae)

Description

This summer annual grass has reclining 30–60 cm long stems which root at the lower nodes. The leaf blades are flat, thick, 5–10 mm wide and 3–10 cm long. The inflorescence a small panicle with two to six short racemes, each 4–8 cm long; spikelets are in two rows on one side of the winged axis. Seeds are 3 mm long and finely roughened. Reproduction is by seeds and somewhat by stem sections. Flowering occurs from June to October.

Habitat

This grass, which is native to North America, occurs in many cultivated fields especially those planted in corn, cotton, and soybeans.

Suggested Control

Cropland—Use clean cultivation or a herbicide. Adequate herbicides are available so that a good crop rotation can be maintained and still have good crop tolerance for each rotational crop. Herbicides which specifically include this weed on the label are alachlor, EPTC, fluchloralin, fluometuron, linuron, metolachlor, oryzalin, napropamide, pebulate, pendimenthalin, or trifluralin.

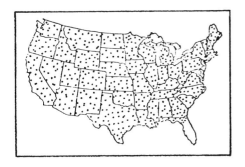

3H
Bromus japonicus Thunb.
Japanese brome
Grass family (Gramineae)

Description

A winter annual grass occurring across most of the United States. Its smooth erect stems are 30–90 cm tall and grow in tufts. Sheaths and blades are softly and densely hairy and the latter are 2–4 mm wide. The inflorescence is a loose, open panicle, 10–20 cm long whose spreading drooping slender branches are much longer than the spikelets. Spikelets are large, mostly 7–10 flowered, hairless, or nearly so, with more or less twisted awns that are divergent when dry. The lowest is 2.5–5 mm long, the uppermost 8.5–12 mm long. Reproduction is by seeds. Flowers appear in May and June.

Habitat

Japanese brome is widely distributed in small grain fields, pastures, roadsides, and waste places. It is native of Europe.

Suggested Control

Cultivated Fields—Crop rotation to include row crops such as corn or soybeans; use herbicides recommended for the crop for grass control such as alachlor, butylate, EPTC, metolachlor, pendimethalin, pronamide, or trifluralin. *Established Forage Legumes without Grass Companion Crop* —Maintain a thick stand of forage, and apply pronamide or simazine in the fall to late winter. *Meadows*—Mow before seed head forms to prevent seed production. *Fence Rows, Waste Areas, etc.*—Spot spray with dalapon or glyphosate. *Industrial Areas*—Use a soil sterilant such as bromacil, hexazinone, or tebuthiuron.

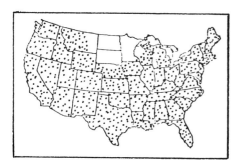

3I
Bromus secalinus L.
Cheat
Grass family (Gramineae)

Description

This tufted winter annual grass has erect stems from 0.4–1.2 m tall. Leaves are flat, smooth to slightly hairy on top with smooth and strongly veined sheaths. The inflorescence is a loose and open panicle, 10–30 cm long with the branches spreading upwardly. Spikelets are born on shorter and more upright pedicels than are those of Japanese brome (*Bromus japonicus*), and have straight, shorter awns, 1–6 mm long. Cheat reproduces only by seeds and flowers from May to July.

Habitat

Cheat occurs in small grain fields, along roadsides, in meadows, and in waste ground. It is also a native of Europe.

Suggested Control

Cultivated Fields—Crop rotation to include row crops such as corn, potatoes or soybeans; use herbicides recommended for the crop for grass control such as alachlor, benefin, butylate, EPTC, metolachlor, pendimethalin, pronamide, trifluralin, or vernolate. *Established Forage Legumes without Grass Companion Crop*—maintain a thick stand of forage, and apply pronamide or simazine in the fall to late winter. *Meadows*—Mow before seed head forms to prevent seed production. *Fence Rows, Waste Areas, etc.*—Spot spray with dalapon, fluazifop-butyl, glyphosate, or sethoxydim. *Industrial*—Use a soil sterilant such as bromacil, hexazinone, or tebuthiuron.

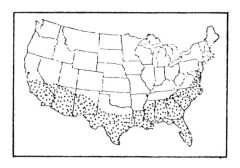

4A
Cenchrus echinatus L.
Southern sandbur
Grass family (Gramineae)

Description

Southern sandbur is a summer annual grass. Stems are compressed, round in cross-section, branched at base, have variable hairiness and are 25–60 cm tall. Leaf blades are hairy on the upper surface near the base, 3–8 mm wide and 5–25 cm long. Sheaths are flattened and slightly hairy on the margins near the summit. The inflorescence is a raceme 3–10 cm long, with burs 4–7 mm long, blunt on the base, globose, and hairy. The spine tips usually turn purple with age. Reproduction is by seeds. Flowers appear from June to September.

Habitat

This weed infests cultivated fields, roadsides, and waste places. It is native to tropical America.

Suggested Control

Home Lawns—Increase level of turf management to provide a thick competitive turf through proper pH adjustment, adequate fertilization, proper mowing height, etc., and use a preemergence herbicide such as benefin, bensulide, DCPA, or siduron to prevent establishment of new seedlings. Remove escaped plants by hand. Protect hands with heavy gloves. *Cultivated Crops*—Prevent establishment and seed formation by cultivation and/or using a preemergence herbicide such as alachlor, diphenamid, EPTC, isopropalin, metolachlor, pendimethalin, terbacil, and trifluralin. *Pastures*—Increase level of pasture management by proper pH and fertilization adjustment, rotational grazing and mowing after grazing. *Waste Areas*—Spot spray with dalapon or paraquat.

4B
Cenchrus longispinus (Hack.)
Fern.
Longspine sandbur
Grass family (Gramineae)

Description

This summer annual grass forms clumps. The 10–80 cm long stems are erect, coarse, round in cross-section, often rooting at lower nodes when in contact with soil. Leaf blades are 4–8 mm wide by 6–20 cm long and smooth, twisted, and rough. Leaf sheaths are hairy on the margins and strongly keeled. The inflorescence is a compact, short spike, 4–10 cm long, composed of spikelets enclosed in sharp, spiny burs. Each bur containing one to three small seeds. Reproduction is by seeds. Flowers appear between June and August.

Habitat

Longspine sandbur occurs in cultivated soils, lawns, roadsides, and waste grounds. The burs cause great discomfort to people and livestock. It is native of western Europe, Africa, and Australia.

Suggested Control

Home Lawns—Increase level of turf management to provide a thick competitive turf through proper pH adjustment, adequate fertilization, adequate water, proper mowing height to prevent scalping, etc., and use a preemergence grass herbicide such as DCPA, benefin, or bensulide. Remove escaped plants by hand-digging. Protect hands with heavy gloves. *Cultivated Crops*—Prevent establishment and seed formation by cultivation and/or by using a preemergence herbicide such as alachlor, diphenamid, EPTC, isopropalin, metolachlor, pendimethalin, terbacil, and trifluralin. *Pastures*—Increase level of pasture management by proper pH and fertilization adjustment, rotational grazing, and clipping after mowing. *Waste Areas*—Spot spray with paraquat or dalapon.

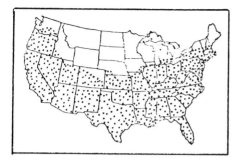

4C
Cynodon dactylon (L.) Pers.
Bermudagrass
Grass family (Gramineae)

Description

This perennial grass forms an extensive mat of surface-creeping stems and rootstocks. Stems are of three kinds: vegetative, surface-creeping, stems extensively rooting at nodes; flowering stems, erect or ascending 20–40 cm tall; and, underground stems, scaly, tough, sharp-pointed, called rootstocks or rhizomes. The flat leaf blades are about 3 mm wide, either sparsely hairy or smooth, usually gray-green in color with a ring of white hairs at the base. The inflorescence is borne at end of the erect flowering stems and has three to seven fingerlike spikes, each 2–7 cm long. Seeds are produced in spikelets arranged in two rows on one side of the axis. Reproduction is by seeds, by surface-creeping stems, and by rootstocks. Flowers are produced from July to September.

Habitat

Bermudagrass is a warm-season grass that occurs in pastures, lawns, gardens, cultivated fields, roadsides, and waste places. It is native of Africa.

Suggested Control

Home Gardens—Use clean cultivation, remove all plant parts. *Home Lawns*—Spray with glyphosate or dalapon, allow sufficient time for die down and herbicide breakdown, remove thatch, and reseed with desired species. *Cultivated Crops*—Along its northern range of adaptation, disk or plow (shallow in the fall of the year to expose the rootstocks to the winter elements of freezing and desiccation) and follow with a clean cultivated crop. In temperate climates, plant row crops and cultivate as necessary. Use fluazifop-butyl and sethoxydim in tolerant crops. Dalapon and glyphosate can be used for spot spraying. *Roadsides and Waste Places*—Treat with dalapon or glyphosate while actively growing. *Industrial Areas*—Use bromacil, hexazinone, or tebuthiuron as soil sterilants.

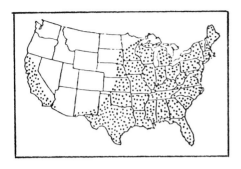

4D
Dactylis glomerata L.
Orchardgrass
Grass family (Gramineae)

Description

Perennial grass with coarse tall (0.4–1.5 m) stems. Stems arise from a central crown to form a bunch or tuft. Leaf blades are broadly linear, 3–8 mm wide. Leaf sheaths are compressed with stiff hairs and long ligules (5–7 mm). The inflorescence is a panicle, 5–25 cm long with few stiff branches. Spikelets are crowded in dense one-sided clusters at the end of the branches, and are either awnless or with very short awns and usually ciliate on the keel. Orchardgrass reproduces by seeds. It is cultivated as a pasture grass and has escaped from cultivation. Flowers appear from May to September.

Habitat

It occurs as a weed in cultivated fields, lawns, roadsides, and waste places. It is native to Europe.

Suggested Control

Home Lawns—Dig out scattered plants, and overseed with a desirable species. *Cultivated Fields*—Plow in the spring or fall, and cultivate during the season. Prevent reinfestation from seed by using a preemergence or preplant herbicide such as alachlor, butylate, EPTC, metolachlor, oryzalin, trifluralin, or vernolate. Dalapon, glyphosate, and pronamide will control established plants. *Roadsides and Waste Places*—If objectionable, spray with dalapon or glyphosate, allow sufficient time for herbicide breakdown and reseed with desirable species.

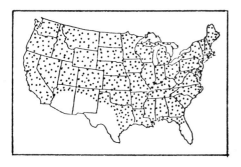

4E
Digitaria ischaemum
(Schreb.) Muhl.
Smooth crabgrass
Grass family (Gramineae)

Description

This summer annual grass has smooth erect stems (10–40 cm long) that become semiprostrate and spreading. Leaf blades are 3–6 mm wide, 5–10 cm long, flat, bluish or occasionally purplish, and have a ring of hairs at the junction with the sheath. The inflorescence is a panicle with two to six spikelike fingers, each 5–10 cm long and green or purple in color. Spikelets are arranged in two rows on one side of the winged axis. Reproduction is by seeds. It flowers from July to October.

Habitat

Smooth crabgrass is a native of Eurasia but presently infests the cultivated fields, gardens, lawns, roadsides, and waste soils of a wide portion of North America.

Suggested Control

Home Gardens—Use various type mulches to shade the soil from light and prevent seed germination, or clean cultivate and hand hoe; use DCPA, diphenamid, or trifluralin before seed germinates on registered crops. *Row Crops*—Cultivate when the weed is small and/or use a crop rotation system with crops tolerant to alachlor, EPTC, fluazifop-butyl, isopropalin, metolachlor, oryzalin, pebulate, pendimenthalin, propachlor, sethoxydin, trifluralin, or vernolate which control this weed. *Waste Areas*—Desiccate with paraquat, DSMA, or dinoseb plus oil. *Industrial*—Use a soil sterilant such as bromacil, hexazinone, or tebuthiuron.

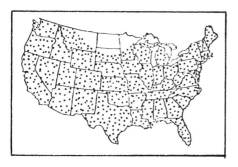

4F
Digitaria sanguinalis (L.)
  Scop.
Large crabgrass
Grass family (Gramineae)

Description

A summer annual grass with erect or prostrate 0.3–1.2 m long stems which are very often purplish in color and root at nodes. Leaf blades are 5–10 mm wide and 5–15 cm long. They are flat and hairy. The leaf sheaths, especially the lower ones, have numerous long hairs. The inflorescence is a panicle with 3 to 10 spikelike fingers, each 5–15 cm long, whorled at the top of stems. Spikelets are on one side of the axis. Reproduction is by seeds. It flowers from June to October.

Habitat

Large crabgrass is a native of Europe which has become a major weed in most cultivated fields, gardens, lawns, pastures, roadsides, and waste places across the United States.

Suggested Control

Turf and Home Lawns—Practice good turf management by maintaining proper pH and fertilization levels, set mower at proper height so as not to scalp the turf, and in early spring about time forsythia blooms apply a preemergence herbicide to prevent crabgrass establishment such as benefin, bensulide or DCPA. *Home Gardens*—Use various types of mulches to shade the soil from light and to prevent seed germination, or clean cultivate and hand hoe, or use DCPA, diphenamid or trifluralin on registered crops. *Row Crops*—Cultivate when the weed is small, before seed is set and/or use a crop rotation with crops tolerant to either alachlor, atrazine, butylate, chloramben, cyanazine, DCPA, diphenamid, EPTC, fluazifop-butyl, isopropalin, linuron, metolachlor, metribuzin, oryzalin, pebulate, propachlor, sethoxydim, terbacil, trifluralin, or vernolate, which can be used to control this weed. *Pastures*—Encourage competition through improved pasture management practices of proper pH adjustment, fertilization, and rotational grazing. *Roadsides and Waste Places*—Mow to prevent excessive growth or dessicate with paraquat or DSMA or if highly objectionable treat with soil sterilant such as bromacil, hexazimone, or tebuthiuron for total vegetation control.

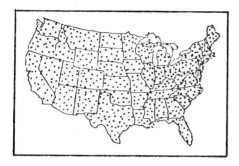

4G
Echinochloa crusgalli (L.)
Beauv.
Barnyardgrass
Grass family (Gramineae)

Description

Summer annual grass with fibrous, shallow roots. Stems are coarse, generally erect but occasionally prostrate, smooth, branching at the base, and 0.8–1.5 m long. Leaf blades are 5–15 mm wide, flat and smooth to slightly roughened. The sheaths are smooth. The inflorescence is an open panicle, green to reddish-purple in color, with 5 to 10 ascending, spreading branches (raceme), 3–5 mm long. Spikelets have conspicuous, short, stiff bristles and often with 10 mm long awn. Seeds are small, rough, brown, ovoid shaped, and ridged. Reproduction is by seeds. Flowers appear from June to October.

Habitat

Barnyardgrass occurs in cultivated soils, ditches, gardens, and bottom lands. It thrives in areas with good soil moisture. It is native of Europe.

Suggested Control

Home Gardens—Improve drainage, clean cultivate, or use various mulches to prevent seed germination. Herbicides such as DCPA, diphenamid, or trifluralin can be used on appropriate crops. *Cultivated Crops*—Clean cultivate or use alachlor, butylate, cyanazine, DCPA, diphenamid, diuron, EPTC, fluazifop-butyl, fluometuron, isopropalin, linuron, metolachlor, methazole, norflurazon, oryzalin, pebulate, pendimethalin, propachlor, propanil, sethoxydim terbacil, trifluralin, or vernolate. *Waste Areas*—Drain and desiccate with paraquat or DSMA. *Industrial*—Use a soil sterilant such as bromacil, hexazinone, or tebathiuron.

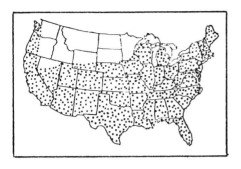

4H
Eleusine indica (L.) Gaertn.
Goosegrass
Grass family (Gramineae)

Description

A summer annual grass whose smooth stems branch at the base. The prostrate to ascending stems are 20–60 cm long and do not root at the nodes. Leaf blades are flat or nearly folded, thick, dark green, smooth to slightly roughened, 4–8 mm wide and 5–25 cm long. Leaf sheaths are compressed, keeled like a boat, and hairy toward the summit. The inflorescence is a panicle with 4 to 10 fingerlike spikes, each being 3–8 cm long. Spikelets are flattened, 3–5 mm long and have three to six seeds along one edge of the winged axis. Seeds are small, 1–1.5 mm long, ridged and reddish brown in color. Flowers appear from July to October.

Habitat

Goosegrass reproduces by seeds and occurs in cultivated fields, lawns, gardens, roadsides, and waste places. It is a native of the Old World.

Suggested Control

Turf and Home Lawns—Practice good turf management by maintaining proper pH and fertilization levels, proper mowing height so as not to scalp the turf, and apply a preemergence herbicide such as benefin, bensulide or DCPA to prevent goosegrass establishment. *Home Gardens*—Use various types of mulches to shade the soil from light and to prevent seed germination, or clean cultivate and hand hoe, or use DCPA, diphenamid, or trifluralin on registered crops. *Row Crops*—Cultivate when the weed is small before seed is set and/or use a crop rotation with appropriate herbicides. Alachlor, atrazine, butylate, chloramben, cyanazine, DCPA, diphenamid, EPTC, fluazifop-butyl, fluchloralin, isopropalin, linuron, metolachlor, metribuzin, oryzalin, pebulate, propachlor, terbacil, sethoxydim, trifluralin, or vernolate are labeled for goosegrass control. *Roadsides and Waste Places*—Mow to prevent excessive growth or dessicate with paraquat or DSMA or if highly objectionable apply a soil sterilant for total vegetation control.

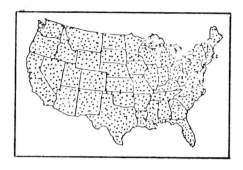

4I
Eragrostis cilianensis (All.)
Lutati
Stinkgrass
Grass family (Gramineae)

Description

This summer annual grass forms dense tufts with many stems arising from a central crown. Slender stems are 30–60 cm tall, erect to ascending and branched at the top. Leaf blades are flat, smooth, 3–6 mm wide, with margins bordered by warty glands. Sheaths have hairs on the upper portion. The open inflorescence is a many-branched panicle, bearing numerous spikelets. Spikelets are 3–12 mm long, flat, dark gray-green to purple and bear 20 to 40 florets or seeds. The orange-red seeds are ovoid and tiny, about 0.7 mm long. Reproduction is by seeds. Flowers appear from June to October.

Habitat

Stinkgrass can be found in cultivated fields, gardens, lawns, and waste places. It is a native of Europe.

Suggested Control

Home Lawns—Practice good turf management by maintaining proper pH and fertility levels, and apply a preemergence herbicide in the early spring to prevent establishment of new seedlings. Possible herbicides are benefin, bensulide, or DCPA. *Gardens*—Use various mulches to prevent seed germination and establishment or clean cultivate and hand hoe to destroy all plants before seed formation, or use DCPA, diphenamid, or trifluralin. *Cultivated Fields*—Cultivate several times in the spring before planting or use alachlor, cyanazine, diphenamid, EPTC, metolachlor, or trifluralin. *Waste Areas*—Dessicate with paraquat or DSMA. *Industrial*—Use a soil sterilant such as bromacil, hexazinone, or tebuthiuron.

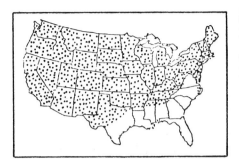

5A
Hordeum jubatum L.
Foxtail barley
Grass family (Gramineae)

Description

A perennial grass that forms clumps and has a densely fibrous root system. The 30–60 cm tall stems are generally erect, but occasionally recline at the base. Leaf blades are rough on the upper surface and 3–6 mm wide. Leaf sheaths are smooth to short hairy. The inflorescence is a 6–12 cm long nodding spike that is enveloped by the sheath at the base and has a rather soft, yellow-green or purplish beard of bristles about 5 cm long. Spikelets with lowermost glumes are bristlelike. Seeds are yellow, hairy, and 3 mm long. Reproduction is by seeds. Flowers appear from June to September.

Habitat

Foxtail barley occurs in pastures, meadows, crop lands, roadsides, and waste places. In irrigated areas of the West, foxtail barley often occurs in poorly drained fields on areas where water is allowed to pond for short periods of time. Native of northeastern North America.

Suggested Control

Cropland—Use a good crop rotation with cultivated row crops. In irrigated areas, improve drainage and use better water management practices to prevent ponding. Herbicides which control new seedlings are alachlor, benefin, butylate, EPTC, metolachlor, pendimethalin, trifluralin, or terbacil. *Established Forage Legumes*—Cultivate with a spring-tooth cultivator in late winter or early spring before regrowth occurs to rip established plants out or apply pronamide or terbacil. *Roadsides and Waste Places*—For burn down, spot spray with dalapon, glyphosate, or paraquat or for total vegetation control use a soil sterilant.

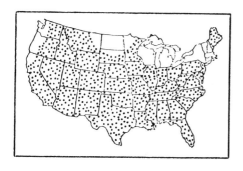

5B
Hordeum pusillum Nutt.
Little barley
Grass family (Gramineae)

Description

This small (20–40 cm tall) tuft grass has stems that recline at first and then become erect. The thin 2–6 mm wide leaf blades stand erect or nearly so and are rough on the upper surface. The leaf sheath is smooth or with short hairs. The inflorescence is a flattened, erect spike, 2–6 cm long, enclosed by a sheath at the base with short (1.5 cm long) stiff bristles. Spikelets with lowermost bracts of two types: bristlelike, and broadened to 1 mm toward the apex; both are only 1–1.5 mm long, much shorter than those of foxtail barley (*Hordeum jubatum*). Seeds are yellow, hairy on top, and 3–7 mm long. Reproduction is by seeds. It flowers from April to June.

Habitat

Little barley can be found in turf, pastures, small grain fields, and waste areas. It is native of Europe.

Suggested Control

Turf—Follow good turf management practices of proper pH adjustment and fertilization and cut regularly to prevent seed formation. This weed does not appear on any herbicide label but preemergence herbicides such as benefin, DCPA, or bensulide used for control of annual grasses generally control little barley. *Small Grains*—Cultivate thoroughly before planting; sow sufficient seed to obtain a dense stand and fertilize sufficiently to allow small grains to grow rapidly and thus offer heavy competition to the weed. *Pastures*—Use good pasture management techniques of proper pH adjustment, fertilization, rotational grazing, and clipping following grazing. *Waste Areas*—For burn down spray with paraquat or for total vegetation control, use a soil sterilant.

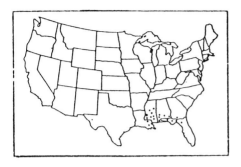

5C
Imperata cylindrica (L.)
P. Beauv.
Cogongrass
Grass family (Gramineae)

Description

Perennial grass that has strongly developed rhizomes. The erect stems have few nodes and are 0.8–1.2 m tall. The flat leaf blades have a white midvein, gradually become more narrow toward the base, and are 5–15 mm wide and up to 150 cm long. Sheaths have long hairs near the leaf base. The inflorescence is a silvery, dense spike-like panicle from 15 to 25 cm long. Reproduction is by seeds and rhizomes. It flowers during the summer months.

Habitat

Cogongrass is a recently introduced species and may be found in pastures, nurseries, and highway rights-of-way. It is native to tropical Asia and is one of the world's worse weeds.

Suggested Control

Because of the importance of this weed in world agriculture, every effort should be made to control the spread of this weed. Preventive measures should be used to prevent introduction of this weed into new areas (see page 2). Seed production must be prevented by destroying the plant before flowering. On a small area, the plants may be dug with a sharp shovel making certain that no rhizome pieces remain in the soil. All parts should be burned. Persistent care must be taken to assure that new plants do not become established. Dalapon and glyphosate have given some control as spot treatments.

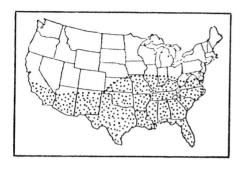

5D
Leptochloa filiformis (Lam.)
Beauv.
Red sprangletop
Grass family (Gramineae)

Description

Summer annual grass with erect stems that branch at base and are often dwarfed (0.3–1.2 m tall). The thin flat leaf blades are soft on the surface but rough to the touch on the edges, thin and 5–10 mm wide. Sheaths are usually overlapping and covered with long, bulbous-based hairs. The inflorescence is a panicle, somewhat sticky, purplish, 20–50 cm long, and has many slender and spreading branches (racemes) that are 5–15 cm long. Spikelets are two to four flowered or seeded, small, reddish-brown or purple and slightly hairy. It reproduces by seeds. It flowers from July to October.

Habitat

Red sprangletop is found in cultivated fields, gardens, roadsides, and fence rows. It is native of tropical America.

Suggested Control

Home Gardens—Use various mulches to prevent seed germination and establishment or clean cultivate and hand hoe to destroy all plants before seed formation or use trifluralin on properly labeled crops. *Cultivated Crops*—Use good crop rotation practices. While this weed is not included on any herbicide label except pronamide and trifluralin, other herbicides such as alachlor, butylate, EPTC, fluazifop-butyl, oryzalin, pendimethalin, propachlor, sethoxydim, and vernolate will probably control this weed. *Fence Rows and Waste Areas*—Burn down with paraquat and/or use a soil sterilant.

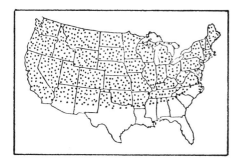

5E
Lolium multiflorum Lam.
Italian ryegrass
Grass family (Gramineae)

Description

This short-lived perennial grass has 30–80 cm tall stems that are usually rough below the spike. The flat leaf blades are 2–4 mm wide and rough on the surface. The inflorescence is an erect elongated spike. Each joint is rough on the side opposite the spikelets. Spikelets are 1–2 cm long and have 6–15 florets or seeds. The bracts (glumes) are about 7 mm long and have slender awns up to 8 mm long, though sometimes they are awnless. Seeds are narrowly oval, brownish and usually have a short-beard at the tip. Reproduction is by seeds. Flowers appear from May to June.

Habitat

Italian ryegrass occurs in small grain fields, pastures, especially those planted to orchardgrass and tall fescue, roadsides, gardens, and waste places. It is native to Europe.

Suggested Control

Home Gardens—Thorough land preparation in the fall or spring followed by cultivation and hand hoeing of scattered plants. Various mulches can be used with success. Possible herbicides are dalapon to control established plants, and trifluralin on registered crops to prevent seedling establishment. *Small Grains and Grass Crops*— Prepare a good seed bed before planting. Sow sufficient seed to obtain a dense stand and fertilize so that the crop can offer heavy competition with the weed. Use a crop rotation with broadleaf crops where a herbicide for control of grasses such as alachlor, benefin, diphenamid, fluazifop-butyl, isopropalin, metolachlor, pronamide, propachlor, sethoxydim, or terbacil can be used. *Roadside and Waste Places*—Use dalapon for selective control or paraquat for burn down or a soil sterilant for total vegetation control.

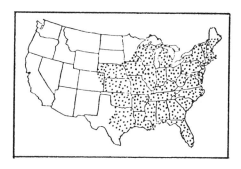

5F
Muhlenbergia schreberi
J. F. Gmel.
Nimblewill
Grass family (Gramineae)

Description

This summer-growing perennial has a hard crown and rooting runners. A single plant usually forms a wide patch more than 30 cm in diameter. Very slender, smooth stems recline at the base, branch throughout, and root at the lower nodes and are up to 30 cm long. The flat, smooth leaf blades are 4 mm wide and 5 cm long. Leaf sheaths are loose and smooth. The inflorescence is a nodding, slender panicle, 5–20 cm long, with loosely arranged spikelets. The spikelets are single-flowered or seeded with a delicate bristle or awn, 2–4 mm long. Reproduction is by seeds and small runners. It flowers in late summer from August to October.

Habitat

Nimblewill occurs in shaded lawns and pastures, around buildings and under shrubbery. It is native to North America.

Suggested Control

Lawns, Shrubbery, etc.—Thorough removal of all plant parts including root stalks, selective killing with glyphosate using caution to prevent misapplication on desirable plants by using a shielded sprayer or wiper type applicator. After killing the weed reseed area with desirable grass or ground cover. *Waste Areas and Fence Rows*—Use a soil sterilant such as bromacil or tebuthiuron.

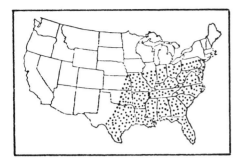

5G
Panicum anceps Michx.
Two-edge panicgrass
Grass family (Gramineae)

Description

A summer growing perennial that has an extensive underground system of thick, scaly rootstocks. The erect 0.5–1.0 m tall stems arise from a central tuft. Leaf blades are flat, smooth on both surfaces or with a few hairs and are 6–12 mm wide and 20–40 cm long. Leaf sheaths are smooth to slightly hairy. The inflorescence is an open panicle, 10–40 cm long and pyramid-shaped with many spreading or ascending branches. The spikelets are single-flowered with a single, ovoid seed, arching away from the axis and surrounded by hardened floral bracts. Reproduction occurs by seeds and rootstocks. Flowering is from June to October.

Habitat

Two-edge panicgrass is a native of North America and occurs in pastures, lawns, fairways, fence rows, cultivated fields, and waste places.

Suggested Control

Lawns and Turf—Thorough removal of all plant parts including rootstalks or selective killing with glyphosate. Reseed areas with desirable grass followed by good turf management techniques. *Pastures*—Use good pasture management techniques of adequate pH adjustment and fertilization, rotational grazing and mowing after grazing. Spot spray with dalapon or glyphosate and reseed with desired grass. *Fence Rows and Waste Areas*—Use dalapon or glyphosate for control of existing plants or a soil sterilant.

5H
Panicum capillare L.
Witchgrass
Grass family (Gramineae)

Description

This summer annual grass has fibrous roots. Erect or ascending stems are branched from the base, spreading, and up to 70 cm tall. The leaves and especially the leaf sheaths are covered with dense soft hairs. The inflorescence is a diffusely branched panicle, that becomes lax and open at maturity, often breaking from stem and being blown about by wind. It is usually two-thirds as long as the entire plant. Spikelets are single-flowered on long pedicels, 2–3 mm long, with a single shiny, smooth, greenish to grayish seed, surrounded by a hardened floral bract (lemma). Reproduction is by seeds. Flowers appear from July to September.

Habitat

Witchgrass can be found in cultivated fields, roadsides, meadows, and waste places. It is native of North America.

Suggested Control

Cropland—Clean cultivate and do not allow seed to form. Use either alachlor, benefin, butylate, chloramben, diphenamid, EPTC, fluazifop-butyl, metolachlor, pendimethalin, sethoxydim, simazine, or trifluralin to control this weed in labeled crops. *Fence Rows and Waste Places*—Prevent seed formation and weed establishment by cultivation, hand hoeing, etc., or spray with dalapon, glyphosate, paraquat, or with a soil sterilant.

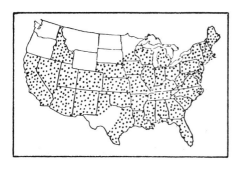

51
Panicum dichotomiflorum
　Michx.
Fall panicum
Grass family (Gramineae)

Description

Fall panicum is a summer annual grass that branches extensively from the base and nodes. Smooth, slightly flat stems are 0.4–1.0 m long and mainly erect though lower nodes may be somewhat reclining. Leaf blades are smooth though may be sparsely hairy on the upper surfaces, with a prominent midrib, 5–15 mm wide and 12–60 cm long. Inflorescences are open panicles, 12–20 cm long, both terminal and axillary. Spikelets are single-flowered with a single smooth, yellow seed, about 2 mm long, surrounded by a hardened floral bract (lemma). It reproduces by seeds. Flowers emerge from July to September.

Habitat

Fall panicum is native to North America. It can be found in cultivated fields especially corn and soybeans, roadsides, fence rows, and waste places.

Suggested Control

Cultivated Fields—Use a crop rotation where it is possible to cultivate the crop until late in the season to prevent seed formation and maturation and/or a crop where it is possible to use one of the following herbicides: alachlor, benefin, butylate, EPTC, fluazifop-butyl, metolachlor, napropamide, oryzalin, pendimethalin, trifluralin, or vernolate. Also under certain conditions, one of the urea-type herbicides or a combination of atrazine plus cyanazine or simazine will give adequate control. *Roadsides, Fence Rows, or Waste Areas*—Use close mowing until late in the season to prevent seed production, or paraquat for chemical burn down, or a soil sterilant.

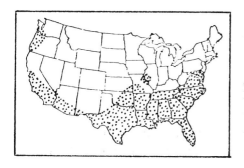

6A
Paspalum dilatatum Poir.
Dallisgrass
Grass family (Gramineae)

Description

This tufted summer-growing perennial grass grows from a hardy crown. The smooth stems are 0.4 to 1.7 m tall. The flat slightly hairy leaves are 4–12 mm wide and 10–30 cm long. The inflorescence has three to five fingerlike branches (racemes), each is 4–15 cm long, growing at the ends of stems. The spikelets are fringed with silky hairs and are 3 mm long, borne in pairs on one side of the raceme, and contain one ovoid seed. Many times a small brownish black ergot hangs from each seed. Reproduction is by seeds and rootstocks. Flowers appear from May to October.

Habitat

This introduced grass is native to Uruguay and Argentina. It infests lawns, cultivated soils, roadsides, pastures, and ditchbanks. It is a problem weed in lawns because the flower stalk re-grows rapidly after mowing, giving the appearance of many defiant flags waving over the well-trimmed sod.

Suggested Control

Home Lawns and Turf—Destroy established plants before turf is established or by selectively removing with a shovel from an established turf. Repeated spot applications of DSMA, MSMA, or glyphosate may be used to destroy established plants, followed by reseeding of the desired grass in the treated areas. Many of the herbicides used to prevent germination of crabgrass in turf will also prevent dallisgrass germination. *Pastures*—Rotate with a cultivated crop or physically remove with a grubbing hoe or spot treatment with glyphosate to destroy existing plants. *Roadsides or Ditchbanks*—Use glyphosate as a spot treatment to destroy existing plants or use a soil sterilant such as tebuthiuron for a total vegetation.

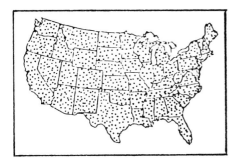

6B
Poa annua L.
Annual bluegrass
Grass family (Gramineae)

Description

Annual bluegrass is a small tufted grass. Germination may occur in late fall or early spring. Stems are few to several, prostrate, reclining and ascending but rarely erect and are up to 30 cm long, though generally much shorter. Leaf blades are soft, and 2–3 mm wide. Sheaths are loose and keeled with a boat-shaped tip. The inflorescence is a panicle, 2–8 mm long, with a few ascending branches bearing crowded spikelets above the middle. The 3–5 mm long spikelets are green, slightly fattened, and have three to six flowers and seeds. Seeds are small and yellow or tan in color. Reproduction is by seeds. Flowers appear from April to June.

Habitat

Annual bluegrass occurs mainly in lawns and gardens. It is native to Eurasia.

Suggested Control

Home Lawns and Turf—Improve turf management practices such as proper fertilization, pH adjustment, higher mowing height with no scalping and planting a turfgrass better suited to the environment. Apply benefin, bensulide, DCPA, or oxadiazon in early spring or late August before annual bluegrass germinates. *Home Gardens*—Prevent establishment and seed production by clean cultivation and hand hoeing or use chloramben, DCPA, diphenamid, or trifluralin on nonsusceptible-labeled crops.

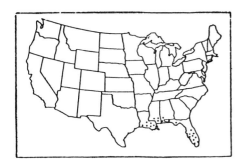

6C
Rottboellia exaltata (L.) L.f.
Itchgrass
Grass family (Gramineae)

Description

Tufted, erect growing annual grass that has stilt roots. The smooth stems are robust and 1.0–3.0 m tall. The leaf blades are flat, rough on both surfaces, 1.0–2.5 cm wide and 20–60 cm long. The leaf sheaths have bristly stinging hairs that break off on contact. The inflorescence is a solitary raceme at the top of each stem. Spikes are cylindrical and 10–15 cm long. Spikelets are sessile, 5–7 mm long and fall off successively at maturity, starting from the apex. Reproduction is by seeds. It flowers during July and August.

Habitat

Itchgrass may be found growing in cultivated fields, along ditchbanks, and in waste places along the gulf coast in the southeastern states. It is native to India.

Suggested Control

Cropland—This weed should be controlled and its spread halted. A crop–herbicide rotation system should be implemented where either pendimethalin or trifluralin can be applied prior to planting the crop followed by fluazifop-butyl or sethoxydim applied postemergence to control any escaped plants. *Noncropland Areas*— In limited research, sulfometuron has given excellent control.

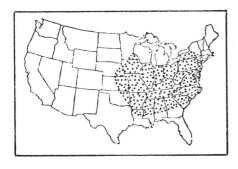

6D
Setaria faberi Herrm.
Giant foxtail
Grass family (Gramineae)

Description

An annual grass that branches at the base and has tall (0.8–1.8 m) weak stems that are often bent over. The broad (7–17 mm) leaf blades are softly pubescent to hairless beneath and have straight, stiff hairs on the upper surface. The leaf sheaths are hairy at the top. The inflorescence is a dense, cylindric, spikelike panicle, 7–20 cm long, many times conspicuously nodding. Spikelets are 3 mm subtended by three to six bristles that are 3–10 mm long. The seeds are mostly green and are intermediate in size between seeds of green and yellow foxtails. It reproduces by seeds. Flowers are produced from June to September.

Habitat

This native of China occurs over a large area of the eastern United States and can be found in crop fields, gardens, roadsides, hay fields, and waste places.

Suggested Control

Home Gardens—Prevent seed production by cultivation and hand hoeing of scattered plants. Mulches can be used with good success to prevent seed germination and establishment. Possible herbicides are DCPA, diphenamid, and trifluralin. *Cropland*—Prepare a well-tilled seedbed before planting and cultivate thereafter. Foxtail is included on many herbicide labels. Possible herbicides include alachlor, ametryn, atrazine, butylate, chloramben, cyanazine, DCPA, DSMA, diphenamid, diuron, EPTC, fluazifop-butyl, fluometuron, isopropalin, linuron, metolachlor, metribuzin, MSMA, oryzalin, paraquat, pebulate, pendimenthalin, prometryn, propachlor, propazine, sethoxydim, simazine, terbacil, trifluralin, and vernolate. *Hayfields*—Mow before weed can produce seed. Use an appropriate herbicide in early spring or after cutting to prevent seed germination. *Waste Places and Roadsides*—Burn down with paraquat or apply residual soil sterilant before seed germination.

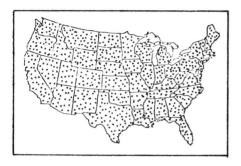

6E
Setaria glauca (L.) Beauv.
Yellow foxtail
Grass family (Gramineae)

Description

This fibrous-rooted, summer annual grass has multiple branches at the base. Its stems are erect or slightly prostrate, tufted, and 0.4–1.0 m tall. The blue-green leaf blades are flat, occasionally with a spiral twist and have many long, soft hairs toward the base on the upper surface. The leaf blade is 4–10 mm wide and about 25 cm long. The leaf sheaths are strongly keeled. The inflorescence is an erect dense, cylindric, spikelike panicle, that turns yellow at maturity. It is 9–14 mm thick and 2–12 cm long with the axis being densely hairy. Spikelets are about 3–3.5 mm long and subtended by five or more bristles that are 3–10 mm inch long. Reproduction is by seeds. Flowers appear from July to September.

Habitat

Yellow foxtail infests cultivated soils, gardens, roadsides, fence rows, and waste grounds. It is a native of Europe.

Suggested Control

Home Gardens—Prevent seed production by cultivation and hand hoeing of scattered plants. Mulches can be used with good success to prevent seed germination and establishment. Possible herbicides are DCPA, diphenamid, and trifluralin. *Cropland*—Prepare a well-tilled seedbed before planting and cultivate thereafter. Foxtail is included on many herbicide labels. Select a herbicide labeled for the desired crop and recommended by the local agricultural extension service. Possible herbicides include alachlor, ametryn, atrazine, butylate, chloramben, cyanazine, DCPA, DSMA, diphenamid, diuron, EPTC, fluazifop-butyl, flumeturon, isopropalin, linuron, metolachlor, metribuzin, MSMA, oryzalin, paraquat, pebulate, pendimethalin, prometryn, propachlor, propazine, sethoxydim, simazine, terbacil, trifluralin, and vernolate. *Hayfields*—Mow before weed can produce seed. Use an appropriately labeled herbicide in early spring or after cutting to prevent seed germination. *Waste Places and Roadsides*—Burn down with paraquat or apply residual soil sterilant before seed germination.

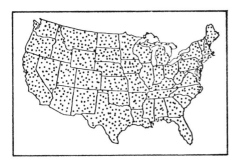

6F
Setaria viridis (L.) Beauv.
Green foxtail
Grass family (Gramineae)

Description

An annual grass where stems are usually branched and often jointed at the base. Leaf blades are flat, hairless on upper surface, and usually less than 10 mm wide. Sheaths are short and hairy. The inflorescence is a dense, 1–7 cm long cylindric, spikelike panicle that stands erect and is green to light brown or purple. Spikelets are about 2–2.5 mm long and are subtended by one to three bristles that are 2–10 mm long. Seeds are green and 2 mm long, but uniformly smaller than those of the giant foxtail. Reproduction is by seeds. Flowers occur from June to September.

Habitat

Green foxtail occurs in cultivated fields, roadsides, lawns, gardens, and waste places. It is native of Eurasia.

Suggested Control

Home Gardens—Prevent seed production by cultivation and hand hoeing of scattered plants. Mulches can be used with good success to prevent seed germination and seedling establishment. Possible herbicides are DCPA, diphenamid, and trifluralin. *Cropland*—Prepare a well-tilled seedbed before planting and cultivate thereafter. Foxtail is included on many herbicide labels. Select a herbicide labeled for the desired crop and recommended by the local agricultural extension service. Possible herbicides include alachlor, ametryn, atrazine, butylate, chloramben, cyanazine, DCPA, DSMA, diphenamid, diuron, EPTC, fluazifop-butyl, fluometuron, isopropalin, linuron, metolachlor, metribuzin, MSMA, oryzalin, paraquat, pebulate, pendimethalin, prometryn, propachlor, propazine, sethoxydim, simazine, terbacil, trifluralin, and vernolate. *Hayfields*—Mow before weed can produce seed. Use an appropriately labeled herbicide in early spring or after cutting to prevent seed germination. *Waste Places and Roadsides*—Burn down with paraquat or apply residual soil sterilant before seed germination.

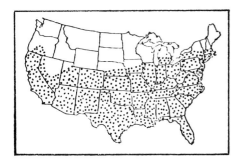

6G
Sorghum halepense (L.) Pers.
Johnsongrass
Grass family (Gramineae)

Description

This coarse summer-growing perennial grass reproduces by both seeds and large rhizomes. The stems are erect, thick, and 0.5–2.0 m tall. Leaf blades are smooth, 10–30 mm wide and 20–50 cm long. The purplish inflorescence is a large 20–50 cm long open panicle. Spikelets are sessile, ovoid, reddish-brown, 4–5 mm long and have an easily broken awn that is 1 cm long, twisted at base and bent at the top. Seeds are almost 3 mm long, oval, reddish-brown and have fine lines on the surface. Flowering occurs from June to October.

Habitat

Johnsongrass was introduced as a pasture grass and has become one of our most tenacious weeds. It may be found in gardens, cultivated fields, fence rows, roadsides, and waste areas. It is a native of the Mediterranean region.

Suggested Control

Home Gardens—Hand hoeing and cultivation can be used to control the rhizome system, but green growth should never be allowed to reach 8 in. in height, thus preventing food storage and causing eventual starvation. Dalapon and glyphosate can be used for spot treatment. *Cropland*—Each control system must include methods for controlling both seedlings and rhizomes. Foliar applications of dalapon, fluazifop-butyl, glyphosate, and sethoxydim will control plants originating from seed or rhizomes. DSMA and MSMA will control seedlings. When used according to specific label instructions, butylate, EPTC, pendimethalin, and trifluralin will control seedling and rhizome johnsongrass. They must be fortified with liberal cultivation. Also, alachlor, metolachlor, oryzalin, and pendimethalin will control seedling johnsongrass. *Fence Rows, Roadsides, etc.*—Apply dalapon or glyphosate. *Industrial Sites*—Use bromacil, sulfometuron, or tebuthiuron.

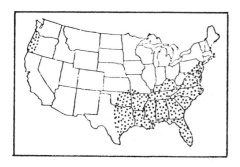

6H
Sporobolus poiretii
(R. & S.) Hitchc.
Smutgrass
Grass family (Gramineae)

Description

Smutgrass is a summer-growing perennial bunchgrass. Its wiry erect stems may be solitary or in tufts. They have only two or three leaves and are 30–90 cm tall. Leaf blades are flat or slightly rolled inward, 2–5 mm wide and 10–30 cm long, and taper to a fine point. The inflorescence is a cylindric, stiff, 10–40 cm long panicle whose branches may be ascending but are usually close to the central axis. Spikelets are one-seeded, greenish in color, about 2 mm long and crowded on the slender erect branches. Reproduction is by seeds. It flowers from May to October.

Habitat

This native of tropical America now infests pastures, roadsides, fence rows, and waste places in the Southeastern and Northwestern States.

Suggested Control

Pastures—Completely renovate pasture and rotate to a cultivated crop for several years. If not possible, destroy existing stand by discing or applying dalapon or glyphosate and replanting a desirable pasture species. Active research is being conducted in several areas. Contact local agricultural extension service for latest recommendations. *Fence Rows and Waste Places*—Spot spray with dalapon or glyphosate to control existing plants and apply a soil sterilant to prevent reinfestation.

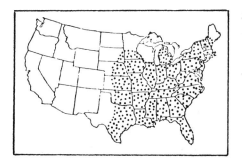

6I
Tridens flavus (L.) Hitchc.
Purpletop
Grass family (Gramineae)

Description

A summer-growing perennial bunchgrass that has stems up to 1.5 m tall. The stems are erect and are sticky or greasy below the inflorescence. Leaf blades are 3–8 mm wide, smooth, rolled inward, and tapered. Leaf sheaths are compressed, keeled at the base, and bearded at the summit. The inflorescence, an open panicle, is purple to black in color and 15–35 cm long. Its branches are distant, drooping, the lower portion is naked, and the swelling at the base of the branches is bearded. Spikelets have five to eight seeds and are 6–9 mm long. Seed is its only mode of reproduction. Flowers appear from July to October.

Habitat

Purpletop is a weed in pastures, roadsides, fence rows, and waste areas. It is a native of North America.

Suggested Control

Pastures—Plow or mechanically till and rotate pasture with a cultivated crop, and use appropriate herbicides for preventing re-establishment of grasses from seed. If in permanent pasture, use good management practices, i.e., adjust soil pH, fertilize, rotate pasture grazing, clip pastures after grazing, graze or mow often enough to prevent seed production; spot spray with dalapon or glyphosate for selective control and reseed with desired species. *Roadsides, Fence Rows and Waste Places*—Apply dalapon or glyphosate for control of existing vegetation or bromacil, or tebuthiuron for residual vegetation control.

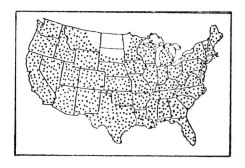

7A
Cyperus esculentus L.
Yellow nutsedge
Sedge family (Cyperaceae)

Description

This perennial sedge has numerous threadlike stolons, each ending in a small tuber. Stems are erect, triangular in cross section, solid and 20–60 cm tall. Leaves are three-ranked, narrow, arise from the base and are grasslike. The terminal inflorescence radiates from one point, with numerous yellow-brown, widely spaced, extremely narrow spikelets, each 8–30 mm long, all are subtended as a group by 3 to 9 conspicuous leafy bracts, one or more of which exceed the length of the inflorescence. Seeds are elliptic-oblong, yellow-brown, three-angled, 1.2–2 mm long. It reproduces by seeds and stolons terminated by hard tubers. Flowers appear from July to September.

Habitat

Yellow nutsedge is one of the most troublesome weeds in the world. It can be found in many cultivated soils, pastures, gardens, and waste places. It is native of North America.

Suggested Control

Home Gardens—Constant, persistant, clean cultivation and hand hoeing at weekly intervals throughout the season to prevent seed and nutlet formation, or hire a professional to use a soil fumigant such as methyl bromide to kill seed and nutlets in the soil. *Cropland*—Improve drainage and rotate crops so as to use herbicides that will control yellow nutsedge. Effective herbicides are butylate, EPTC, pebulate, and vernolate, applied preplant incorporated, and bentazon applied postemergence. *Fence Rows, Waste Areas and Industrial Sides*—Apply a soil sterilant labeled for nutsedge control such as bromacil or sulfometuron.

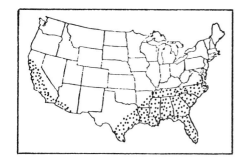

7B
Cyperus rotundus L.
Purple nutsedge
Sedge family (Cyperaceae)

Description

This perennial herb has numerous stolons bearing numerous small tubers in chains. Erect stems are 10–40 cm tall, triangular and solid. Leaves are narrow, 3–6 mm wide, grasslike, and arise from the base. The terminal inflorescence has numerous, widely spaced, extremely narrow, 8–25 mm long chesnut-brown to purple spikelets radiating from one point. All are subtended as a group by three to six conspicuous leafy bracts, none of which is longer than the inflorescence. The three-angled seeds are linear-oblong, olive gray-brown in color and approximately 1.5 mm long. Purple nutsedge is one of the world's worst weeds and reproduces by seeds and tubers. Flowers appear from July to October.

Habitat

Purple nutsedge is found in cultivated sandy fields, gardens, lawns, and waste places in the warmer areas of the United States. It is a native of Eurasia.

Suggested Control

Home Gardens—Use constant, persistant (every 10 days) clean cultivation and hand hoeing throughout the season to induce germination of tubers in the soil and to prevent seed and tuber formation, or hire a professional to use a soil fumigant such as methyl bromide to kill the seed and tubers in the soil. *Cropland*—Rotate crops so as to use herbicides that will control purple nutsedge, i.e., butylate, EPTC, pebulate, and vernolate (bentazon will not control purple nutsedge). *Fence Rows, Waste Areas and Industrial Sites*—Use a soil sterilant labeled for nutsedge control, such as sulfometuron.

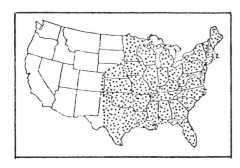

7C
Scirpus americanus Pers.
American bulrush
Sedge family (Cyperaceae)

Description

Perennial aquatic or marsh herb arises from an enlogate rhizome. Its triangular erect stems are 1–6 mm thick and 0.6–1.2 m tall. They are occasionally twisted and have concave sides. Its linear elongate, 5–60 cm long leaves are sharp pointed and arise near the base of the stems. The terminal inflorescence has several red-brown, densely clustered, elliptic spikelets, each 5–20 mm long and the group is subtended by a single erect, 3–12 cm long bract that appears to be a continuation of the stem. The smooth brown seeds are obovoid, short-tipped and 2.5–3 mm long. Reproduction is by seeds and rhizomes. It flowers from June to September.

Habitat

American bulrush occurs in the shallow water of marshes and ponds and along lake and stream banks. It is a native of Eurasia.

Suggested Control

Aquatic—Deepen the edges of the pond or lake or spray 2,4-D or diquat directly on the plant or apply dichlobenil in early spring before growth is initiated.

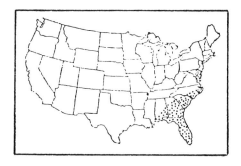

7D
Pistia stratioites L.
Waterlettuce
Arum family (Araceae)

Description

Waterlettuce is a free floating perennial aquatic herb, with a tuft of long, unbranched fibrous roots extending from an underwater rhizome. The light green, spongy inflated leaves are softly hairy and form a rosette. They are up to 50 cm long and have strong veination from the base. Numerous, small, inconspicuous flowers are borne in the center of the plant. Seed production is limited under natural conditions. Most reproduction occurs vegetatively by buds. Waterlettuce flowers from May to September.

Habitat

This native of tropical Asia may be found in still waters of ponds and lakes or slow-flowing streams and canals in the southeastern states.

Suggested Control

Aquatic—Do not introduce into your aquatic areas. If already infested, treat with copper sulfate plus diquat or diquat alone.

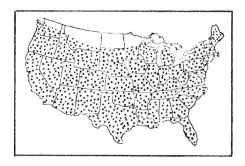

7E
Lemna minor L.
Common duckweed
Duckweed family
(Lemnaceae)

Description

Common duckweed is an annual, free-floating aquatic weed. Its small round leaves are approximately 2–4 mm in diameter and somewhat elliptic or obovate in shape, commonly keeled on the back and generally grouped or attached in pairs. Sometimes a colony of more than two, generally five to eight leaves are attached as a result of vegetative reproduction. A single root generally extends from a small pouch on the lower surface of the leaf. Flowers are very small and are borne on a tiny stalk arising from the leaf edge. This flower produces some seeds. Reproduction occurs by seeds, budding, and breaking apart of leaves.

Habitat

This small plant may be found in the still waters of ponds, lakes, and very slow-moving streams and canals. It can form extensive vegetative mats that may completely cover the water surface. It is native of both the New and Old World.

Suggested Control

Aquatic—Cut brush and trees around the edge of lake or pond and clear logs, emerged weeds, etc., from water surface to allow wind to blow duckweed onto the shores, or keep six to eight tame ducks per surface acre of pond and thus biologically control duckweed, or spray with diquat or 2,4-D in accord with label restrictions.

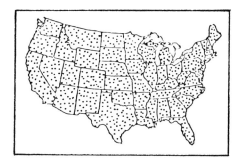

7F
Spirodela polyrhiza (L.)
   Schleid.
Giant duckweed
Duckweed family
(Lemnaceae)

Description

This annual free-floating aquatic herb has ovate leaves that are pur-ple-red on the lower surface and dark green on the upper surface. They have 5 to 11 palmately arranged veins and are about 6 mm wide and 3–10 mm long. Small roots (4–9) protrude from the lower surface of each leaf. This plant occurs in colonies of two or more leaves attached together as a result of budding. Very small flowers form, one on each lateral leaf margin, but flower formation is rare. Reproduction is mainly by vegetative budding.

Habitat

Giant duckweed may form extensive mats via budding that may com-pletely cover the surface of stagnant waters of lakes and ponds. It is a native of tropical Asia.

Suggested Control

Aquatic—Cut brush and trees around the edge of lake or pond and clear logs, emerged weeds, etc., from water surface to allow wind to blow duckweed onto shores, or keep six to eight tame ducks per surface acre of pond and thus biologically control duckweed, or spray with diquat or 2,4-D in accord with label restrictions.

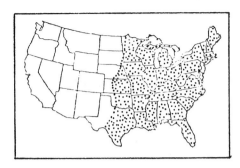

7G
Wolffia columbiana Karst.
Watermeal
Duckweed family
(Lemnaceae)

Description

This tiny annual free-floating aquatic herb is probably the smallest flowering plant and weed. The individual plants look like small globular particles of ground grain. The light green, round or elliptic leaves are commonly 0.3–1 mm long and nearly as wide. There are no roots. Rarely tiny flowers are produced that break through the upper leaf surface. The plants generally float on the water surface or just below, but may be found up to 30 cm below the surface. Vegetative budding is the major means of reproduction. The plants may lie dormant on rather dry soil along a pond shore and grow again when the water is available.

Habitat

Watermeal occurs in still waters of ponds and small lakes where it forms a thick green mat on the water surface making the water green. It is a native of tropical America.

Suggested Control

Aquatic—Remove all restrictions such as brush, trees, logs, weeds, trash, etc., from the shallow water around the edges of the pond or lake so that the wind and wave action can move weeds onto shores, or biologically control weed by keeping six to eight tame ducks per surface acre of pond or physically remove watermeal with a fine mesh seine.

1A *Chara* spp. (Musk-grass)

1B *Pithophora* spp. (Pithophora)

1C *Equisetum arvense* L. (Field horsetail)

1D *Pteridium aquilinum* (L.) Kuhn (Bracken)

1E *Azolla caroliniana* Willd. (Atlantic azolla)

1F *Salvinia rotundifolia* Willd. (Salvinia)

1G *Typha latifolia* L. (Common cattail)

1H *Potamogeton crispus* L. (Curlyleaf pondweed)

1I *Potamogeton illinoensis* Morong (Illinois pondweed)

2A *Potamogeton nodosus* Poir.
(American pondweed)

2B *Potamogeton pectinatus* L.
(Sago pondweed)

2C *Potamogeton pusillus* L.
(Small pondweed)

2D *Najas guadalupensis*
Magnus (Southern naiad)

2E *Najas minor* All.
(Naiad)

2F *Sagittaria calycina* Engelm.
(California arrowhead)

2G *Sagittaria graminea* Michx.
(Coastal arrowhead)

2H *Sagittaria latifolia* Willd.
(Common arrowhead)

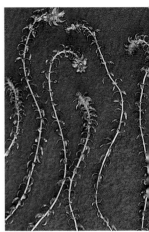

2I *Egeria densa* Planch.
(Egeria)

3A *Elodea canadensis* Michx. (Elodea)

3B *Hydrilla verticillata* (L. F.) Casp. (Hydrilla)

3C *Limnobium spongia* (Bosc.) Steud. (Frogbit)

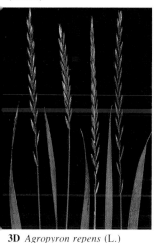

3D *Agropyron repens* (L.) Beauv. (Quackgrass)

3E *Andropogon virginicus* L. (Broomsedge)

3F *Avena fatua* L. (Wild oats)

3G *Brachiaria platyphylla* (Griseb.) Nash (Broadleaf signalgrass)

3H *Bromus japonicus* Thunb. (Japanese brome)

3I *Bromus secalinus* L. (Cheat)

4A *Cenchrus echinatus* L.
(Southern sandbur)

4B *Cenchrus longispinus* (Hack.)
Fern. (Longspine sandbur)

4C *Cynodon dactylon* (L.) Pers
(Bermudagrass)

4D *Dactylis glomerata* L.
(Orchardgrass)

4E *Digitaria ischaemum* (Schreb.)
Muhl. (Smooth crabgrass)

4F *Digitaria sanguinalis* (L.)
Scop. (Large crabgrass)

4G *Echinochloa crusgalli* (L.)
Beauv. (Barnyardgrass)

4H *Eleusine indica* (L.) Gaertn.
(Goosegrass)

4I *Eragrostis cilianensis* (All.)
Link (Stinkgrass)

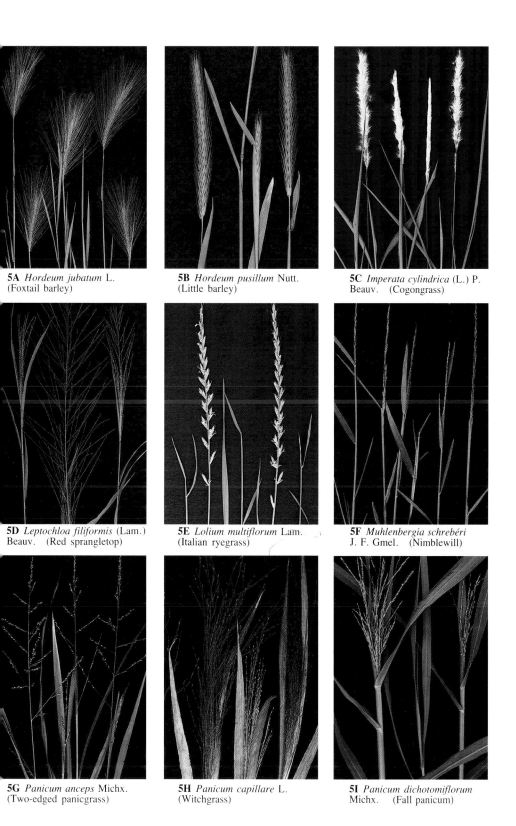

5A *Hordeum jubatum* L.
(Foxtail barley)

5B *Hordeum pusillum* Nutt.
(Little barley)

5C *Imperata cylindrica* (L.) P.
Beauv.　(Cogongrass)

5D *Leptochloa filiformis* (Lam.)
Beauv.　(Red sprangletop)

5E *Lolium multiflorum* Lam.
(Italian ryegrass)

5F *Muhlenbergia schrebéri*
J. F. Gmel.　(Nimblewill)

5G *Panicum anceps* Michx.
(Two-edged panicgrass)

5H *Panicum capillare* L.
(Witchgrass)

5I *Panicum dichotomiflorum*
Michx.　(Fall panicum)

6A *Paspalum dilatatum* Poir.
(Dallisgrass)

6B *Poa annua* L.
(Annual bluegrass)

6C *Rottboellia exaltata* (L.)
L. f.   (Itchgrass)

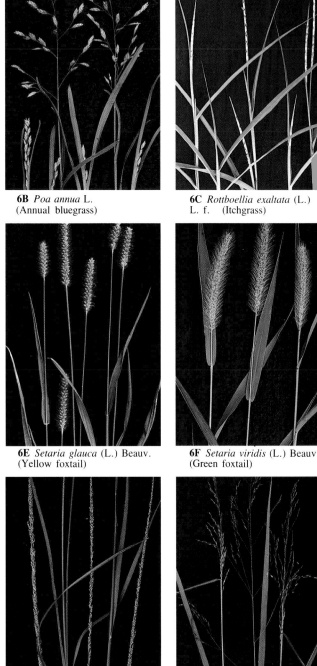

6D *Setaria faberi* Herrm.
(Giant foxtail)

6E *Setaria glauca* (L.) Beauv.
(Yellow foxtail)

6F *Setaria viridis* (L.) Beauv.
(Green foxtail)

6G *Sorghum halepense* (L.)
Pers.   (Johnsongrass)

6H *Sporobolus poiretii* (R. &
S.) Hitchc.   (Smutgrass)

6I *Tridens flavus* (L.) Hitchc.
(Purpletop)

7A *Cyperus esculentus* L.
(Yellow nutsedge)

7B *Cyperus rotundus* L.
(Purple nutsedge)

7C *Scirpus americanus* Pers.
(American bulrush)

7D *Pistia stratioites* L.
(Waterlettuce)

7E *Lemna minor* L.
(Common duckweed)

7F *Spirodela polyrhiza* (L.)
Schleid.   (Giant duckweed)

7G *Wolffia columbiana* Karst.
(Watermeal)

7H *Commelina communis* L.
(Dayflower)

7I *Eichhornia crassipes* (Mart.)
Solms   (Waterhyacinth)

8A *Pontederia cordata* L. (Pickerelweed)

8B *Pontederia lanceolata* Nutt. (Pickerelweed)

8C *Juncus effusus* L. (Soft rush

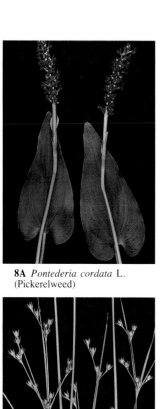

8D *Juncus tenuis* Willd. (Slender rush)

8E *Allium vineale* L. (Wild garlic)

8F *Smilax glauca* Walt. (Cat greenbrier)

8G *Dioscorea batatas* Dcne. (Cinnamon-vine)

8H *Cannabis sativa* L. (Hemp)

8I *Parietaria pensylvanica* Mu (Pennsylvania pellitory)

9A *Brunnichia cirrhosa* Gaertn. (Redvine)

9B *Fagopyrum esculentum* Moench (Buckwheat)

9C *Polygonum aviculare* L. (Prostrate knotweed)

9D *Polygonum convolvulus* L. (Wild buckwheat)

9E *Polygonum cuspidatum* Sieb. & Zucc. (Japanese knotweed)

9F *Polygonum hydropiper* L. (Marshpepper smartweed)

9G *Polygonum pensylvanicum* L. (Pennsylvania smartweed)

9H *Polygonum persicaria* L. (Ladysthumb)

9I *Rumex acetosella* L. (Red sorrel)

10A *Rumex conglomeratus*
Murr.   (Cluster dock)

10B *Rumex crispus* L.
(Curly dock)

10C *Rumex obtusifolius* L.
(Broadleaf dock)

10D *Chenopodium album* L.
(Common lambsquarters)

10E *Chenopodium ambrosioides* L.
(Mexicantea)

10F *Kochia scoparia* (L.) Roth.
(Kochia)

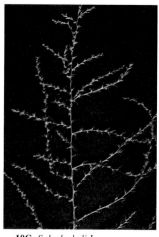

10G *Salsola kali* L.
(Russian Thistle)

10H *Alternanthera philoxeroides*
(Mart.) Griseb   (Alligstorweed)

10I *Amaranthus albus* L.
(Tumble pigweed)

11A *Amaranthus hybridus* L.
(Smooth pigweed)

11B *Amaranthus palmeri* S.
Wats.   (Palmer amaranth)

11C *Amaranthus retroflexus* L.
(Redroot pigweed)

11D *Amaranthus spinosus* L.
(Spiny amaranth)

11E *Phytolacca americana* L.
(Common pokeweed)

11F *Mollugo verticillata* L.
(Carpetweed)

11G *Portulaca oleracea* L.
(Common purslane)

11H *Agrostemma githago* L.
(Corn cockle)

11I *Arenaria serpyllifolia* L.
(Thymeleaf sandwort)

12A *Cerastium viscosum* L.
(Sticky chickweed)

12B *Cerastium vulgatum* L.
(Mouseear chickweed)

12C *Holosteum umbellatum* L.
(Jagged chickweed)

12D *Lychnis alba* Mill.
(White cockle)

12E *Saponaria officinalis* L.
(Bouncingbet)

12F *Scleranthus annuus* L.
(Knawel)

12G *Silene antirrhina* L.
(Sleepy catchfly)

12H *Spergula arvensis* L.
(Corn spurry)

12I *Stellaria media* (L.) Cyrillo.
(Common chickweed)

13A *Certophyllum demersum* L.
(Common coontail)

13B *Cabomba caroliniana* Gray
(Cabomba)

13C *Nelumbo lutea* (Willd.) Pers.
(American lotus)

13D *Nuphar advena* (Ait.)
Ait. f.   (Spatterdock)

13E *Nymphaea odorata* Ait.
(Fragrant waterlily)

13F *Ranunculus abortivus* L.
(Smallflower buttercup)

13G *Ranunculus acris* L.
(Tall buttercup)

13H *Ranunculus bulbosus* L.
(Bulbous buttercup)

13I *Ranunculus repens* L.
(Creeping buttercup)

14A *Cocculus carolinus* (L.) DC.
(Redberry moonseed)

14B *Papaver dubium* L.
(Field poppy)

14C *Barbarea vulgaris* R. Br.
(Yellow rocket)

14D *Brassica kaber* (DC.) L.C.
Wheeler   (Wild mustard)

14E *Brassica nigra* (L.) Koch
(Black mustard)

14F *Brassica rapa* L.
(Birdsrape mustard)

14G *Camelina microcarpa*
Andrz.   (Smallseed falseflax)

14H *Capsella bursa-pastoris*
(L.) Medic. (Shepherdspurse)

14I *Cardamine hirsuta* L.
(Hairy bittercress)

15A *Cardaria draba* (L.) Desv.
(Hoary cress)

15B *Coronopus didymus* (L.) Sm.
(Swinecress)

15C *Lepidium campestre* (L.)
R. Br.   (Field pepperweed)

15D *Lepidium virginicum* L.
(Virginia pepperweed)

15E *Raphanus raphanistrum* L.
(Wild radish)

15F *Sisymbrium officinale* (L.)
Scop.   (Hedge mustard)

15G *Thlaspi arvense* L.
(Field pennycress)

15H *Duchesnea indica* (Andr.)
Focke. (India mockstrawberry)

15I *Potentilla canadensis* L.
(Common cinquefoil)

16A *Potentilla norvegica* L.
(Rough cinquefoil)

16B *Potentilla recta* L.
(Sulfur cinquefoil)

16C *Rosa multiflora* Thunb.
(Multiflora rose)

16D *Rosa setigera* Michx.
(Prairie rose)

16E *Rubus argutus* Link.
(Blackberry)

16F *Albizzia julibrissin* Durazzi
(Mimosa)

16G *Cassia fasciculata* Michx.
(Partridgepea)

16H *Cassia obtusifolia* L.
(Sicklepod)

16I *Cassia occidentalis* L.
(Coffee senna)

17A *Desmodium canadense* (L.)
DC.   (Hoary tickclover)

17B *Lespedeza striata* (Thunb.)
H. & A. (Common lespedeza)

17C *Medicago lupulina* L.
(Black medic)

17D *Melilotus alba* Desr.
(White sweetclover)

17E *Melilotus officinalis* (L.)
Lam.   (Yellow sweetclover)

17F *Pueraria lobata* (Willd.)
Ohwi   (Kudzu)

17G *Sesbania exaltata* (Raf.) Cory
(Hemp sesbania)

17H *Trifolium procumbens* L.
(Low hop clover)

17I *Trifolium repens* L.
(White clover)

18A *Vicia angustifolia* L.
(Narrowleaf vetch)

18B *Vicia dasycarpa* Tenore
(Winter vetch)

18C *Vicia grandiflora* Scop.
(Yellow vetch)

18D *Oxalis stricta* L.
(Common yellow woodsorrel)

18E *Erodium cicutarium* (L.)
L'Her.   (Redstem filaree)

18F *Geranium carolinianum* L.
(Carolina geranium)

18G *Geranium molle* L.
(Dovefoot geranium)

18H *Tribulus terrestris* L.
(Puncturevine)

19A *Acalypha ostryaefolia*
Riddell (Hophornbeam copperleaf)

19B *Acalypha virginica* L.
(Virginia copperleaf)

19C *Croton capitatus* Michx.
(Woolly croton)

19D *Croton gladulosus* L.
(Tropic croton)

19E *Croton monanthogynus*
Michx.   (Prairietea)

19F *Euphorbia corollata* L.
(Flowering spurge)

19G *Euphorbia dentata* Michx.
(Toothed-leaf poinsettia)

19H *Euphorbia maculata* L.
(Spotted spurge)

19I *Euphorbia supina* Raf.
(Prostrate spurge)

20A *Rhus glabra* L.
(Smooth sumac)

20B *Rhus radicans* L.
(Poison ivy)

20C *Rhus toxicodendron* L.
(Poison oak)

20D *Ampelopsis arborea* (L.)
Koehne   (Peppervine)

20E *Parthenocissus quinquefolia*
(L.) Planch. (Virginia creeper)

20F *Vitis rotundifolia* Michx.
(Muscadine grape)

20G *Abutilon theophrasti*
Medic.   (Velvetleaf)

20H *Anoda cristata* (L.)
Schlecht.   (Spurred anoda)

20I *Hibiscus trionum* L.
(Venice mallow)

21A *Malva neglecta* Wallr.
(Common mallow)

21B *Sida spinosa* L.
(Prickly sida)

21C *Hypericum perforatum* L.
(St. Johnswort)

21D *Viola papilionacea* Pursh
(Meadow violet)

21E *Passiflora incarnata* L.
(Maypop passionflower)

21F *Opuntia humifusa* Raf.
(Spreading pricklypear)

21G *Jussiaea leptocarpa* Nutt.
(Primrose willow)

21H *Jussiaea repens* L.
(Creeping waterprimrose)

21I *Oenothera biennis* L.
(Common eveningprimrose)

22A *Oenothera laciniata* Hill
(Cutleaf eveningprimrose)

22B *Myriophyllum brasiliensis*
Camb. (Parrotfeather)

22C *Myriophyllum heterophyllu*
Michx. (Broadleaf watermilfoil)

22D *Myriophyllum spicatum* L.
(Eurasian watermilfoil)

22E *Chaerophyllum tainturieri*
Hook (Chervil)

22F *Cicuta maculata* L.
(Spotted waterhemlock)

22G *Conium maculatum* L.
(Poison hemlock)

22H *Daucus carota* L.
(Wild carrot)

22I *Hydrocotyle umbellata* L.
(Water pennywort)

23A *Pastinaca sativa* L.
(Wild parsnip)

23B *Anagallis arvensis* L.
(Scarlet pimpernel)

23C *Lysimachia nummularia* L.
(Moneywort)

23D *Apocynum cannibinum* L.
(Hemp dogbane)

23E *Ampelamus albidus* (Nutt.)
Britt.   (Honeyvine milkweed)

23F *Asclepias incarnata* L.
(Swamp milkweed)

23G *Asclepias syriaca* L.
(Common milkweed)

23H *Asclepias tuberosa* L.
(Butterfly milkweed)

23I *Asclepias verticillata* L.
(Eastern whorled milkweed)

24A *Convolvulus arvensis* L.
(Field bindweed)

24B *Convolvulus sepium* L.
(Hedge bindweed)

24C *Cuscuta pentagona* Engelm
(Field dodder)

24D *Ipomoea coccinea* L.
(Scarlet morningglory)

24E *Ipomoea hederacea* (L.)
Jacq. (Ivyleaf morningglory)

24F *Ipomoea lacunosa* L.
(Pitted morningglory)

24G *Ipomoea pandurata* (L.)
G. F. W. Meyer
(Bigroot morningglory)

24H *Ipomoea purpurea* (L.)
Roth. (Tall morningglory)

24I *Ipomoea quamoclit* L.
(Cypressvine morningglory)

25A *Echium vulgare* L.
(Blue thistle)

25B *Heliotropium indicum* L.
(Indian heliotrope)

25C *Lithospermum arvense* L.
(Corn gromwell)

25D *Verbena hastata* L.
(Blue vervain)

25E *Verbena simplex* Lehm.
(Narrow-leaved vervain)

25F *Glechoma hederacea* L.
(Ground ivy)

25G *Lamium amplexicaule* L.
(Henbit)

25H *Lamium purpureum* L.
(Red deadnettle)

25I *Mentha piperita* L.
(Peppermint)

26A *Monarda fistulosa* L.
(Wild bergamot)

26B *Perilla frutescens* (L.) Britt.
(Purple mint)

26C *Prunella vulgaris* L.
(Healall)

26D *Salvia lyrata* L.
(Lyre-leaved sage)

26E *Datura stramonium* L.
(Jimsonweed)

26F *Physalis heterophylla* Nee
(Clammy groundcherry)

26G *Solanum carolinense* L.
(Horsenettle)

26H *Solanum dulcamara* L.
(Bitter nightshade)

26I *Solanum nigrum* L.
(Black nightshade)

27A *Linaria vulgaris* Hill
(Yellow toadflax)

27B *Striga lutea* Lour.
(Witchweed)

27C *Verbascum blattaria* L. forma
blattaria Brug. (Moth mullein)

27D *Verbascum blattaria* L. forma
erubescens Brug. (Moth mullein)

27E *Verbascum thapsus* L.
(Common mullein)

27F *Veronica arvensis* L.
(Corn speedwell)

27G *Veronica hederaefolia* L.
(Ivy speedwell)

27H *Veronica officinalis* L.
(Common speedwell)

27I *Veronica peregrina* L.
(Purslane speedwell)

28A *Veronica persica* Poir.
(Bird's-eye speedwell)

28B *Campsis radicans* (L.)
Seem   (Trumpetcreeper)

28C *Utricularia inflata* Walt.
(Floating bladderwort)

28D *Plantago aristata* Michx.
(Bracted plantain)

28E *Plantago lanceolata* L.
(Buckhorn plantain)

28F *Plantago major* L.
(Broadleaf plantain)

28G *Plantago virginica* L.
(Paleseed plantain)

28H *Diodia teres* Walt.
(Poorjoe)

28I *Diodia virginiana* L.
(Virginia buttonweed)

29A *Galium aparine* L.
(Catchweed bedstraw)

29B *Richardia scabra* L.
(Florida pusley)

29C *Sherardia arvensis* L.
(Field madder)

29D *Lonicera japonica* Thunb.
(Japanese honeysuckle)

29E *Valerianella radiata* (L.)
Dufr. (Cornsalad)

29F *Dipsacus sylvestris* Huds.
(Teasel)

29G *Sicyos angulatus* L.
(Burcucumber)

29H *Specularia perfoliata*
(L.) A. DC. (Venus lookingglass)

29I *Acanthospermum hispidum*
DC. (Bristly starbur)

30A *Achillea millefolium* L.
(Common yarrow)

30B *Ambrosia artemisiifolia* L.
(Common ragweed)

30C *Ambrosia trifida* L.
(Giant ragweed)

30D *Anthemis arvensis* L.
(Corn chamomile)

30E *Anthemis cotula* L.
(Mayweed)

30F *Arctium minus* (Hill.)
Bernh.   (Common burdock)

30G *Artemisia vulgaris* L.
(Mugwort)

30H *Aster pilosus* Willd.
(White heath aster)

30I *Bidens bipinnata* L.
(Spanishneedles)

31A *Bidens frondosa* L.
(Devils beggarticks)

31B *Bidens pilosa* L. var. *radiata*
Sch. Bip. (Hairy beggarticks)

31C *Bidens polylepis* Blake
(Coreopsis beggarticks)

31D *Carduus acanthoides* L.
(Plumeless thistle)

31E *Carduus nutans* L.
(Musk thistle)

31F *Centaurea cyanus* L.
(Cornflower)

31G *Chrysanthemum
leucanthemum* L. (Oxeye daisy)

31H *Cichorium intybus* L.
(Chicory)

31I *Cirsium arvense* (L.) Scop.
(Canada thistle)

32A *Cirsium vulgare* (Savi.)
Tenore (Bull thistle)

32B *Coreopsis tinctoria* Nutt.
(Plains coreopsis)

32C *Eclipta alba* (L.) Hassk.
(Eclipta)

32D *Erigeron annus* (L.) Pers.
(Annual fleabane)

32E *Erigeron canadensis* L.
(Horseweed)

32F *Erigeron philadelphicus* L
(Philadelphia fleabane)

32G *Galinsoga ciliata* (Raf.)
Blake (Hairy galinsoga)

32H *Helenium amarum* (Rafin.)
H. Rock (Bitter sneezeweed)

32I *Helenium autumnale* L.
(Common sneezeweed)

33A *Helianthus annuus* L.
(Sunflower)

33B *Hieracium pratense* Tausch
(Yellow hawkweed)

33C *Lactuca canadensis* L.
(Tall lettuce)

33D *Lactuca serriola* L.
(Prickly lettuce)

33E *Pyrrhopappus carolinianus*
DC.   (Carolina falsedandelion)

33F *Rudbeckia hirta* L.
(Hairy coneflower)

33G *Senecio glabellus* Poir.
(Cressleaf groundsel)

33H *Senecio smallii* Britt.
(Small's ragwort)

33I *Solidago canadensis* L.
(Canada goldenrod)

34A *Sonchus asper* (L.) Hill
(Spiny sowthistle)

34B *Sonchus oleraceus* L.
(Annual sowthistle)

34C *Taraxacum officinale*
Weber   (Dandelion)

34D *Tragopogon dubius* Scop.
(Western salsify)

34E *Verbesina alternifolia* (L.)
Britt.   (Wingstem)

34F *Verbesina encelioides* Gray
(Crownbeard)

34G *Verbesina occidentalis* (L.)
Walt.   (Western crownbeard)

34H *Vernonia altissima* Nutt.
(Tall ironweed)

34I *Xanthium pensylvanicum*
Wallr.   (Common cocklebur)

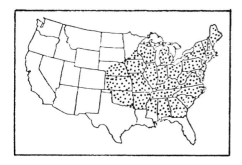

7H
Commelina communis L.
Dayflower
Spiderwort family
(Commelinaceae)

Description

An annual, slender-rooted herb with smooth, succulent, decumbent stems that root at the lower nodes and are up to 80 cm long. Fleshy, lance-shaped smooth or minutely hairy leaves are 4–12 cm long. Leaf sheaths are hairless on the edges and summit. Bracts sheathing the inflorescence are broadly heart-shaped, 12–25 mm long, smooth, and its edges are free to the base. The posterior flower of the inflorescence protrudes from the bract on long stalks. Its petals are clawed, pale violet-blue, 1–1.5 cm long. The flower has six anthers. Seeds are wrinkled and about 4 mm long. Reproduction is by seeds. Flowers appear from June to October.

Habitat

Dayflower may be found in many agricultural settings such as crop lands, undisturbed shady gardens, vineyards, and waste soils. It is a native of tropical America.

Suggested Control

Home Garden—Hoe or pull before early flowering stage or use mulches or soil fumigation to prevent seed germination. *Cropland*—Use mechanical control methods. This weed is listed on the bentazon label. *Industrial*—Use a soil sterilant for total vegetation control.

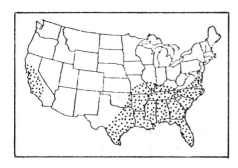

7I
Eichhornia crassipes (Mart.)
  Solms
Waterhyacinth
Pickerelweed family
(Pontederiaceae)

Description

Perennial, free-floating, aquatic plant with stems that produce long pendent roots at the nodes. The bright-green, shiny, smooth leaves have greatly inflated, spongy petioles and radiate in a basal rosette. Leaf blades are entire, circular or kidney-shaped and 4–12 cm long. The inflorescence is a panicle borne at the end of a long stalk higher than the leaves. Each plant may have several showy flowers with five to seven lilac to bluish-purple petals. The upper petal is mottled by yellow surrounded by a dark-blue margin. The fruit is a capsule with many seeds. Waterhyacinth reproduces by seeds and vegetatively by rooted stem sections or stolons. It flowers from May to October.

Habitat

Waterhyacinth invades ponds, lakes, sluggish streams, rivers, and canals. It is a native of South America.

Suggested Control

Aquatic—In small areas, waterhyacinth can be mechanically harvested with a rake, net, and boat, or it can be controlled on small or large areas by spraying with 2,4-D or diquat.

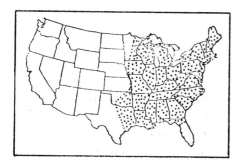

8A
Pontederia cordata L.
Pickerelweed
Pickerelweed family
(Pontederiaceae)

Description

A perennial aquatic herb has a creeping rootstock and erect or ascending smooth stems that are 50–100 cm tall. Basal leaves and lower stem leaves are similar, up to 18 cm long, with thick and firm blades and long petioles. The upper stem leaves have 4–5 cm long petioles. Inflorescence is a densely flowered 5–15 cm long spike, loosely sheathed by a large leafy bract. The violet-blue flowers have funnel-shaped corolla that is 5–7 mm long. Seeds are 3.5–4.5 mm long. Reproduction is by seeds and by rootstocks. It flowers from May to November.

Habitat

Pickerelweed may be found in shallow waters of ponds and ditches and along lake margins. It is native of South America.

Suggested Control

Aquatic—Pickerelweed can be controlled by deepening the edges of the pond or drainage ditch to 0.6–1 m or by spraying with 2,4-D.

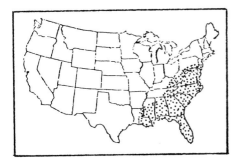

8B
Pontederia lanceolata Nutt.
Pickerelweed
Pickerelweed family
(Pontederiaceae)

Description

A perennial aquatic herb that has thick, creeping rootstocks. Its firm, simple, erect leaves have lance-oblong- to lance-linear-shaped leaf blades that narrow at the base and are up to 8 cm wide. Blue or violet flowers are borne on rather loose spikes. The buds conspicuously glandular and the glands commonly are persistent on the mature flowers. The fruit is a single-seeded utricle, 5–6 mm long and as broad as it is long or broader. Seeds are 2.5–3.0 mm long and 2 mm in diameter. Reproduction is by seeds and rootstocks. It flowers from May to September.

Habitat

This native of the tropical world may be found in shallow water, in marshes, ponds and lakes.

Suggested Control

Aquatic—Pickerelweed can be controlled by deepening the edges of the pond or drainage ditch to 0.6–1.0 m or by spraying with 2,4-D.

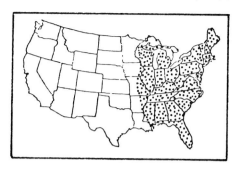

8C
Juncus effusus L.
Soft rush
Rush family (Juncaceae)

Description

A perennial emerged aquatic plant that arises from a short coarse rhizome. Pale green stems are round, soft, and easily compressed and are densely clumped. They continue above the inflorescence and are up to 1.5 m tall. Leaf sheaths are brown, basal and without blades, about 20 cm long, and have a slender bristle at the end. The dense inflorescence is loosely branched, emerges on the side of the stem, about 8–16 cm from the tip, and is up to 10 cm long. Green to brown flowers, not showy, are only 1.5–4.5 mm long. Reproduction is both by seeds and rootstocks. Flowers appear from June to August.

Habitat

This cosmopolitan plant may be found in wet soils in meadows, shallow drainage areas, waste areas, or in the wet areas around ponds and lakes.

Suggested Control

Meadows and Pastures—Improved drainage is an absolute requirement before other controls are initiated. After drainage, improved production of desirable species should be encouraged through improved management techniques of pH adjustment, proper fertilization, and rotational grazing and mowing. *Drainageways and Shorelines*—Increase the depth of the water and make periodic applications of 2,4-D, MCPA, or diquat in accord with label restrictions.

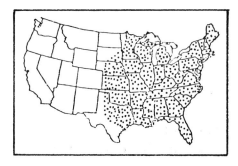

8D
Juncus tenuis Willd.
Slender rush
Rush family (Juncaceae)

Description

A cosmopolitan perennial plant that lives in many areas from marshes and dry lands. It has slender hollow, round, wiry stems that are densely or loosely clumped, branched at the top, and 10–60 cm tall. Leaves arise from the base and have blades a third to half as long as the stems. They are narrow, flat and grasslike. Leaf sheaths are prolonged, 1–4 mm beyond the base of the blade. The 4–10 cm long inflorescence is in loose clusters and subtended by leafy bracts that are longer than the inflorescence. The nonshowy flowers are green to brown and 3.0–4.5 mm long. The fruit is a thin-walled capsule shorter than the perianth, with tiny brown seeds. Reproduction is by seeds. Flowers appear from June to August.

Habitat

Slender rush will grow along paths, roadsides, cultivated fields, pastures, and bottom lands.

Suggested Control

Cropland—Improve drainage, adopt a crop rotation system where the land is plowed periodically followed with row crops that are cultivated. *Pastures*—Improve drainage and increase the vigor of desirable species by adopting improved management techniques of renovation, pH adjustment, proper fertilization, rotational grazing, and mowing. This will allow desirable species to successfully compete with slender rush.

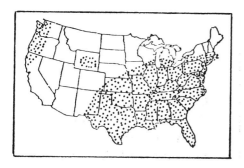

8E
Allium vineale L.
Wild garlic
Lily family (Liliaceae)

Description

This biennial aromatic bulbous herb has smooth, waxy, erect stems that are stiff and leafy in the middle portion and 30–120 cm tall. Hollow, slender, round leaves are attached to the lower half of stem and are two-ranked with sheath at base. Smooth, shiny aerial bulblets are produced during spring and borne at the end of a long and stiff stalk with as many as 300 in a cluster. Purplish flowers are sometimes borne above the cluster of bulblets. The small (2 mm) black seeds are flat on one side and only rarely are produced. If seed production occurs it will be in the spring and then the seed will germinate the following fall. Two types of asexually produced bulblets, hard and soft, are found clustered around the central basal bulb. Reproduction is from basally produced hard and soft bulblets, from aerial produced bulblets and from seed. This weed flowers from May to June.

Habitat

Wild garlic is a native of Eurasia and infests gardens, lawns, pastures, hay and cultivated fields. Aerial bulblets are often contaminants in small grains and give wheat flour a garlicky taste.

Suggested Control

Home Gardens—Remove all bulbs with a shovel, carefully separate from the soil and destroy. Clean cultivate and hand hoe to control any escapees. Hardshell bulbs will remain dormant in soil for 5 or 6 years. Maintain vigilance against reinfestation. *Home Lawns*—Manually remove all plant parts or spray with 2,4-D low volatile ester in three successive growth periods, i.e., fall-spring-fall or spring-fall-spring. *Small Grains*—Spray with 2,4-D low volatile ester when small grains are in the full tiller stage. This will not control the plant but will cause the stem bearing the bulblets to twist downward thus preventing a number of aerial bulblets from being harvested and possible dockage. The sicklebar on the combine should be set high enough to avoid the bulblets. Also chlorsulfuron shows promise for wild garlic control. *Pastures and Waste Areas*—Spray with 2,4-D low volatile ester in three successive growth periods.

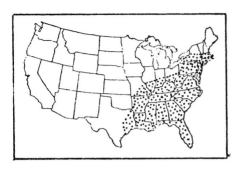

8F
Smilax glauca Walt.
Cat greenbrier
Lily family (Liliaceae)

Description

A perennial, woody, tendril-bearing vine that arises from a deep, tough, gnarled rootstock. The climbing stems are round or obscurely four-angled, often with scattered thorns. The short petioled, 5–9 cm long leaves are waxy on the lower surface with variable shapes, from triangular-ovate to nearly triangular. Mature leaves are leathery in nature. Flower stalks are 2–4 cm long and bear a compact head type inflorescence. Fruits are waxy, black berries. Reproduction is by seeds and rootstocks. Flowers occur from April to June.

Habitat

This native to North America may be found in pastures, newly cleared lands, fence rows, and woodlots.

Suggested Control

Pastures—Mow after each grazing rotation. Rootstalks should be dug out where possible. *Newly Cleared Land*—Use a crop rotation which includes land management by plowing and cultivation. *Fence Rows*—Spray with tebuthiuron. *Woodlots*—Manually remove total plant including rootstalk or overgraze with cattle or goats for several years.

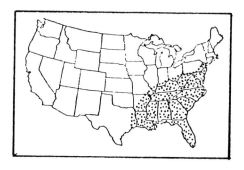

8G
Dioscorea batatas Dcne.
Cinnamon-vine
Yam family (Dioscoreaceae)

Description

A perennial herbaceous vine that arises from a large starchy tuber. Smooth climbing stems are 1–5 m long. The shiny, heart-shaped leaves are simple, alternate, opposite, or whorled and have seven to nine conspicuous veins. Often small tubers resembling very miniature potatoes are borne in axils of the leaves. Small, white, unisexual flowers are borne on separate plants. The female flowers are borne at each node in short spikes while the male flowers are in loose panicles. Fruits are rarely produced. Reproduction is vegetatively by small deciduous, axillary tubers and the large underground tubers which sprout in spring. Tubers are produced in midsummer and flowering occurs from July to November.

Habitat

This plant is native to China and may be found growing along fences or in gardens, pastures, and waste areas.

Suggested Control

Home Gardens and Cropland—Use clean cultivation to prevent seed production and aerial and subterranean tuber development. This weed does not appear on any specific herbicide label. However, it may be susceptible to higher rates of 2,4-D, dicamba, or glyphosate. *Fence Rows and Waste Areas*—This plant may be susceptible to sulfometuron or tebuthiuron. Use on a trial basis initially.

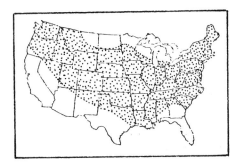

8H
Cannabis sativa L.
Hemp
Hemp family
(Cannabinaceae)

Description

This annual bushy herb is an escape from man's efforts to produce fiber and drugs. Its erect, simple or much branched, coarse, rough, and hairy stems are slightly grooved and 0.5–2.5 m tall. The upper leaves are alternate, palmately divided, with five to nine hairy leaflets with toothed edges. The flowers are small and greenish and the male and female flowers are borne on separate plants (dioecious). Male flowers are borne on panicles in the axils of the upper leaves, and female flowers are borne on spikelike clusters in the leaf axils. The fruit is a yellow, round achene. The oval seeds have a distinctly netted surface, a distinct edge, and are about 3 mm long. Reproduction is by seeds. Flowering is from June to October.

Habitat

Hemp is the source of marijuana and hemp fibers. It is native of Asia and may be found growing as single plants or in patches along fence rows, drainage ways, creeks, ditches, or roadsides, or occasionally in old fields and around farmyards.

Suggested Control

Farmyards, Roadsides, Fence Rows, Ditches—Prevent seed production by pulling, hand hoeing, cultivation, or spraying with 2,4-D when plants are 15 to 20 cm tall or with paraquat or glyphosate at any stage.

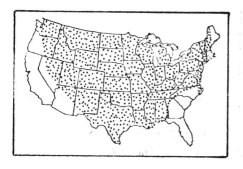

8I
Parietaria pensylvanica
 Muhl.
Pennsylvania pellitory
Nettle family (Urticaceae)

Description

An annual herb that has erect, simple stems or sparingly branched stems with ascending branches. Stems are covered with minute hairs and are 10–40 cm tall. The simple, entire, thin, slender-petioled leaves are roughened on the upper surface and have opaque dots. The middle and upper blades are oblong-lanceolate, 2–7 cm long and tapered. The blade is several times longer than the petiole. Flowers are borne in clusters at the middle to upper leaf axils. They are without stalks and are subtended by bracts twice or thrice longer than the mature calyx. The fruits contain one smooth, egg-shaped seed that is about 1 mm long. Reproduction is by seeds. Flowers appear from May to August.

Habitat

Pennsylvania pellitory may occur in gardens, lawns, cropland, fence rows, and waste places. It is a native of North America.

Suggested Control

Home Gardens—Prevent seed germination by heavy mulching or soil fumigation. If established, hoe or pull before flowering. *Home Lawns*—Use good management techniques such as proper fertilization, proper pH adjustment, etc., to maintain a thick competitive turf; and spray in the spring with a mixture of 2,4-D, dicamba, and mecoprop. *Cropland*—Use methods normally used for control of broadleaf weeds, including good land preparation, cultivation if needed, and on labeled crops use a herbicide such as atrazine, cyanazine, diuron, fluometuron, 2,4-D, linuron, metribuzin, or simazine. *Fence Rows and Noncrop Areas*—Use paraquat for temporary control or a nonselective soil sterilant for longer control.

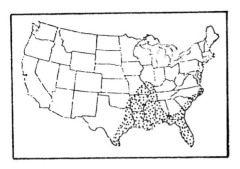

9A
Brunnichia cirrhosa Gaertn.
Redvine
Buckwheat family
(Polygonaceae)

Description

This perennial woody tendril-bearing vine has branched climbing stems up to 4 m long. Leaves are simple, alternate, and 5–15 cm long. Inflorescences are solitary spikes, arising from the leaf axils or lower stem, or open panicles borne on the upper stem. Flowers are winged and whitish to greenish. Fruit is a brown, teardrop-shaped achene, 5–7 mm wide, and 3 cm long and are surrounded by dried floral parts. Reproduction is by seeds and rootstocks. Flowers appear from May to September.

Habitat

Redvine is a native of the tropics but may occur in the Southeastern States and up the Mississippi river valley. It is generally found in cultivated fields, river banks, roadsides, and waste places.

Suggested Control

Cropland—Use clean cultivation and hand hoe escaped plants. Never allow plants to become more than 30 cm in length. If mechanical control is not practical, spot spray with glyphosate (this will also kill the existing crop). *Noncropland*—Apply glyphosate in early summer or a nonselective soil sterilant applied in early spring before growth is initiated.

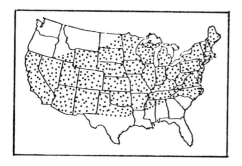

9B
Fagopyrum esculentum
Moench
Buckwheat
Buckwheat family
(Polygonaceae)

Description

This annual herb is an escape from cultivation. Its erect, branched, 20–60 cm long stems are smooth, hairless on the lower portion, and have small fine hairs in rows on the upper portion. Leaves are simple, alternate, and triangular with basal lobes. The lower leaves have long petioles, the upper leaves have short petioles. Flower clusters are usually crowded, compact, and located at the end of the stems or arise from the upper leaf axils. Seeds are smooth, shiny, about 7 mm long, three-angled and only one is produced per flower. Reproduction is by seeds. Flowering occurs from June to September.

Habitat

Buckwheat may be found in small grain and general crop fields and waste areas. It is a native to Central Asia.

Suggested Control

Small Grains—Apply 2,4-D or MCPA in combination with dicamba before small grain initiates jointing stage. *Other Crops*—Use a good crop rotation, stimulate seed germination through tillage prior to planting the crop. If area is heavily infested, plant corn and apply atrazine, cyanazine, or simazine preemergence followed by dicamba postdirected. In soybeans, metribuzin may provide some control. *Waste Areas*—Apply a mixture of 2,4-D plus dicamba.

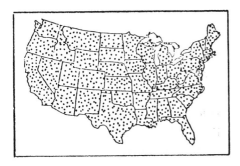

9C
Polygonum aviculare L.
Prostrate knotweed
Buckweat family
(Polygonaceae)

Description

This summer annual herb has prostrate or loosely ascending well-branched stems. Leaves are simple, alternate, elliptic or oblong, 1–8 mm wide and 1–3 cm long. They are weakly veined, pointed, or rounded at the tip and somewhat narrowed toward the base. Flowers are small, greenish in color with white or pink edges. Seeds are triangular, dark red-brown to black, 2–2.5 mm long and only one per flower. Reproduction is by seeds. Flowering occurs from June to September.

Habitat

Prostrate knotweed occurs in lawns, pastures, cropland, and waste areas. It is a native of North America.

Suggested Control

Home Lawns—Use improved management techniques such as pH adjustment, adequate fertilization, proper mowing height, so as to maintain a vigorous, healthy turf capable of strong competition. Spray with a mixture containing 2,4-D plus dicamba. *Cropland*—Maintain a good crop rotation, use clean cultivation and apply atrazine, chlorpropham, cyanazine, or terbacil in appropriate crops. *Waste Areas*—Treat with a mixture of 2,4-D plus dicamba.

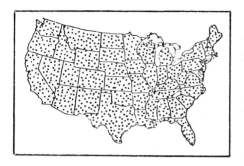

9D
Polygonum convolvulus L.
Wild buckwheat
Buckwheat family
(Polygonaceae)

Description

An annual twining herb that has stems up to 1 m long. Its viney stems climb on adjacent plants for support. Very fine rough hairs are on the stems, petioles, and leaf veins. Leaves are simple, alternate, and triangular with heart-shaped bases and have smooth, sheathing stipules (ocreae). The inflorescence is an axillary or terminal raceme and is 2–6 cm long. The small white flowers are in clusters of three to six. The seeds are triangular, dull-black and about 3 mm long. Reproduction is by seeds. It flowers from June to September.

Habitat

Wild buckwheat is commonly found in fields where spring planted grains are grown and occasionally along roadsides and in waste areas. It is a native of Europe and was probably introduced as a contaminant in small grain seed.

Suggested Control

Small Grains—Plant clean seed but if weed becomes established apply dicamba plus MCPA or 2,4-D, or bromoxynil plus MCPA. *Non-crop Areas*—Spray with either dicamba, or bromoxynil in combination with 2,4-D or MCPA for selective control without injury to grasses. Apply a soil sterilant if it is desirable to control all vegetation.

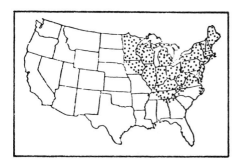

9E
Polygonum cuspidatum
Sieb. & Zucc.
Japanese knotweed
Buckwheat family
(Polygonaceae)

Description

A perennial herb that has coarse underground rootstocks and coarse, erect, waxy, bushy-branched stems up to 2.5 m tall. The simple, alternate, leaves are 5–12 cm wide and 8–15 cm long. They have wavy edges, are more or less square at the base and are abruptly pointed at the lip. The inflorescence is a panicle borne on a short stalk in the leaf axils and 8–15 cm long. Flowers are numerous, greenish or white, and 8–9 mm long. Seeds are about 3 mm long, triangular, shiny brown to black; one seed is produced per flower. Reproduction is by seeds and rootstocks. Flowers are produced during August and September.

Habitat

Japanese knotweed may be found in fence rows and thickets, along roadsides or in waste areas. It is a native of eastern Asia.

Suggested Control

Fence Rows, Roadsides, Waste Places—Frequent cultivation or selective grubbing is needed to destroy underground rhizome. Do not allow this plant to produce seed. Chemical control might be accomplished by spraying with a mixture of dicamba plus 2,4-D or picloram plus 2,4-D.

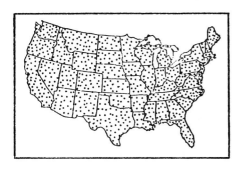

9F
Polygonum hydropiper L.
Marshpepper smartweed
Buckwheat family
(Polygonaceae)

Description

This annual aquatic or marshy herb has erect or spreading, simple or branched, smooth and often reddish stems. Its simple, alternate, narrowly lanceolate leaves are either smooth or have short hairs on the veins. The inflorescence is a terminal or axillary raceme. Flowers are greenish and have four perianth segments that are usually white-bordered. Seeds are 2–3 mm long, dark-brown to black and flat or more commonly triangular, with round angles. Reproduction is by seeds. Flowers occur from June to October.

Habitat

Marshpepper smartweed may occur in damp soils found in swamps, pastures, and bottom lands. It is a native of Europe.

Suggested Control

Cropland—Improve drainage to reduce infestation and use clean cultivation. Herbicides that may give satisfactory control are atrazine, dicamba, fluometuron, glyphosate, metribuzin, methazole, propazine, simazine, and terbacil. *Pastures and Waste Areas*—Provide proper drainage, mow frequently and treat periodically with dicamba.

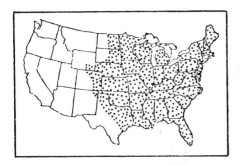

9G
Polygonum pensylvanicum L.
Pennsylvania smartweed
Buckwheat family
(Polygonaceae)

Description

An annual herb that has freely branched and erect or ascending stems up to 1.8 m tall. Leaves are simple, alternate, lanceolate with long tapered sheathing stipules (ocreae). The inflorescence is composed of axillary or terminal racemes. They are 1.5–3.0 cm long, commonly cylindrical in shape, and blunt on the end. Perianth segments are rose to white and are slightly longer than the seed (achene) at maturity. Seeds are lens-shaped, flat on one side, 2.6–3.4 mm long and almost as wide. One is produced per flower. Reproduction is by seeds. Flowers appear from May to frost.

Habitat

Pennsylvania smartweed may occur in cultivated fields, damp soils, and waste areas. It is native to North America.

Suggested Control

Cropland—Leave areas infested with smartweed until other areas have been planted to allow time for seed germination. Completely destroy all vegetation by thorough disking and seedbed preparation, and use clean cultivation as needed during the season. Herbicides that are labeled for control of smartweed are acifluorfen, alachlor, ametryn, atrazine, bentazon, chlorsulfuron, cyanazine, dicamba, dinoseb, fluometuron, glyphosate, linuron, metribuzin, methazole, norflurazon, oxyfluorfen, pendimethalin, prometryn, propazine, pyrazon, simazine, and terbacil. *Pastures and Waste Areas*—Control by frequent mowing and annual spring application of dicamba. *Industrial Areas*—Use a soil sterilant such as a high rate of atrazine or simazine or bromacil, hexazinone, or tebuthiuron.

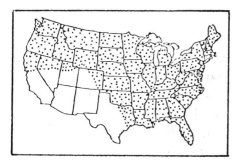

9H
Polygonum persicaria L.
Ladysthumb
Buckwheat family
(Polygonaceae)

Description

A summer annual herb with erect or ascending, simple or commonly many-branched, stems that may be up to 80 cm tall. They are smooth or sparsely hairy. Leaves are simple, alternate, narrowly lanceolate and often have a dark blotch in the center. The sheathing stipules (ocreae) are membranous, minutely hairy, and ciliate toward the base. The inflorescence is in a dense axillary or terminal, cylindric spike that is 7–12 mm thick and 1–4 cm long. The perianth segments are pink or purplish. Seeds are mostly flat but occasionally triangular, smooth, shiny, black and 1.8–2.5 mm long. One is produced per flower. Reproduction is by seeds. Flowers appear from June to October.

Habitat

Ladysthumb is a common weed that occurs in home gardens, damp clearings, cultivated fields, pastures, along stream banks, and in moist waste places. It is native to Europe.

Suggested Control

Home Gardens—Use clean cultivation and hand hoeing. Prevent seed production. *Cropland*—In heavily infested areas delay planting sufficiently to allow several thorough cultivations to destroy early emerging seedlings. Then follow a program of timely cultivation as needed coupled with chemical control. Herbicides that may be used are ametryn, atrazine, bentazon, bromacil, bromoxynil, chlorosulfuron, cyanazine, dicamba, dichloroprop, glyphosate, linuron, metribuzin, pyrazon, and terbacil. This weed is highly resistant to 2,4-D. *Pastures, Roadsides and Waste Areas*—Use frequent mowing plus treatment with dicamba. *Industrial Areas*—Sterilize the soil with bromacil, hexazinone, or tebuthiuron.

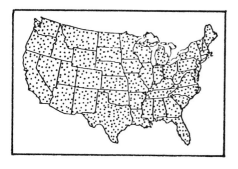

91
Rumex acetosella L.
Red sorrel
Buckwheat family
(Polygonaceae)

Description

A perennial herb that spreads by extensive, though shallow, rhizomes. Erect, simple, or branched stems are 10–40 cm tall. Leaves are simple, alternate, and usually three-lobed. The terminal lobe is narrowly elliptic to oblong. The lateral lobes are triangular and much smaller. The leaf base below the lobes is long and wedge-shaped. The inflorescence is a panicle, sometimes half as long as the plant. The outer perianth segments are yellow to red. Seeds are 1.5 mm long, shiny, golden-brown and one per flower. Reproduction is by seeds and spreading rhizomes. Flowering occurs from June to August. Some say it is poisonous.

Habitat

This weed may occur in gardens, cultivated fields, pastures, and waste places. It is a native of Eurasia.

Suggested Control

Home Gardens—Buy clean transplants, especially strawberries. Do not introduce this weed. If present, use clean cultivation, destroy all plant parts, and prevent all seed production. *Home Lawns and Pastures*—Apply a mixture of 2,4-D and dicamba or glyphosate when weed is young and actively growing; use repeated applications if necessary. *Cultivated Cropland*—Thoroughly till the soil and use clean cultivation throughout the season. On labeled crops use diphenamid, dicamba, 2,4-D, diuron, glyphosate, or terbacil. *Waste Places*—Apply 2,4-D or dicamba for selective control or glyphosate for nonselective control. Repeat if necessary or use a soil sterilant for total vegetation control.

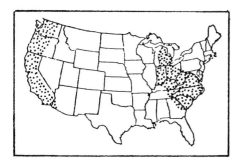

10A
Rumex conglomeratus Murr.
Cluster dock
Buckwheat family
(Polygonaceae)

Description

A perennial herb with slender stems that are up to 1 m tall and often has vegetative axillary leaf tufts. It has simple, alternate leaves; the larger ones are oblong and heart-shaped at the base. Leaves may be 6–20 cm long; a membranaceous sheath surrounds the stems at the base of the leaf. The inflorescence is a large clustered panicle making up as much as half the plant. The middle and lower clusters of flowers are usually subtended by leaves. Pedicels of individual flowers are 1–2 mm long and jointed near the base. There are usually three seeds per flower. Reproduction is by seeds. It flowers from June to August.

Habitat

Cluster dock often occurs in lawns, pastures, fence rows, and waste places. It is native of Europe.

Suggested Control

Home Lawns—Mechanically remove larger plants with a spade. Young plants (before large taproot develops) can be controlled with a mixture of 2,4-D plus dicamba. *Cropland*—Till the soil thoroughly to destroy well-established plants, include small grains or corn in rotation, and treat with 2,4-D plus dicamba at the correct crop stage while new seedlings are small. *Pastures*—Mechanically remove scattered plants, or rotate to a clean cultivated crop for one or two years, or use repeated applications of 2,4-D plus dicamba. *Fence Rows and Waste Places*—Mechanically remove established plants or treat with glyphosate or a mixture of 2,4-D plus dicamba, or for total vegetation control use sulfometuron or tebuthiuron.

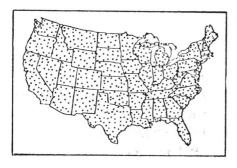

10B
Rumex crispus L.
Curly dock
Buckwheat family
(Polygonaceae)

Description

A perennial herb that has a large, fleshy, branched taproot. Stems are erect, unbranched, and up to 1 m tall. The leaves are simple, alternate, and have puckered or wavy margins. The larger leaves are lance-shaped and 15–30 cm long. The inflorescence is large, with many ascending or erect branches and becomes compact at maturity. Pedicels of individual flowers are 5–10 mm long, spreading to drooping and jointed near the base. There are three seeds per flower. Reproduction is by seeds and root segments. Flowering occurs from June to September.

Habitat

Curly dock occurs in lawns, old fields, pastures, and waste areas. It is a native of Europe.

Suggested Control

Home Lawns—Mechanically remove larger plants with a spade. The taproot must be cut off well below the soil surface (15+cm). Young plants (before large taproot develops) can be controlled with a mixture of 2,4-D plus dicamba. *Cropland*—Till the soil thoroughly to destroy well-established plants, include small grains or corn in rotation and treat with 2,4-D and dicamba at the correct crop stage while new seedlings are small. *Pastures*—Mechanically remove scattered plants with a spade or rotate to a clean cultivated crop for one or two years, or use repeated applications of 2,4-D plus dicamba. *Fence Rows and Waste Places*—Mechanically remove established plants or treat with glyphosate or a mixture of 2,4-D plus dicamba, or for total vegetation control use sulfometuron or tebuthiuron.

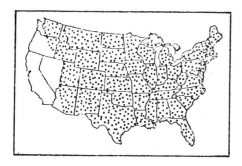

10C
Rumex obtusifolius L.
Broadleaf dock
Buckwheat family
(Polygonaceae)

Description

A perennial herb that has bitter foliage and coarse stems. Its tall, up to 1.2 m stems, are erect and unbranched to the inflorescence. The lower leaves are often up to 15 cm wide and 15–25 cm long and have smooth, nonpuckered margins. The leaf veins are minutely hairy underneath. The upper leaves are much smaller. The inflorescence is a narrow, freely branched, terminal panicle. Lower whorls of flowers are commonly separate and have leafy bracts. The upper whorls are closer together. Pedicels of individual flowers are longer than the fruit and are jointed below the middle. Perianth segments are triangular and have spiny teeth on each margin. There is usually one seed per flower. Reproduction is by seeds and root sections. Flowers appear from June to September.

Habitat

Broadleaf dock may be found in pastures, cultivated fields, fence rows, and along roadsides. It is a native of Europe.

Suggested Control

Home Lawns—Mechanically remove larger plants with a spade. The taproot must be cut off well below the soil surface (15+cm) Young plants (before large taproot develops) can be controlled with mixture of 2,4-D and dicamba. *Cropland*—Till the soil thoroughly to destroy well-established plants, include small grains or corn in rotation, and treat with 2,4-D or dicamba at the correct crop stage while new seedlings are small. *Pastures*—Mechanically remove scattered plants, or rotate to a clean cultivated crop for 1 or 2 years, or use repeated applications of 2,4-D plus dicamba. *Fence Rows and Waste Places*—Mechanically remove established plants or treat with glyphosate or a mixture of 2,4-D plus dicamba. For total vegetation control use sulfometuron or tebuthiuron.

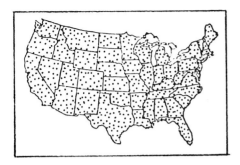

10D
Chenopodium album L.
Common lambsquarters
Goosefoot family
(Chenopodiaceae)

Description

An annual herb that has many branched erect stems. The stems are smooth, often groved with red and green streaks and are 30–180 cm tall. The leaves are light green on the surface and more or less white with mealy pustules especially on the underside when young. The leaves often turn red in the fall. The inflorescence is a rather large terminal panicle, with a mealy surface and dense clusters of variously arranged tiny flowers. The fruit has a thin wall that is papery when dry. The seeds are less than 1.5 mm across and are black, smooth, and finely grooved. Reproduction is by seeds. Flowering occurs from June to October.

Habitat

This weed may occur in or around most cultivated sites. It is commonly used for greens while a young plant. It is a native of North America and Eurasia.

Suggested Control

Home Garden—Clean cultivation and hand hoeing. Use mulches to prevent seedling establishment. *Cropland*—Use cultivation with or without the use of a variety of herbicides. Select one of the following herbicides according to labeled tolerance for desired crop: alachlor, ametryne, atrazine, bentazon, bromoxynil, chloramben, chlorosulfuron, chloroxuron, cyanazine, DCPA, dinoseb, diphenamid, diuron, EPTC, ethafluralin, fluometuron, isopropalin, linuron, metribuzin, methazole, oryzalin, oxyfluorfen, pebulate, pendimethalin, profluralin, prometryn, propachlor, propazine, pyrazon, simazine, terbacil, trifluralin, vernolate, MCPA, and 2,4-D. Any postemergence herbicide such as ametryn, bentazon, 2,4-D, MCPA, etc., must be applied while the plant is young as it rapidly becomes woody and resistant. *Pastures*—Sheep will eat young plants but cattle will not unless feed is scarce. Apply 2,4-D when plants are young. *Industrial*—Use atrazine, bromacil, hexazinone, simazine, sulfumeturon, or tebuthiuron.

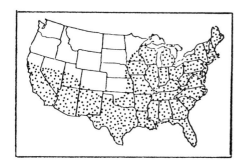

10E
Chenopodium
ambrosioides L.
Mexicantea
Goosefoot family
(Chenopodiaceae)

Description

This annual or perennial plant is an unpleasantly aromatic herb. The stems are erect, up to 1.5 m tall, well-branched, and have numerous leaves. The stems and leaves have minute yellow glands. Leaves are up to 12 cm long, short petioled, and oblong to lance-shaped. Leaves may have deeply toothed margins, although the higher they are located on the stem the less toothed they are and may even have entire leaf margins. The inflorescence is composed of densely flowered spikes, intermixed with leaves forming a pyramidal panicle. The fruit has a thin glandular-dotted wall. Seeds are 0.8 mm across, dark brown and shiny. Reproduction is by seeds. It flowers from July to September.

Habitat

Mexicantea may occur around barnyards, in cultivated fields, and waste areas. It is a native of tropical America.

Suggested Control

Home Gardens—Hoe or pull plants before early flowering stage or use a mulch before seed germination. *Cropland*—Use mechanical control methods; this weed does not appear on specific herbicide labels, but herbicides used for control of common lambsquarters may be a possibility. *Industrial*—possibly controlled by atrazine, bromacil, hexazinone, simazine, sulfometuron, or tebuthiuron.

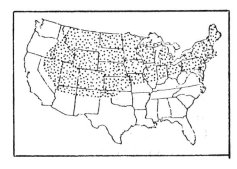

10F
Kochia scoparia (L.) Roth.
Kochia
Goosefoot family
(Chenopodiaceae)

Description

An annual herb with erect, much branched, slender, green stems that are 30 to 100 cm tall. Its simple, pale green, alternate, leaves are sessile, linear or narrowly lance-shaped, and more or less hairy. Flowers are greenish, without petals and are borne in axillary spikes forming a terminal panicle. Seeds are about 2 mm long, dull brown, marked with yellow, oval shaped and flattened with a groove on each side. Reproduction is by seeds. It flowers from July to September.

Habitat

Kochia may be found in cultivated fields, pastures, rangelands, and waste areas. It is native to Europe.

Suggested Control

Cultivated Crops—Use cultivation to prevent seed formation and to control escaped plants. Use a crop and herbicide rotation system as part of normal weed management program. Herbicides that include kochia on their label are atrazine, cyanazine, dicamba, diuron, EPTC, fluometuron, pendimethalin, simazine, trifluralin, and terbacil. *Pastures*—Mow periodically to prevent seed production and use improved pasture management practices. *Fence Rows, Waste Places, and Industrial*—If burn down is desired, use paraquat or glyphosate, or if residual control is desired, use a soil sterilant.

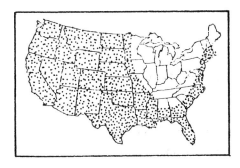

10G
Salsola kali L.
Russian thistle
Goosefoot family
(Chenopodiaceae)

Description

This annual herb has a spreading taproot. The erect stems are profusely branched, bushy, rigid, spiny, and 30–80 cm tall. Leaves are
alternate, semicylindric, sharp-pointed, dull green or grayish, and
turn red when mature. The green or pinkish flowers are axillary and
without petals. The fruit is surrounded by the five enlarged sepals.
The seeds are cone-shaped and about 2 mm broad. The plants break
off near the ground when mature and will tumble in the wind thus
spreading their seed. It flowers from July to October.

Habitat

This weed is very common on the over-grazed ranges of the moun-
tain west and also occur in small grain fields, legume seedings, and
waste areas. It is native of Central Asia.

Suggested Control

Cultivated Crops—Use cultivation if needed and a good crop–herbicide rotation, which includes atrazine, cyanazine, dicamba, diuron,
fluometuron, simazine, or trifluralin. *Fence Rows, Waste Places, and
Industrial*—For burn down use paraquat or glyphosate and for residual control use one of soil sterilants.

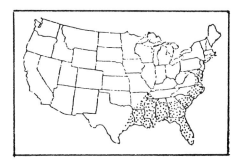

10H
Alternanthera philoxeroides
   (Mart.) Griseb.
Alligatorweed
Amaranth family
(Amaranthaceae)

Description

This perennial aquatic herb has erect, prostrate, or decumbent stems that are smooth and hollow. The prostrate stems may produce two shoots at each node, which form a mat of vegetation interwoven with other stems. The ascending stems are often 20 to 60 cm tall. Leaves are simple, opposite, lance-shaped, slightly hairy, sessile on the stem, and 6–12 cm long. The flower head is a globose spike 13 mm in diameter and borne on long peduncles 2–7 cm long. Individual florets are silvery-white and 6 to 20 form a head. Seeds are rarely produced in the United States. Reproduction is vegetatively by axillary buds and rarely by seeds. It flowers from May to October.

Habitat

Alligatorweed may occur in wet areas along drainage ways, ditches, or free floating in ponds, lakes, and canals. It is native to South America.

Suggested Control

Through cooperating agricultural agencies obtain the release of alligatorweed beetle (*Agasicles hyprophila*), alligatorweed thrips (*Amynothrips andensoni*), and a stem-boring moth (*Vogtia mallei*), for biological control. Also multiple applications of 2,4-D applied in spring or summer will control the weed. In rice, glyphosate applied preplant will control the weed.

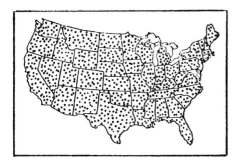

10I
Amaranthus albus L.
Tumble pigweed
Amaranth family
(Amaranthaceae)

Description

An annual, bushy-branched herb that is up to 80 cm tall. Stems are pale-green or whitish, erect or ascending and smooth. Leaves are pale green, with veiny blades, 1 to 8 cm long, and the long base tapers into a long petiole. Flowers are unisexual and grouped in short, dense axillary clusters. Bracts are rigid and about twice as long as the flowers. Female flowers commonly have three oblong sepals. The seed is a very small (1 mm), round, lens-shaped shiny-black disk. Reproduction is by seeds. Flowers appear from July to October.

Habitat

Tumble pigweed may occur in any cultivated or waste area. It is a native of North America.

Suggested Control

See suggestions under redroot pigweed control, page 122.

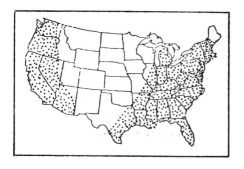

11A
Amaranthus hybridus L.
Smooth pigweed
Amaranth family
(Amaranthaceae)

Description

An annual herb with many branches that grows up to 2 m tall. Stems are coarse and erect. Leaves are oval to oblong and 8–15 cm long. The inflorescence is composed of numerous cylindric spikes about 1 cm thick. The lateral spikes are up to 8 cm long, and the terminal spike is up to 15 cm long. Together they form an erect panicle. Also solitary spikes are commonly found in the upper leaf axils. Bracts are nearly twice as long as the short-pointed sepals. Sepals of the female flowers are equal or slightly longer than the fruit and are minutely bristled at the apex. The fruit is about 1.5 to 2 mm long. The seeds are very small, 1 mm in diameter and disk-shaped. Seed is the only method of reproduction. It flowers from July to November.

Habitat

Smooth pigweed may be found in most any type of cultivated or disturbed area. It is a native of tropical America.

Suggested Control

See suggestions under redroot pigweed control, page 122.

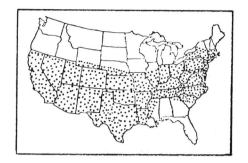

11B
Amaranthus palmeri
S. Wats.
Palmer amaranth
Amaranth family
(Amaranthaceae)

Description

A summer annual herb that has erect branched stems up to 100 cm tall. Leaves are long-petioled, oval to lance-shaped, and about 4 to 10 cm long. The apex is rounded with a small pointed tip. The blades are dark green, with prominent veins on the bottom side. The inflorescence is an open panicle with the terminal branch up to 50 cm long and 1.5 cm thick. The lateral branches are much shorter or absent. Bracts of the female flowers are narrow and 3–6 mm long, while those of the male flowers are thinner and about 3–4 mm long and have a slender awn. The seed is brown and disk-shaped. Reproduction is by seeds. The illustration (plate 11B) shows both male and female plants. It flowers from August to October.

Habitat

Palmer amaranth can be found in cultivated fields, barnyards, and waste areas. It is native to southwestern North America.

Suggested Control

See suggestions under redroot pigweed control, page 122.

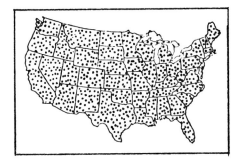

11C
Amaranthus retroflexus L.
Redroot pigweed
Amaranth family
(Amaranthaceae)

Description

An annual, erect, branched herb that has coarse, finely hairy, up to 2 m tall stems. The lower stem and upper root are generally distinctly red in color. Leaves are dull-green, long petioled, oval shaped and up to 10 cm long. The inflorescence is a panicle made up of clusters of small flowers. The terminal branch is short, 5–20 cm long, densely crowded; smaller branches are produced from the upper axils. Flowers are subtended by three spiny bracts, 4–8 mm long, much exceeding the sepals. The female flowers have five sepals that are much longer than the fruit. The fruit is flattened and about 2 mm long. The seeds are small (1.2 mm in diameter), brownish-black disks. Reproduction is by seeds. It flowers from July to November.

Habitat

Redroot pigweed is commonly found in most cultivated areas, home gardens, and around barnyards. It is native to tropical America.

Suggested Control

Pigweed is listed on herbicide labels with no species differentiation. Susceptibility of most species is similar, so control measures are listed under the most common species. Some biotypes of pigweeds are resistant to triazine-type herbicides. If this is the case, use a nontriazine-type herbicide. *Home Gardens*—Clean cultivate several times in spring before planting vegetables to stimulate seed germination, followed by careful weeding during the summer. Organic and inorganic mulches may be used with good success. Possible herbicides include DCPA, diphenamid, and trifluralin. *Cropland*—Use delayed planting and multiple shallow, tillage operations to stimulate seed germination and control young seedlings as well as an effective herbicide for residual activity. Possible herbicides include acifluorfen, alachlor, ametryn, atrazine, bromoxynil, chlorsulfuron, cyanazine, diuron, EPTC, fluchloralin, fluometuron, isopropalin, linuron, metolachlor, metribuzin, methazole, MSMA, napropamide, norflurazon, oryzalin, oxyfluorfen, pebulate, pendimethalin, prometryn, propazine, simazine, trifluralin, vernolate, MCPA, 2,4-D, and dicamba. *Industrial*—Use paraquat for burn down or a soil sterilant for residual control.

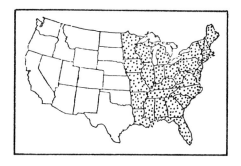

11D
Amaranthus spinosus L.
Spiny amaranth
Amaranth family
(Amaranthaceae)

Description

A summer annual herb that has a smooth erect, grooved stem with a pair of divergent spines, 5–10 mm long protruding from most leaf axils. The plant may grow up to 1.2 m tall. Leaves are oval to lance-shaped, 3–6 cm long and have a short-pointed tip. The inflorescence is a panicle that is 5–15 cm long and composed of numerous branches. The terminal branches bear male flowers and the basal and axillary branches bear female flowers. Bracts are awl-shaped and are about the same length as the five bristle-tipped sepals. The fruit is about 2 mm in diameter. Seeds nearly circular and 0.8–1 mm wide. Reproduction is by seeds. It flowers from June to October.

Habitat

Spiny amaranth may occur in cultivated fields, gardens, barnyards, and waste areas. It is native to tropical America.

Suggested Control

See suggestions under redroot pigweed control, page 122.

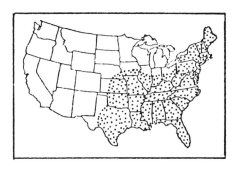

11E
Phytolacca americana L.
Common pokeweed
Pokeweed family
(Phytolaccaceae)

Description

A coarse perennial herb that has a very large, fleshy taproot. Stems are erect, smooth, fleshy, and multiple-branched at the top. They are 2–3 m tall, often clumped and arched. The smooth leaves alternate on the stem. Leaves are simple, petioled, and somewhat heart-shaped to oblong and lance-shaped. They have entire margins and are 10–30 cm long. The inflorescence is a raceme, 10–20 cm long, borne either on terminal stalk or on lateral stalk, opposite a leaf. Flowers are white or greenish. Mature fruit is a dark purple, 10-seeded berry, about 7 mm in diameter. Seeds are small, flat, shiny-black, hard, and about 3 mm in diameter. Reproduction is by seeds and parts of the tap root. Flowers appear from July to October. Very young plants are eaten for greens, but mature foliage and roots are poisonous.

Habitat

This plant may be found in fields under conservation tillage, pastures, fence rows, borders of fields, roadsides, and waste areas. It is a native of North America.

Suggested Control

Cultivated Fields—Use thorough tillage including fall or spring plowing followed by clean cultivation. Spot spray with 2,4-D plus dicamba when plants are small. *Fence Rows and Waste Areas*—Remove the large perennial rootstalk with a sharp spade or other device. Young plants up to about 0.6 meter tall can be controlled with 2,4-D plus dicamba.

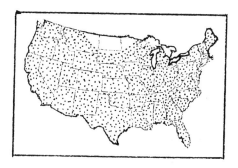

11F
Mollugo verticillata L.
Carpetweed
Carpetweed family
(Aizoaceae)

Description

An annual, prostrate herb that has many branched, smooth stems up to 40 cm long, and forms large, green, flat mats on the soil surface. Leaves are in whorls of three to eight at each node and are 1–2.3 cm long. They are narrowly to broadly oblaceolate and the petiole is scarcely differentiated. The small, pale-green or white flowers are borne on short stalks with two to five per node. Flowers have five petals, five oblong sepals and three or four stamens. The oval-shaped fruit has three locules and three valves and is 3 mm long. The seeds are small, kidney-shaped and orange-red. It reproduces by seeds. It flowers from June to November.

Habitat

Carpetweed may be found in gardens, crop lands, lawns, and waste areas. It is apparently native to tropical America.

Suggested Control

Home Gardens—Prevent seed production by cultivation and hand-hoeing of scattered plants. Organic and inorganic mulches can be used with good success. Possible herbicides are DCPA, diphenamid, and trifluralin. *Cropland*—Use clean cultivation or select a herbicide that is labeled for carpetweed control and has the crop selectivity needed. Possible herbicides include acifluorfen, atrazine, cyanazine, DCPA, diphenamid, EPTC, fluchloralin, linuron, metolachlor, metribuzin, pendimethalin, propazine, trifluralin, and vernolate. *Industrial*—Use paraquat for burn down or a soil sterilant for residual control.

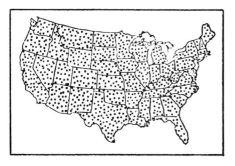

11G
Portulaca oleracea L.
Common purslane
Purslane family
(Portulacaceae)

Description

An annual herb that has prostrate, very fleshy stems, 20–50 cm long. Stems are smooth, green or purplish red, multiple branched, and tend to form a large mat. Leaves are succulent and have smooth margins. They are 1–3 cm long, sessile, generally alternate on the stem but sometimes nearly opposite and often are in clusters at the ends of the branches. The flower has 6 to 10 stamens, four to six styles, and the lower portion of the calyx is fused with the ovary. The fruit is a globe-shaped, many seeded capsule, 4–8 mm long that splits open around the middle. The seeds are very small, black and rough textured. Reproduction is by seeds. Flowers appear from August to October.

Habitat

Common purslane may be found in gardens, cultivated fields especially those planted to vegetables, and around barnyards. It is a native to Western Asia.

Suggested Control

Home Gardens—Use periodic cultivation and hand hoeing to control this weed in the seedling stage. If allowed to grow much over 5 cm, the cut plant can reroot. If the plant has initiated flowers, remove cut plants and destroy them as seed will mature while the plant is drying. Pigs are fond of this weed. *Cropland*—Use a preemergence or postemergence herbicide coupled with cultivation if necessary. Herbicides that include purslane on the label are acifluorfen, atrazine, bentazon, chloramben, cyanazine, DCPA, diphenamid, diuron, EPTC, fluometuron, isopropalin, linuron, metribuzin, methazole, norflurazon, oryzalin, pebulate, pendimethalin, perfluidone, prometryn, propachlor, pyrazon, simazine, trifluralin, and terbacil.

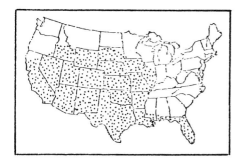

11H
Agrostemma githago L.
Corn cockle
Pink family
(Caryophyllaceae)

Description

A winter annual herb with erect, simple, or sparingly branched stems that are up to 1 m tall and covered with silky white hairs. Leaves are opposite, almost grasslike, 6–12 mm wide and 8–12 cm long. Flowers are 3–4 cm in diameter, solitary at the ends of the branches on 10–20 cm long pedicels. The calyx has five united sepals with long narrow lobes and the corolla has five red or purple petals that are 2–3 cm long. The fruit is a 12–16 mm long capsule. It reproduces by seeds. Flowering occurs from May to August.

Habitat

Corn cockle may occur in small-grain and hay fields and along roadsides and in waste areas.

Suggested Control

Small grains—Use a good crop rotation and alternate small grains with cultivated row crops; use only clean noncontaminated seed, spray small grains in spring before wheat is in the jointing stage with MCPA. Do not substitute 2,4-D for MCPA as a pronounced difference in susceptibility has been reported. *Hay Fields, Roadsides, and Waste Places*—Mow periodically to prevent seed production, apply MCPA in the spring when corn cockle plants are small. Be careful to prevent herbicide drift.

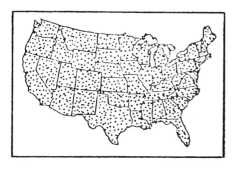

11I
Arenaria serpyllifolia L.
Thymeleaf sandwort
Pink family
(Caryophyllaceae)

Description

A diffuse, delicate, wiry-stemmed, minutely hairy annual herb that is up to 20 cm tall. It has 8 to 10 leaf pairs that are 3–5 mm long and have sparse stiff hairs and frequently a somewhat pimply surface. The inflorescence is usually small, with leafy bracts. Flowers are white with very short and thin pedicels. The sepals are about 3 mm long, lance-shaped and have three to five nerves. The sepals are usually shorter than the sepals. The fruit is an egg-shaped capsule slightly longer than the sepals and breaks open along six equal teeth. The seeds are very small, kidney-shaped, and gray-black. It reproduces by seeds. It flowers from May to August.

Habitat

This small weed may occur in lawns and waste areas. It is a native of Eurasia.

Suggested Control

Turf—Good turf management techniques including proper turf grass selection, fertilization, pH adjustment, and mowing height and frequency will allow the turf to successfully compete with this weed. Apply a mixture of 2,4-D, mecoprop, and dicamba in the spring, and if necessary the application may be repeated. *Waste Areas*—For selective control in grass apply a mixture of 2,4-D, mecoprop, and dicamba; for burn down apply paraquat; for complete vegetation control apply a soil sterilant.

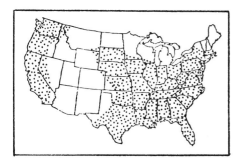

12A
Cerastium viscosum L.
Sticky chickweed
Pink family
(Caryophyllaceae)

Description

An annual herb with spreading, tufted, ascending, gummy, hairy stems that are 10–30 cm long. Leaves are commonly 1–2 cm long, somewhat oval in shape, and the lower ones are sometimes pointed. The inflorescence is a compact cluster of white flowers. The flowers have short pedicels and green, lance-shaped hairy sepals that are rather strongly single-nerved at base and translucent at the edges. The flower has five white petals that are about as long as the sepals. The fruit is 6–10 mm long, cylindric, and sometimes rather curved. The seeds are pale reddish and very small. Reproduction is by seeds. Flowers appear from April to July.

Habitat

Sticky chickweed may be found in lawns, pastures, and hay fields. It is a native of Eurasia.

Suggested Control

Turf—Use good turf management techniques including proper turf grass selection, fertilization, pH adjustment, and mowing height and frequency so that the turf can successfully compete with this weed. Apply a mixture of 2,4-D, mecoprop, and dicamba in the spring; if necessary the application should be repeated. *Pastures and Hay Fields*—Use good pasture management practices of proper fertilization and pH adjustment to maintain a competitive stand of grass or hay. If clovers or alfalfa are not part of the pasture then apply a mixture of 2,4-D, mecoprop, and dicamba in the early spring.

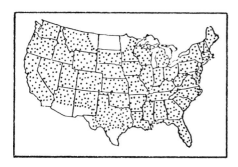

12B
Cerastium vulgatum L.
Mouseear chickweed
Pink family
(Caryophyllaceae)

Description

A perennial herb with spreading, tufted stems that are 15–30 cm long, ascending or erect, and covered with short, gummy hairs. Leaves are oblong to lance shaped, 1–2 cm long, single-nerved, and somewhat hairy. The inflorescence is rather open. The mature flower is on a 5–12 mm long pedicel. Sepals are 4–6 mm long, oblong-lanceolate, hairy, rather strongly one-nerved and have translucent edges. Petals are longer than the sepals. The fruit is a 8–10 mm long, cylindric, curved capsule opening by short teeth. The seeds are reddish brown and very small. Reproduction is by seeds. Flowers occur from April to July.

Habitat

This weed is found in lawns, pastures, cropland, and waste areas. It is a native of Eurasia.

Suggested Control

Turf—Practice good turf management techniques including proper turf grass selection, fertilization, pH adjustment, and proper mowing height and mowing frequency to allow the turf to successfully compete with this weed. Apply a mixture of 2,4-D, mecoprop, and dicamba in the spring, and repeat if necessary. *Cropland*—With proper seedbed preparation before planting and periodic crop rotation, this weed will not persist. *Waste Places*—For selective control in grass apply a mixture of 2,4-D, mecoprop, and dicamba; for total vegetation control use a soil sterilant.

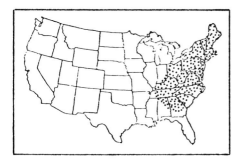

12C
Holosteum umbellatum L.
Jagged chickweed
Pink family
(Caryophyllaceae)

Description

Winter annual herb with tufted, unbranched, 10–30 cm long stems that are smooth or nearly so below on the lower portion and hairy on the upper portion. Most of the leaves occur at the base of the plant and only a few, 1–2.5 cm long leaves occur on the stems. The inflorescence is a cluster of flowers (3–8) borne at the end of a long stalk. The flowers are white, borne on a slender 2–3 cm long pedicel. The sepals are rounded and translucent at the edges. The petals are 2–3 mm long and ragged toward the apex. There are three to five stamens and three styles. The fruit is an egg-shaped, one-celled, many-seeded, capsule opening at the top by six teeth. Reproduction is by seeds. Flowers occur from March to June.

Habitat

Jagged chickweed may occur in lawns, pastures, small grains, and some cultivated fields. It is a native of Eurasia.

Suggested Control

Turf—Practice good turf management techniques including proper turf grass selection, proper fertilization, pH adjustment, and proper mowing height and mowing frequency to allow the turf to successfully compete with this weed. Apply a mixture of 2,4-D, mecoprop, and dicamba in the spring, and repeat the application if necessary. *Cropland*—With proper seedbed preparation before planting and periodic crop rotation, this weed will not persist. *Pastures and Small Grains*—Apply a mixture of 2,4-D and dicamba in the early spring.

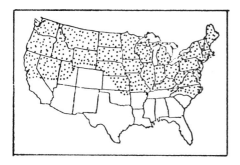

12D
Lychnis alba Mill.
White cockle
Pink family
(Caryophyllaceae)

Description

An annual or perennial herb that arises from a coarse root. Each plant has either male or female flowers. The stems are 40–120 cm tall, coarsely hairy, and are glandular on the upper portion. There may be as many as 10 pairs of stem leaves that are more or less lance-shaped. Leaves are 3–10 cm long, pointed, three- to five-nerved and finely to stiffly hairy. The lower blades have petioles but the upper ones are without petiole. The inflorescence is many branched with leafy bracts. Flowers are white and unisexual. The calyx is tubular and 15–20 mm long. There are 10 nerves in the male flower and 20 nerves in the female flowers. Petals are 2–4 cm long and ragged on the margins. The fruit is an egg-shaped capsule that is 10–15 mm long and splits by 10 spreading teeth. Reproduction is by seeds. Flowers are produced from June to August.

Habitat

White cockle may occur in cropland and hayfields. It is a native of Europe.

Suggested Control

Cropland—Use clean seed if planting small seeded legumes and small grains. The weed is controlled by good cultivation techniques and crop rotation in row crops. Herbicides that may control white cockle are bentazon, bromoxynil, chlorsulfuron, methazole, terbacil, and terbutryn. *Hayfields*—Use good management practices of proper fertilization and pH adjustment and if clover or alfalfa is not present, apply a mixture of 2,4-D plus dicamba in the spring.

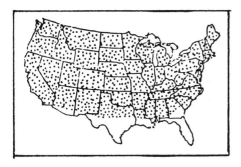

12E
Saponaria officinalis L.
Bouncingbet
Pink family
(Caryophyllaceae)

Description

Erect, perennial herb that arises from a horizontal rhizome and is found in extensive colonies. The smooth, simple or branched, coarse stems are 40–80 cm tall. The leaves are opposite, pointed at the tip, smooth, 2–4 cm wide and 7–10 cm long. The inflorescence is congested and up to 15 cm long. Primary bracts are leafy and subsequent bracts are more membranous. The flowers are fragrant. The calyx is cylindric and the lobes are triangular and drawn out. The petals are white or pinkish. The fruit is a capsule splitting by four apical teeth. Reproduction is mainly by seeds but sometimes by rhizome pieces. Flowers occur from July to September.

Habitat

This weed is not common in cultivated fields but is along fence rows, roadsides, railroad ballast, and in waste areas. It is a native of Eurasia.

Suggested Control

Cropland—With proper crop management including proper seedbed preparation and periodic crop rotation coupled with herbicides normally used for control of broadleaf weeds, this weed will not persist. *Noncropland*—Apply bromacil, sulfometuron, or tebuthiuron if complete vegetation control is desired or 2,4-D plus dicamba if only grass is desired.

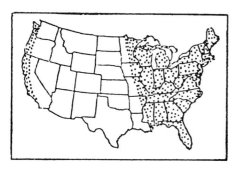

12F
Scleranthus annuus L.
Knawel
Pink family
(Caryophyllaceae)

Description

A low, spreading winter and spring annual that has diffuse, smooth or finely pubescent stems up to 15 cm tall. The leaves are more or less awl-shaped, green, narrow, opposite, and bent downward. The flowers are inconspicuous, greenish, and are borne on the side of the stem. The calyx lobes are equal or longer than their tube and five to ten stamens are usually present. The small 1–1.3 mm long seeds are straw-colored. It reproduces by seeds. Flowers occur from March to June.

Habitat

Knawel occurs in cultivated fields, especially those with a long history of small grain production and along roadsides and waste areas. It is a native of Eurasia.

Suggested Control

Cropland—Good crop rotation and clean cultivation will do much to reduce infestation. Knawel is susceptible to atrazine, bromoxynil, linuron, metribuzin, paraquat, and simazine so include crops such as soybeans, corn, or potatoes where these herbicides can be used in your crop rotation. *Roadsides and Waste Places*—Burn down with paraquat or apply atrazine, bromacil, simazine, or tebuthiuron if total vegetation control is desired.

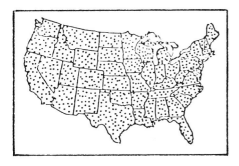

12G
Silene antirrhina L.
Sleepy catchfly
Pink family
(Caryophyllaceae)

Description

This plant is an annual or biennial, depending on the climatic zone where it is growing. Its smooth to finely hairy stems are 20–80 cm tall, simple to branched, erect to decumbent and usually have glandular zones below the upper nodes. The basal leaves are oblanceolate and the stems leaves are oblanceolate to linear. They are 3–6 cm long and finely hairy and the margins are cilliate near the base. The inflorescence is a panicle with variable branching that is greatly influenced by growing conditions. The calyx is 4–10 mm long and 10-nerved. The petals are white or pink, two-lobed, equal or exceeding the calyx in length. The fruit is an egg-shaped capsule, 4–10 mm long. The seeds are very small and have three or four rows of tiny protrusions. Reproduction is by seeds. Flowers appear from May to September.

Habitat

Sleepy catchfly may occur in small grain fields, newly seeded pastures, hay fields, and waste areas. It is a native of North America.

Suggested Control

Small Grains—Prepare a good seedbed prior to seeding and harrow lightly after crop emergence. Possible herbicides would be chlorsulfuron, dicamba, 2,4-D, or MCPA applied when small grains are in the tiller stage of development. *Pastures*—Use good pasture management techniques of pH adjustment, fertilization, rotational grazing and clipping following grazing. Apply 2,4-D or dicamba while weed is young and actively growing. *Waste Places*—Apply a mixture of 2,4-D plus dicamba for selective control in grass or apply atrazine, bromacil, or tebuthiuron for total vegetation control.

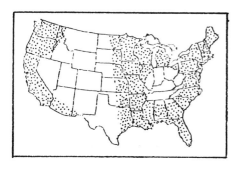

12H
Spergula arvensis L.
Corn spurry
Pink family
(Caryophyllaceae)

Description

An annual herb with small weak stems that are bright green, erect or spreading and 15–45 cm tall. The leaves are 2–5 cm long, bright green, threadlike, and are clustered at the nodes in two opposite sets of six to eight each, that appear to be in a whorl. The flowers are small, white, with five petals and borne in a terminal cluster. The fruit is a single-celled capsule that breaks into five sections with many seeds. The rough dull-black seeds are 1–2 mm wide and have narrow white wings. Reproduction is by seeds. Flowering occurs from March to October.

Habitat

Corn spurry may be found in small grain fields and other cultivated lands. It is a native of Europe.

Suggested Control

Cultivated Crops—Use a crop rotation coupled with cultivation and one of the following herbicides: atrazine, cyanazine, dicamba, diuron, EPTC, fluometuron, linuron, propachlor, and simazine. *Small grains*—Apply dicamba during the full tiller stage and immediately after harvest, destroy all vegetation by cultivation. Rotate small grains with a clean cultivated crop. *Fence Rows and Waste Places*—Apply dicamba for selective control in grass, paraquat for burn down, or a soil sterilant if complete vegetation control is desired.

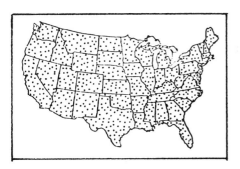

12I
Stellaria media (L.) Cyrillo.
Common chickweed
Pink family
(Caryophyllaceae)

Description

A weak, tufted, annual that has trailing to ascending stems. The 30–40 cm long stems are finely pubescent and branched. The smooth leaves are 1–3 cm long and ovate or elliptic. The upper leaves have no petioles, whereas, the lower leaves may have petioles that are longer than the blades. There may be a few hairs toward the base of the leaf. Flowers are solitary or in clusters of a few flowers and are borne at the end of a stalk. The lance-shaped or oblong sepals are 3.5–6 mm long and more or less hairy. The white petals are shorter than the sepals. The fruit is an egg-shaped capsule that opens by splitting down the sides. The small seeds are reddish brown. Reproduction is by seeds. Flowers occur from February to July.

Habitat

Common chickweed is a pest in lawns and may also occur in pastures, small grains, and hay fields. It is a native of Eurasia.

Suggested Control

Turf—Apply a mixture of 2,4-D plus mecoprop plus dicamba in the early spring when plants are small. *Row Crops*—Select the proper herbicide for the crop desired. Chickweed is included on the labels of atrazine, benefin, chloramben, chloroxuron, chlorpropham, chlorsulfuron, cyanazine, DCPA, dinoseb, diphenamid, duron, DSMA, endothall, EPTC, linuron, methazole, MSMA, metribuzin, monuron, napropamide, oryzalin, paraquat, pronamide, simazine, terbacil, terbutryn, and trifluralin. *Small grains*—Sow adequate seed and apply sufficient fertilizer to provide a highly competitive crop cover. In some climatic areas linuron or terbutryn may be applied. *Alfalfa*—Apply chlorpropham, metribuzin, pronamide, or terbacil in late winter or early spring according to the label.

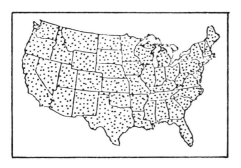

13A
Ceratophyllum demersum L.
Common coontail
Hornwort family
(Ceratophyllaceae)

Description

Submersed aquatic herb that forms large vegetative mats and generally has no roots. The stems are up to 80 cm long, cordlike, flexible, and branched. The leaves are in whorls of 5 to 12 and are finely dissected into two or three narrow, blunt-toothed segments. They are about 0.5 mm wide and 1–3 cm long. Flowers are minute, borne in the leaf axils and generally difficult to locate. The fruit is single-seeded, compressed, smooth, about 5 mm long and has two basal spines. Reproduction is by seeds and stem sections that break loose from the parent plant. Flowers may be found from July to October.

Habitat

Common coontail may be present in quiet fresh water ponds, lakes, or canals. It is a cosmopolitan plant.

Suggested Control

Aquatic—Apply 2,4-D, diquat, or endothall in the spring or early summer as the weeds start to grow. The following herbicides may be used for control of common coontail: 2,4-D, dichlobenil, diquat, endothall, and simazine.

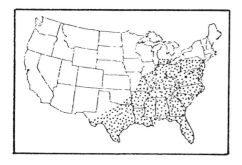

13B
Cabomba caroliniana Gray
Cabomba (Fanwort)
Water-lily family
(Nymphaeaceae)

Description

An aquatic rooted submersed perennial herb that has delicate stems up to 2 m long. The stems are slender, much branched, and may be covered with a thin gelatinous coating. This plant has two types of leaves. Submersed leaves are most common and are opposite or whorled, palmately dissected, fan-shaped, and have 1–2 cm long petiole. Floating leaves are few in number, alternate, 6–20 mm long, and slightly constricted at the middle. The flowers are white, have a peduncle, and are borne on the same axis as the floating leaves. Reproduction is by seeds and vegetative fragmentation. Flowers appear from May to September.

Habitat

This aquatic weed occurs in acidic lakes, ponds, and quiet streams. It is a native to North America.

Suggested Control

Aquatic—If possible use a water level fluctuation program with a drawdown time of 4 months. Good control has also been obtained with endothall and simazine.

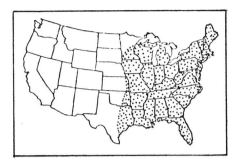

13C
Nelumbo lutea (Willd.) Pers.
American lotus
Water-lily family
(Nymphaeaceae)

Description

A perennial, aquatic herb that has thick rhizomes or edible tuberous rootstocks. Leaves are borne at ends of long, coarse petioles that lift the blade high above the water surface. The circular leaf blades have entire leaf margins and are 30–60 cm in diameter. They are softly pubescent, bluish-green, and the center is depressed, forming a cup or bowl. The young leaves usually lie on the water surface. The flowers are pale-yellow, 8–10 cm in diameter, and have more than 20 petals and sepals. The fruits are acornlike, 1 cm in diameter, and borne on a spongy, prolonged, cone-shaped, fruiting receptable that is about 10 cm wide on the end of the flower stalk. Reproduction is by seeds and rootstocks. It flowers from July to September.

Habitat

This plant may be found in the muddy and shallow waters of sluggish canals and along the shores of ponds and lakes. It is a native of North America.

Suggested Control

Aquatic—The edges of the pond or lake may be deepened and canals should be dried out periodically. Chemical control may be obtained with dichlobenil, 2,4-D, or endothall.

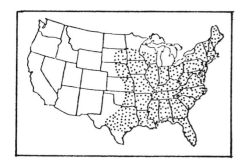

13D
Nuphar advena (Ait.) Ait. f.
Spatterdock
Water-lily family
(Nymphaeaceae)

Description

A perennial, emersed, aquatic plant that has thick 5–30 cm long rhizomes. Leaves arise directly from the rhizomes on long, coarse petioles. The leaf blades are circular and extend above the water, though they may be submersed or floating when young, or in periods of high water. Mature leaves are 20–40 cm in diameter and have a conspicuous midvein and a broad V-shaped cleft at the base. Flowers are yellow, 4–5 cm in diameter, borne at end of a long and erect stalk, and raised above the water surface. The fruit is green, furrowed, 2–5 cm high with a rayed disk that is up to 2.5 cm wide on the top. Reproduction is by seeds and rootstocks. It flowers from May to October.

Habitat

Spatterdock may occur in alluvial ponds and shallow waters along the rivers and particularly in sluggish canals. It is a native of North America.

Suggested Control

Aquatic—Make the pond deeper especially around the edges to prevent rooting on the bottom. Chemical control may be obtained with dichlobenil, 2,4-D, or endothall.

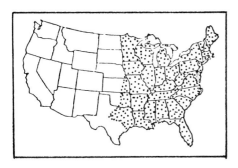

13E
Nymphaea odorata Ait.
Fragrant waterlily
Water-lily family
(Nymphaeaceae)

Description

A perennial emersed aquatic plant that has horizontal, elongated rhizomes without tubers. Leaves arise from the rhizomes on long, purplish-green petioles that are attached to the center of the blade. The leaf blades are circular, split to the middle, and generally lie flat on the water surface. They are 15–30 cm wide, green on the top and purplish on the bottom. The white flowers are solitary, borne at end of a long stalk, and rise a little above the water surface. They are very fragrant, and open only during the morning hours. The fruit matures under water. Seeds are 1.5–2.3 mm long and are borne in a fleshy saclike structure. Reproduction is by seeds and rootstocks. Flowers are present from June to September.

Habitat

This waterlily occurs in the still or stagnant waters of lakes and ponds, and in sluggish streams. It is a native of North America.

Suggested Control

Aquatic—Refrain from introducing into a farm pond or lake regardless of its beauty. If it is already established, methodically remove all parts each time a new plant appears or treat with dichlobenil, 2,4-D, or endothall.

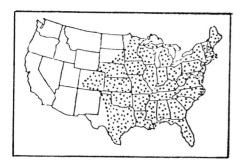

13F
Ranunculus abortivus L.
Smallflower buttercup
Crowfoot family
(Ranunculaceae)

Description

A short-lived perennial that has a slender, fibrous root system. The stems are erect, branched, smooth or very nearly so, and 20–50 cm tall. Basal leaves are kidney-shaped to round and are more or less heart-shaped at base. They may be slightly toothed or more often variously lobed or divided. Stem leaves have sheathing leaf bases. The blades are usually divided into three to five segments, which vary in size and shape. The flowers are small with five yellow petals that are less than 3 mm long. Many small teardrop-shaped seeds form in a cluster. Reproduction is by seeds. It flowers from March to June.

Habitat

Smallflower buttercup is common in lawns, hay fields, waste areas, and along roadsides. It is a native of North America.

Suggested Control

Pastures, Lawns, Roadsides and Waste Areas—Individual plants can be removed mechanically with a sharp shovel, or the young plants can be controlled with a mixture of 2,4-D plus dicamba. Buttercups are more prolific in poorly drained areas; therefore, improve drainage and use improved pasture management with proper fertilization and pH adjustment to help pasture grasses compete with this weed and gradually reduce the stand.

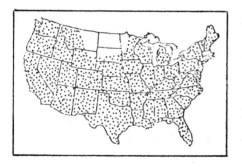

13G
Ranunculus acris L.
Tall buttercup
Crowfoot family
(Ranunculaceae)

Description

Perennial herb that has a short, thick, fibrous system. The stems are erect, branched above, slender, more or less hairy, tufted, and up to 100 cm tall. Leaves are alternate, hairy, palmately divided into three main segments, which in turn are deeply divided. Flowers are bright yellow to cream, shining as though varnished, and have many stamens about 2.5 cm across. The five petals are notched at the tip and are up to 1.5 cm long. The fruit is a cluster of subglobose, sharp-pointed 2–3 mm long achenes whose surface is minutely pitted. This weed reproduces by seeds. Flowers appear from May to August. This plant is poisonous to livestock.

Habitat

Tall buttercup may be found in lawns, pastures, meadows, cultivated fields, and moist places. It is a native of Europe.

Suggested Control

Pastures, Lawns, Roadsides, and Waste Areas—Buttercups thrive in areas of poor drainage and poor management, therefore, improved drainage, proper pH adjustment, and fertilization encourage desirable plants and increase plant competition. Seed production is prevented by cutting or mowing before flowering. If infestation is sparse or the area is small, scattered plants may be removed mechanically by digging below the crown with a sharp shovel. Young plants can be controlled with 2,4-D plus dicamba.

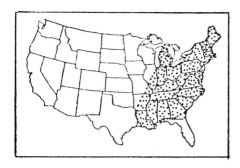

13H
Ranunculus bulbosus L.
Bulbous buttercup
Crowfoot family
(Ranunculaceae)

Description

A short-lived perennial that has a thickened bulbous base. The stems are erect, branched, pubescent and 20–60 cm tall. Basal leaves are long-petioled and in three three-part segments. The terminal segment has a stalk. All segments are deeply lobed. Stem leaves are few, smaller, less divided, and have clasping leaf bases. Flowers are terminal on a long-peduncle. The shiny yellow petals are 8–14 mm long and longer than the sepals. The seeds are numerous and are borne on an extended floral axis. They are 2.5–3.5 mm long, sharply margined and have coarse and curved beaks. Reproduction is by seeds. Flowers appear from March to June. This plant is poisonous to livestock.

Habitat

This weed may occur in lawns, pastures, and hay fields. It is a native of Europe.

Suggested Control

Pastures, Lawns, Roadsides and Waste Areas—Individual plants can be removed mechanically with a sharp shovel, or the young plants can be controlled with a mixture of 2,4-D plus dicamba. Buttercups are more prolific in poorly drained areas, therefore, drainage should be improved and better fertilization and pH adjustment should be practiced.

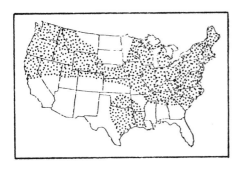

13I
Ranunculus repens L.
Creeping buttercup
Crowfoot family
(Ranunculaceae)

Description

A perennial, trailing, creeping herb with stems that are branched, creeping, rarely ascending, or erect. The stems often root at the nodes. The leaves are three-parted or lobed. Each segment is coarsely toothed, petioled, hairy, or dark green, sometimes has light spots. The glossy, golden-yellow flowers are about 1–1.2 cm across. They have five to nine round to obovate-shaped petals that are 8–15 mm long and have numerous stamens. The fruit is a cluster of achenes that are sharply but narrowly margined and have prominent triangular beaks. Reproduction is by seeds and runners. Flowers appear from May to July. This plant is poisonous to livestock.

Habitat

Creeping buttercup may be found in lawns, cultivated fields, pastures, moist meadows, and along roadsides. It is a native of Europe.

Suggested Control

Pastures, Lawns, Roadsides, and Waste Areas—Heavily infested pastures should be rotated to a clean cultivated crop for two or three years. If crop rotation and cultivation are not possible, management practices should be improved. Proper fertilization, pH adjustment, and rotational grazing encourage desirable pasture species. Scattered plants can be removed with a sharp shovel. Young plants can be controlled with 2,4-D plus dicamba.

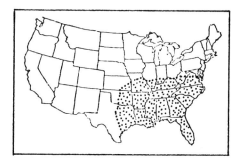

14A
Cocculus carolinus (L.) DC.
Red-berry moonseed
Moonseed family
(Menispermaceae)

Description

This semiwoody perennial vine has climbing stems that are 2–3 m long. The simple alternate, triangular to ovate, 5–15 cm long leaves are pointed, entire or three-lobed and have a heart-shaped base and are downy on the lower surface. The inflorescences are composed of unisexual flowers in axillary panicles or racemes. Male and female flowers are on separate plants. Flowers are greenish-white and 3–4 mm wide. The fruit is a red drupe about the size of a pea. Seeds are flat, wrinkled, grooved, and crescent-shaped. Reproduction is by seeds. It flowers from July to September.

Habitat

This vine may occur in fence rows, pastures, and waste places. It is a native of North America.

Suggested Control

Pastures—A good pasture management program including proper pH adjustment and fertilization to maintain a healthy, productive pasture coupled with rotational grazing and clipping after each grazing will do much to control this weed. *Fence Rows and Waste Places*—Grub the root out with a heavy hoe, or use a combination of 2,4-D plus dicamba on a trial basis.

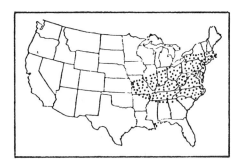

14B
Papaver dubium L.
Field poppy
Poppy family (Papaveraceae)

Description

This spring or winter annual herb has colored juice. Its stems are erect, simple, or sparingly branched, bristly, waxy and 30–60 cm tall. The leaves are pinnately compound with toothed to deeply incised segments, bristly surfaces, and on a rather long petiole. Flowers are solitary, borne at its end of a long, bristly stalk that is a continuation of the main plant axis. The corolla is showy, light scarlet to red and has four petals that are 2 cm long. The fruit is a club-shaped, smooth, waxy capsule, with five to nine stigmatic rays on the flat top. Reproduction is by seeds. Flowering is during May and June.

Habitat

Field poppy may occur in cultivated fields, pastures, hay fields, and waste places. It is a native of Europe and was probably introduced as a garden flower.

Suggested Control

Cultivated Fields—Established plants can be destroyed by plowing and cultivation. Do not allow scattered plants to seed. Use a crop rotation. This weed is susceptible to 2,4-D, ametryn, atrazine, chlorpropham, dichlobenil, dinoseb, linuron, and simazine. *Pastures and Hay Fields*—Use improved management practices such as pH adjustment, adequate fertilization, rotational grazing, etc., to thicken the crop stand and to provide increased competition. Remove scattered plants with a hand spade or spot spray of 2,4-D. *Waste Areas*—If objectionable, remove scattered plants with a spade or spray with 2,4-D.

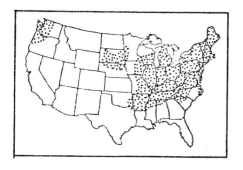

14C
Barbarea vulgaris R. Br.
Yellow rocket
Mustard family (Cruciferae)

Description

A biennial or short-lived perennial has a long taproot. The stems are erect, branched above, and 20–80 cm tall. The basal leaves are petioled and have one to four pairs of small, elliptic to ovate, lateral lobes and a large rounded terminal lobe. The stem leaves become progressively smaller and have shorter petioles. The upper ones are sessile, clasping, and are angulately toothed to entire. The flowers are yellow, 8 mm wide and crowded. The fruit is square in cross section and the body is 2.5–5.0 cm long with a beak that is up to 3 mm long. The seeds are gray to yellow-brown, wrinkled and 1–1.5 mm long. Reproduction is by seeds. It flowers from April to June.

Habitat

Yellow rocket may occur in gardens, small grain fields, hay fields, and pastures. It is a native of Europe.

Suggested Control

Home Gardens—Purchase clean vegetable seeds. Prevent seed production of any established plants by pulling, hand hoeing, and/or clean cultivation. *Cropland*—This weed is mainly a problem in small grains; therefore, purchase clean seed and then apply 2,4-D in early spring when small grains are in the well-tillered stage of growth and before jointing begins. Also, small grains can be rotated with other crops, where atrazine, cyanazine, EPTC, fluometuron, linuron, metribuzin, propazine, or simazine can be used to control this weed. *Pastures and Hay Fields*—Apply 2,4-D before seed is formed.

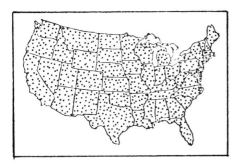

14D
Brassica kaber (DC.) L. C.
Wheeler
Wild mustard
Mustard family (Cruciferae)

Description

This annual herb has 20–100 cm tall stems that are usually coarsely hairy on the lower portion. The leaves are obovate and the lower ones are sometimes lobed but more often coarsely toothed. The upper leaves are progressively smaller and coarsely toothed. The yellow flowers are about 15 mm wide. The fruits are round in cross section and the body is 1–2 cm long with a beak about half as long. The seeds are round, black to purplish brown and 1–1.5 mm in diameter. Reproduction is by seeds. Flowers occur from May to July.

Habitat

This weed infests gardens, small grain fields, pastures, hay fields, and waste places. It is native of Europe.

Suggested Control

Home Gardens—Purchase clean vegetative seeds. Prevent seed production of any established plants by pulling, hand hoeing, and/or clean cultivation. *Cropland*—This weed is mainly a problem in small grains; therefore, purchase clean seed. Apply 2,4-D in early spring when small grains are in the well-tillered stage of growth and before jointing begins. Small grains can be rotated with other crops, where atrazine, cyanazine, EPTC, fluometuron, linuron, metribuzin, propazine, or simazine can be used to control this weed. *Pastures*—Apply 2,4-D before new seed is formed. Use improved pasture management practices and mow periodically close to ground to prevent seed maturation. *Fence Rows, Waste Areas, Industrial Sites*—Spray with 2,4-D if selective control is desired in grass, paraquat for immediate burn down of all vegetation, or a soil sterilant for residual total vegetation control.

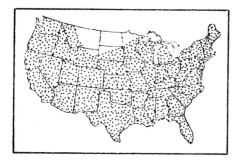

14E
Brassica nigra (L.) Koch
Black mustard
Mustard family (Cruciferae)

Description

An annual or winter annual herb that has a long taproot. The stem is erect, simple or branched, and up to 1.5 m tall. The lower part is usually bristly, while the upper part may be without hairs. The leaves on the lower part of the stems have a petiole, a large terminal lobe, and a few small lateral lobes, while the upper leaves are merely toothed. The four-petaled flowers are bright yellow and 8–10 mm wide. The fruits are four-sided smooth pods lying against the stem and up to 2 cm long. The seeds are brown, somewhat oval, and have a pitted surface. Reproduction is by seeds. Flowers appear from May to July.

Habitat

Black mustard occurs in cultivated fields, pastures, and waste places. It is native of Eurasia.

Suggested Control

Home Gardens—Purchase clean seed, prevent seed production, and eliminate all plants by pulling, hand hoeing, or clean cultivation. *Field Crops*—Rotate small grains with cultivated crops. Spray small grains with 2,4-D in early spring during the well-tillered stage. In other crops, atrazine, cyanazine, EPTC, fluometuron, linuron, metribuzin, propazine, and simazine can be used to control this weed. *Pastures*—Apply 2,4-D before the seed is formed. *Fence Rows, Waste Areas, and Industrial Sites*—Spray with 2,4-D if selective control in grass is desired, paraquat for immediate burn down of all vegetation, or a soil sterilant for residual total vegetation control.

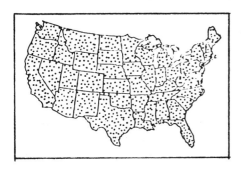

14F
Brassica rapa L.
Birdsrape mustard
Mustard family (Cruciferae)

Description

A biennial succulent herb with erect, glabrous, or very nearly so, branched stems that are up to 1 m tall. The pinnately lobed lower leaves have a petiole, whereas the oblong to lanceolate upper leaves are sessile and clasping and have toothed or entire leaf margins. The pale yellow flowers are about 10 mm wide. The flowering stems rise from a thick round root. Fruits are round in cross section; the body is 3–7 cm long and the beak is 0.8–2 mm long. Seeds are dark brown, 1.5–2 mm long, minutely roughened and round. Reproduction is by seeds. Flowers occur from May to October.

Habitat

This member of the mustard family may be found in small grain fields, newly seeded hay fields, pastures, and waste places. Its origin is unknown.

Suggested Control

Home Gardens—Purchase clean vegetable seeds, prevent seed production of any established plants by pulling, hand hoeing, and/or clean cultivation. *Cropland*—This weed is mainly a problem in small grains; therefore, purchase clean seed and then apply 2,4-D in early spring when small grains are in the well-tillered stage of growth and before jointing begins. Also, small grains can be rotated with other crops, where atrazine, cyanazine, EPTC, fluometuron, linuron, metribuzin, propazine, or simazine can be used to control this weed. *Pastures*—Spray with 2,4-D before seed is formed. Use improved pasture management practices and mow periodically close to ground to prevent seed maturation. *Fence Rows, Waste Areas, Industrial Sites*—Apply 2,4-D, paraquat, or a soil sterilant.

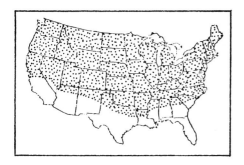

14G
Camelina microcarpa Andrz.
Smallseed Falseflax
Mustard family (Cruciferae)

Description

This herb can be either an annual or winter annual depending on the locale. The erect, simple, or branched stems are coarsely hairy and 30–60 cm tall. The simple, hairy leaves alternate on the stems and clasp it by a broad, arrow-shaped base. The inflorescence is a raceme up to 20 cm long. Flowers are pale yellow. Fruits are erect, rounded, or pear-shaped pods, that are 3–5 mm wide and 6–8 mm long. Several 1 mm long reddish-brown seeds are in each section of the fruit. Reproduction is by seeds. It flowers from May to July.

Habitat

This weed may be found in small grain and flax fields, roadsides, hay fields, and waste places. It is a native of Europe.

Suggested Control

Cropland—In small grains apply 2,4-D in early spring when small grains are well-tillered but before jointing is initiated. Also small grains can be rotated with other crops where control can be obtained with either atrazine, chlorsulfuron, cyanazine, fluometuron, linuron, methazole, metribuzin, propazine, or simazine. *Pastures*— Apply 2,4-D before seed is formed. Use improved pasture management practices and mow periodically close to ground to prevent seed formation. *Fence Rows, Waste Areas, and Industrial Sites*— Spray with 2,4-D, paraquat, glyphosate, or a soil sterilant.

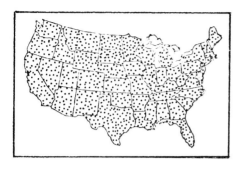

14H
Capsella bursa-pastoris (L.)
Medic.
Shepherdspurse
Mustard family (Cruciferae)

Description

An annual or winter annual herb that has a thin taproot and 10–60 cm tall, sparingly branched stems. The oblong basal leaves are 5–10 cm long and pinnately lobed, while the lanceolate to linear stem-leaves are smaller, entire, or toothed with earlike lobes at the base. The inflorescence is a cluster of congested flowers, but by maturity it is greatly elongated, often forming half the total height of the plant. The flowers are white, about 2 mm wide and the petals are about twice as long as the sepals. The fruits are 5–8 mm long, flat, triangular, and broader at the slightly notched apex (purse-shaped). The seeds are yellow-brown, shiny, and about 1 mm long. Reproduction is by seeds. Flowers occur from March to October.

Habitat

Shepherdspurse may be found in gardens, lawns, hay fields, and small grain fields. It is probably native to Europe, although it is widely scattered throughout the world.

Suggested Control

Home Gardens—Prepare an excellent seed bed in spring to destroy small rosettes and follow by clean cultivation and hand hoeing. Chemical control can be obtained with DCPA, diphenamid, and trifluralin. *Alfalfa and Small Seeded Legumes*—Apply diuron, pronamide, simazine, or terbacil before crop breaks winter dormancy. *Turf*—Improved management practices, i.e., adequate liming, fertilization, etc., and an early spring application of 2,4-D or a mixture of 2,4-D plus dicamba. *Small Grains*—Apply 2,4-D or bromoxynil in the early spring. *Fence Rows and Waste Areas*—Dinoseb, paraquat or a soil sterilant.

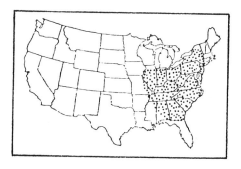

14I
Cardamine hirsuta L.
Hairy bittercress
Mustard family (Cruciferae)

Description

An annual herb that has one to several stems and is 10–40 cm tall. Basal leaves are numerous and conspicuous in comparison to a few small stem-leaves. The terminal leaflet is round to kidney-shaped, entire, toothed, or shallowly lobed. The petioles of the stem-leaves have a few minute white hairs at the base. Flowers are very small and have four white petals. The fruit develops very rapidly, is commonly purple-colored and contains 20–40 seeds. Reproduction is by seeds. Flowering occurs from March and April.

Habitat

This plant is a common weed in lawns and may occur in hay fields, pastures, gardens, and small grain fields. It is a native of the Old World.

Suggested Control

Home Gardens—Excellent seedbed preparation in spring will destroy small rosettes. Follow with clean cultivation and hand hoeing. *Alfalfa and Small Seeded Legumes*—Apply diuron, pronamide, simazine, or terbacil before crop breaks winter dormancy. *Turf*—Improved management practices, i.e., adequate liming, fertilization, etc., and an early spring application of 2,4-D or a mixture of 2,4-D plus dicamba. *Fence Rows and Waste Areas*—Apply paraquat or a soil sterilant.

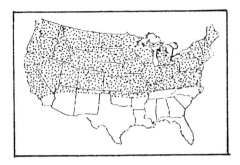

15A
Cardaria draba (L.) Desv.
Hoary cress
Mustard family (Cruciferae)

Description

A perennial herb arising from rootstocks. It is a noxious weed in many states. It has a simple, erect stem that branches at the top and becomes stiff and wiry. It can be up to 60 cm tall. Its sessile stem leaves clasp the stem and are lanceolate. The lower stem-leaves are oblong. The leaf margins are wavy with shallow indentations. The inflorescence is composed of numerous racemes that form a conspicuous large terminal panicle. The numerous small white flowers are borne on slender stalks. The fruits are rounded, heart-shaped pods, 3–5 mm wide and about 3 mm long. The rough oval seeds are reddish brown and about 2 mm long. Reproduction is by seeds and rootstocks. Flowers appear from May to July.

Habitat

This weed has been spread because of its white flowers and has become well-established in many areas of the country. It may be found in pastures, small grain fields, meadows, roadsides, and waste places. It is a native of Eurasia.

Suggested Control

Cropland—Spot spray with glyphosate in early flower bud stage. Wait at least seven days before plowing. *Small Grains*—Apply 2,4-D plus dicamba when small grains are in the full tiller stage. *Pasture*—Apply 2,4-D plus dicamba or picloram. *Noncropland*—Apply amitrole when hoary cress is in the bud stage or a long-lasting soil sterilant in the late fall or early spring for residual control.

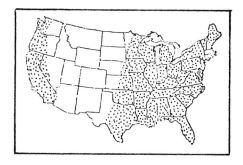

15B
Coronopus didymus (L.) Sm.
Swinecress
Mustard family (Cruciferae)

Description

Annual or biennial herb with prostrate, thinly pubescent, much branched, stems that form mats up to 80 cm across. The alternate leaves are pinnately compound. Margins of the segments are entire or may have a few deep teeth. The lower leaves have petioles, but the upper leaves are sessile. The tiny flowers have small, white petals and are borne in a slender axillary raceme. The fruit is a deeply notched, two-seeded pod. The dull yellow seeds are about 1.5 mm long and roughened by an irregular network of ridges. Reproduction is by seeds. It flowers from March to June.

Habitat

Swinecress may occur in small grain fields, pastures, gardens, and waste places. It is native to Europe.

Suggested Control

Home Gardens—Prepare a well-tilled seedbed to destroy any established plants and prevent further seed production by pulling, hand hoeing, and/or clean cultivation. *Cropland*—Use clean cultivation or a herbicide labeled for the specific crop, such as atrazine, cyanazine, 2,4-D, diphenamid, fluometuron, linuron, metribuzin, paraquat, propazine, simazine, and terbacil. *Pastures*—Use improved pasture management practices, such as pH adjustment, proper fertilization, etc., to encourage pasture species, thus providing strong competition. Apply 2,4-D in early spring before seed maturation. *Waste Places and Industrial Sites*—Burn down with paraquat or apply a soil sterilant.

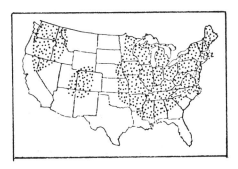

15C
Lepidium campestre (L.) R. Br.
Field pepperweed
Mustard family (Cruciferae)

Description

An annual or winter annual herb that has tiny papery fruits. Erect stems are 20–50 cm tall, simple to much branched, and densely covered with short pubescence. Basal leaves are elongate, oblanceolate, and leaf margins are entire to shallowly lobed. Stem leaves are 2–4 cm long, erect or ascending, lanceolate to narrowly oblong, and their margins are entire or toothed. They are sessile on the stems and clasp around it by pointed, earlike lobes. The small, white flowers are grouped together in many-flowered finely pubescent racemes. The two-seeded fruit is oval shaped, about 4 mm wide and 5–6 mm wide and encircled by a papery wing. The short style is barely exserted. Reproduction is by seeds. Flowers appear during May and June.

Habitat

This weed may be found in gardens, hay fields, pastures, small grain fields, and waste places. It is native of Europe.

Suggested Control

Home Gardens—Prepare a well-tilled seedbed and prevent seed production of any established plants by pulling, hand hoeing, and/or clean cultivation. *Cropland*—This weed is mainly a problem in small grains; therefore, apply 2,4-D in early spring when small grains are in the well-tilled stage of growth and before jointing begins. Also, small grains can be rotated with other crops, where atrazine, cyanazine, EPTC, fluometuron, linuron, metribuzin, propazine, or simazine can be used to control this weed. *Pastures*—Apply 2,4-D before seed is formed. Use improved pasture management practices and mow periodically close to ground to prevent seed maturation. *Fence Rows, Waste Areas*—Spray with 2,4-D if selective control in grass is desired, paraquat for immediate burn down of all vegetation, and a soil sterilant for residual total vegetation control.

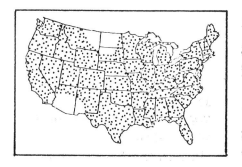

15D
Lepidium virginicum L.
Virginia pepperweed
Mustard family (Cruciferae)

Description

Annual or winter annual herb that has tiny papery fruits. Stems are erect, 10–50 cm tall, and simple to much branched. Basal leaves are oblaceolate in general outline, sharply toothed to pinnatifid, and occasionally twice pinnately. Stem leaves are smaller, oblanceolate to linear, have toothed to entire edges, and are pointed and narrowed at the base. The small white flowers are borne on many-flowered, glabrous racemes. The circular two-seeded fruits are 3 mm wide and 2.5–4.0 mm long and narrowly winged across the apex. The style is included in the notch. Reproduction is by seeds. Flowers appear from May to July.

Habitat

This weed occurs in gardens, pastures, hay fields, lawns, small grain fields, and waste areas. It is native to North America.

Suggested Control

Home Gardens—Prepare a well-tilled seedbed. Mulches can be used to prevent reestablishment. Prevent seed production of any established plants by pulling, hand hoeing, and/or clean cultivation. *Cropland*—This weed is mainly a problem in small grains; therefore, apply 2,4-D in early spring when small grains are in the well-tillered stage of growth and before jointing begins. Also, small grains can be rotated with other crops, where atrazine, cyanazine, EPTC, fluometuron, linuron, metribuzin, propazine, or simazine can be used to control this weed. *Pastures*—Apply 2,4-D before seed is formed. Use improved pasture management practices and mow periodically after rotation to prevent seed maturation. *Fence Rows, Waste Areas*—Use a soil sterilant for residual control.

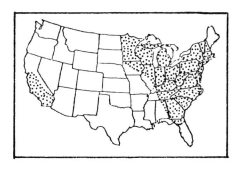

15E
Raphanus raphanistrum L.
Wild radish
Mustard family (Cruciferae)

Description

This herb is either an annual or biennial depending on locale. It has a coarse taproot and an erect stem that branches at the top. The coarse stem is 30–80 cm tall and is sparsely pubescent with stiff hairs on the lower parts. The lower leaves are 10–20 cm long, pinnately divided into 5 to 15 oblong segments with a large rounded terminal segment. The upper leaves are much smaller and mostly undivided, but they do have a few small segments. The four-petaled flowers are 10–15 cm long and may be light yellow, white, pink, or purple. Seed pods are pithy but solid, nearly cylindrical when fresh but becoming constricted when dry. They contain 4 to 10 seeds and are 2–4 cm long. Seeds vary in size and shape but are usually oval and reddish-brown. Reproduction is by seeds. Flowering occurs from June to August.

Habitat

Wild radish may be found in small grain and flax fields, along roadsides, and in waste places. It is native to Eurasia.

Suggested Control

Cropland—This weed is mainly a problem in small grains; therefore, apply 2,4-D in early spring when small grains are in the well-tillered stage of growth and before jointing begins. Also, small grains can be rotated with other crops, where atrazine, cyanazine, EPTC, fluometuron, linuron, metribuzin, propazine, or simazine can be used to control this weed. *Pastures*—Apply 2,4-D before seed is formed. Use improved pasture management practices and mow periodically close to ground to prevent seed maturation. *Fence Rows, Waste Areas, Industrial Sites*—Spray with 2,4-D, paraquat, or a soil sterilant.

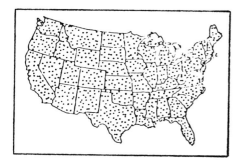

15F
Sisymbrium officinale (L.)
  Scop.
Hedge mustard
Mustard family (Cruciferae)

Description

This pubscent plant may be either a winter annual or a summer annual. Its erect stems may be simple or branched at the top, and it is 30–80 cm tall. The lower leaves are petioled and deeply lobed. The segments or leaflets are oblong to ovate, but the terminal is sometimes rotound and angularly toothed. Stem leaves are sessile or nearly so, and may be either entire or with a few variably shaped lobes. The flowers are bright yellow and about 3 mm wide. Fruits closely appressed to the stiffly erect inflorescence branches and are 1–1.5 mm wide and 10–15 mm long. Reproduction is by seeds. Flowers occur from May to October.

Habitat

Hedge mustard may be found in gardens, lawns, hay fields, pastures, and fence rows. Native of Europe.

Suggested Control

Use control measures listed for *Brassica kaber* (Wild mustard). Cyanazine is the only herbicide specifically labeled for control of hedge mustard.

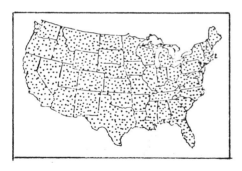

15G
Thlaspi arvense L.
Field pennycress
Mustard family (Cruciferae)

Description

A winter annual herb that has smooth simple to much branched stems. The waxy stems are erect and 10–50 cm tall. The stem leaves are sessile and oblong to lanceolate. The leaf margins are entire or few-toothed and have two narrow, divergent earlike lobes at the base, each 1–5 mm long. The flowers are white and about 3 mm wide with petals twice as long as the sepals. Fruits are circular, 10–14 mm in diameter and winged all around with a deep (2–3 mm) notch. Seeds are 2–2.3 mm long and red-brown to black. Reproduction is by seeds. Flowers occur in May and June.

Habitat

Field pennycress may be found in gardens, lawns, hay fields, roadsides, and waste grounds. It is native to Europe.

Suggested Control

Home Gardens—Mulches can be applied before weed establishment. Established plants should be controlled by pulling, hoeing, or clean cultivation. New seed production should be prevented. *Cropland*—Thoroughly prepare seed bed in spring of year to destroy any small plants that had become established in the fall or early spring. Small grains can be sprayed with 2,4-D before jointing is initiated. Atrazine or cyanazine may be used in corn. Use a good crop rotation system where either cultivation or herbicides that control broadleaf weeds can be used. *Pastures*—Improve management practices such as proper pH adjustment and fertilization, rotational grazing, and proper mowing to prevent seed maturation. Apply 2,4-D in early spring. *Fence Rows, Waste Areas, and Industrial Sites*—Spray with 2,4-D, paraquat, or a soil sterilant.

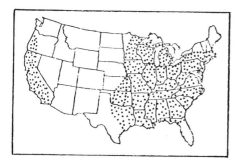

15H
Duchesnea indica (Andr.)
Focke.
Indian mockstrawberry
Rose family (Rosaceae)

Description

This prostrate perennial herb resembles a strawberry. The stems are prostrate, branched, and up to 30 cm long. The leaves are compound, having three leaflets, each 2–4 cm long. Leaflets are ovate or elliptic, bluntly toothed, and sparsely hairy on the bottom side. The yellow flowers are borne singly and are 14–18 mm wide. Large, leafy, three-toothed bracts occur beneath each flower. The red, fleshy fruit is similar to a small strawberry but is dry and seedy, and about 1 cm in diameter. Reproduction is mainly by leafy runners. Flowering is from April to June.

Habitat

This weed occurs mainly in shady areas in gardens, lawns, and under shrubbery. It is a native of Asia.

Suggested Control

Home Gardens—A plastic or organic mulch can be used to control this weed under shrubbery. Hand-hoeing, making certain to remove all plant parts, will control this weed. *Lawns*—Rake thoroughly to raise creeping stems and mow closely, or remove total plant and reseed bare spots. In spring when plant is actively growing it may be controlled with a mixture of 2,4-D plus dicamba. Treatment should be repeated to control escapees. Do not apply inside of drip line of shrubs or trees as some injury may occur.

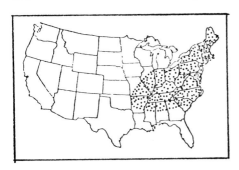

151
Potentilla canadensis L.
Common cinquefoil
Rose family (Rosaceae)

Description

A perennial herb that has a short, thick rhizome and numerous runners. The silky-hairy stems are prostrate and branched. They are ascending and only 5–15 cm long when flowering is initiated but soon elongate greatly and become prostrate. Alternate leaves are palmately compound with five wedge-shaped, 1–3 cm long leaflets. The leaf margins have sharp teeth on the distal half only, while the margins below the teeth are entire. The flowers are yellow; the first ones usually arise at the end of the first well-developed internode. Flower petals are rich yellow and barely 1 cm long. Reproduction is by seeds and runners. Flowers appear from May to July.

Habitat

This weed may occur in gardens, residential areas, hayfields, pastures, and waste places. It is native of North America.

Suggested Control

Home Gardens—Remove the total plant including the rhizomes with a spade, or plow and cultivate. Do not allow new plants to become established. *Lawns and Pastures*—Increase level of management through proper fertilization and pH adjustment to maintain a vigorous, competitive sod. MCPA, 2,4-D, and dicamba can be applied in the spring. Repeat applications may be necessary. *Fence Rows and Waste Areas*—Apply 2,4-D, MCPA, or dicamba for selective control or a soil sterilant for total vegetation control.

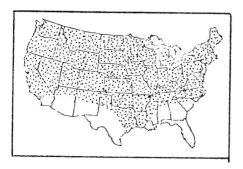

16A
Potentilla norvegica L.
Rough cinquefoil
Rose family (Rosaceae)

Description

Annual or biennial herb that is 30–90 cm tall. Its coarse, leafy, stems are erect or spreading, branched, and have stiff and spreading hairs. Leaves are alternate, palmately divided, and have three obovate leaflets which are usually hairy. Leaf margins are coarsely toothed; the uppermost leaves are sessile and have narrower leaflets. Flowers are terminal and inconspicuous. Their yellow petals are shorter than calyx lobes. There are 15 to 20 stamens. The fruit is a light-brown achene about 1 mm long and has longitudinally curved ridges. Reproduction is by seeds. Flowers are seen from June to October.

Habitat

This native of Eurasia may be found in cultivated fields, pastures, meadows, roadsides, and waste places.

Suggested Control

Cropland—Maintain a good crop rotation with cultivation and the herbicides normally used for control of annual broadleaf weeds. Cultivation and spring or winter tillage should be included to control overwintering plants in areas where cinquefoil acts as a biennial. *Pastures*—Increase the level of management through proper fertilization, pH adjustment, etc., to maintain a vigorous competitive sod. Apply 2,4-D plus dicamba in the early spring after active growth has been initiated. Repeat applications may be necessary. *Fence Rows and Waste Areas*—Apply 2,4-D, MCPA, or dicamba for selective control or a soil sterilant for total vegetation control.

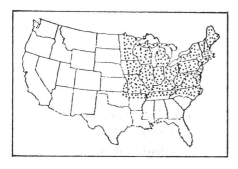

16B
Potentilla recta L.
Sulfur cinquefoil
Rose family (Rosaceae)

Description

The perennial herb has an erect pubescent stem that is 40–80 cm tall and unbranched to the inflorescence. The alternate leaves are digitately compound; the basal and lower leaves have long-petioles and five to seven leaflets, while the upper leaves are short-petioled to sessile, smaller and have only three leaflets. The leaflets are narrowly oblaceolate with deeply toothed edges. Inflorescence is terminal, many-flowered, and flat-topped. Flower petals are about 1 cm long, light sulfur yellow in color and deeply notched at apex. Seeds are striate with low curved ridges. Reproduction is by seeds. Flowers bloom from May to August.

Habitat

Sulfur cinquefoil may be found in pastures, roadsides, fence rows, and waste areas. It is native of Europe.

Suggested Control

Pastures—The level of pasture management should be upgraded through proper fertilization, pH adjustment, rotation grazing, etc. Desirable pasture species should be encouraged to provide strong competition against cinquefoil. Dicamba, plus either 2,4-D or MCPA, may be applied in the spring. Repeat applications may be necessary. *Fence Rows and Waste Areas*—Apply dicamba, 2,4-D, or MCPA.

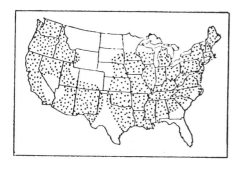

16C
Rosa multiflora Thunb.
Multiflora rose
Rose family (Rosaceae)

Description

A perennial shrub with arched, thorny stems that has been commonly planted in hedge rows. The stems are weakly climbing and covered with many small thorns. Stipules are fused to petioles and conspicuously toothed. Leaves are alternate, pinnately compound, with seven to nine elliptic leaflets. The inflorescence is a panicle with numerous flowers at the ends of branches. Sepals are often elongated and have long points. The white petals are 1–2 cm long. The bright red fruits (hips) are 8 mm in diameter, nearly round, and often last until the following spring. Achenes (seeds) are enclosed in the fleshy calyx tube. Reproduction is by seeds. Flowers appear during June and July.

Habitat

This weed may be found in pastures, fence rows, and clearings and along the borders of woods and roadsides. It is a native of eastern Asia.

Suggested Control

Pastures—The level of pasture management must be increased. An environment for healthy, competitive, desirable species must be provided. Plant improved species, provide adequate fertilization and favorable pH, control stocking rates, and use rotational grazing followed by mowing immediately after each rotation. Rose bushes may be destroyed by persistant mechanical cutting and physically removing the roots from the soil with an ax and shovel, or by applying a foliar spray of glyphosate or picloram or a mixture of 2,4-D and dicamba repeated as necessary.

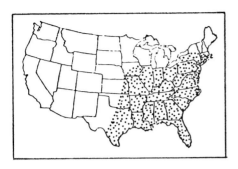

16D
Rosa setigera Michx.
Prairie rose
Rose family (Rosaceae)

Description

A perennial shrub that has awkwardly climbing, thorny stems. The stems are 2–4 m long and are sparsely armed with coarse thorns, though occasionally they are unarmed. The stipules are fused to the petioles and are narrow and entire. The alternating leaves are pinnately compound with three (rarely five) leaflets and sparsely prickly petioles. The leaflets are lanceolate or nearly so; the lateral ones are nearly sessile and the terminal one has a long stalk. Flowers are numerous with 2–3 cm long pink petals. The red fruits (hips) are 8–12 mm in diameter and nearly round. Reproduction is by seeds. Flowering occurs from June to August.

Habitat

Prairie rose may be found in pastures or fence rows, along roadsides, and in waste areas. It is a native of North America.

Suggested Control

Pastures—When this rose occurs in pastures it indicates that the level of management must be increased. If possible, the pasture should be cross-fenced and a schedule of rotational grazing be followed. The pasture should be clipped after each grazing. A proper environment should be provided for desirable species by maintaining good fertilization and a favorable pH. A few scattered rose bushes may be destroyed by persistant mechanical cutting and physically removing the roots from the soil with an ax and shovel, or by applying a foliar spray of glyphosate, picloram, or a repeated mixture of 2,4-D plus dicamba.

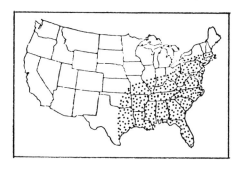

16E
Rubus argutus Link.
Blackberry
Rose family (Rosaceae)

Description

Perennial shrub that has straight or stiffly arching stems. The erect stems are up to 2 m tall, with straight or slightly reflexed, 3–8 mm long thorns. The petioles, flowering branches, pedicels and midveins are commonly armed with smaller spines. The alternating leaves are palmately compound with five leaflets. The terminal one has a long, commonly 8–12 cm, stalk, and the intermediate pair are also stalked. They are oblong or oblong-lanceolate, sharply toothed, widest above the middle and sharply pointed. The flowers have white petals and are borne in short, loose, open racemes. Fruits resemble commercial blackberries and are 1 cm thick. Reproduction is by seeds. Flowering occurs from May to July.

Habitat

Blackberries may be found in pastures, fence rows, roadsides, and waste places. They are a native of North America.

Suggested Control

Pastures—Scattered plants can be removed with a spade. Proper pasture management must be followed maintaining a dense sod through proper fertilization, pH adjustment, and rotational grazing. After each grazing the pasture should be mowed. Dicamba and picloram can be applied for selective control. *Fence Rows and Waste Areas*—Glyphosate can be applied as a spot treatment. If complete vegetation control is desired use a soil sterilant such as sulfometuron or tebuthiuron.

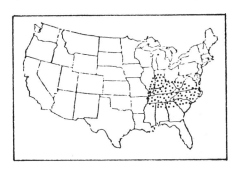

16F
Albizzia julibrissin
  Durazzini
  Mimosa (Silktree albizzia)
  Pulse family (Leguminosae)

Description

A low, widely spreading tree that grows up to 10 m tall. Leaves are twice pinnately compound, 20–50 cm long with 4 to 12 major divisions. Each division has 20 to 30 pairs of oblong leaflets. The inflorescence is an elongated raceme with tiny pink flowers in globose heads on long peduncles. The corolla is 5–8 mm long, funnel-shaped, with five deep lobes. The numerous stamens are exserted and are united at the base of the filaments. The fruit is a wide, broad, flat, several-seeded legume or pod about 2 cm wide and up to 15 cm long. Reproduction is by seeds. Flowering is from June and July.

Habitat

This weedy tree may be found growing in disturbed areas, fence rows, roadsides, and pastures. It is a native of tropical Asia.

Suggested Control

Pastures—Use improved pasture management techniques such as rotational grazing followed by clipping and spraying with 2,4-D–dicamba mixture on a yearly basis to prevent this tree from becoming established. If already present, larger plants should be cut and removed with an axe and grubbing hoe. Smaller plants can be sprayed with 2,4-D–dicamba mixture. *Fence Rows and Roadsides*—Grub out any larger plants or scatter a few tebuthiuron pellets at the base of the tree.

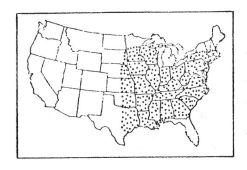

16G
Cassia fasciculata Michx.
Partridgepea
Pulse family (Leguminosae)

Description

A summer annual herb that grows 15–90 cm tall. The stems are erect or ascending, many-branched, and finely hairy. Leaves are compound with 10 to 15 pairs of leaflets. The blades of the leaflets are linear-oblong, longer than they are wide. The very showy flowers are bright yellow with red mottling and 1–2 cm long. The 10 stamens are very unequal in length. The fruit is a flat, straight pod (legume), up to 8 cm long. Seeds are quadrangular, and slightly marked with shallow pits in rows. Reproduction is by seeds. Flowering occurs from July to September.

Habitat

This plant may be found in abandoned fields, poorly managed pastures, fence rows, and roadsides. It is native of North America.

Suggested Control

Cropland—Partridgepea will not persist as a weed if a good crop–herbicide rotation system is followed. Soybeans and peanuts should be excluded. Practices normally used for broadleaf weed control such as cultivation and appropriate herbicide for control of broadleaf weeds should be used. *Pastures and Waste Areas*—Periodic mowing and/or an occasional herbicide application that includes dicamba in the mixture will control any occasional plants.

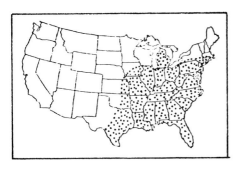

16H
Cassia obtusifolia L.
Sicklepod
Pulse family (Leguminosae)

Description

A summer annual herb that has erect, smooth, branching stems up to 1 m tall. Compound leaves are alternate with two or three pairs of leaflets. The bluntly oval-shaped leaflets are 4–7 cm long, although the lower ones are usually smaller. Flowers are either solitary or in groups of two to three and borne in each upper leaf axil. The petals are bright yellow and 10–15 mm long. The fruit, a cylindric, sickle-shaped pod that is 3–6 mm wide and 10–18 cm long. The seeds are shiny brown to black and obliquely box-shaped. Reproduction is by seeds. Flowering occurs from July to September.

Habitat

This weed may occur in cultivated fields, pastures, fence rows, and waste places. It is native of tropical America.

Suggested Control

Cropland—Prevent infestation by using clean seed and clean harvesting machinery. Use a good crop herbicide rotation and clean cultivation if needed. In corn, use higher rates of atrazine or cyanazine followed by a post-directed application of 2,4-D plus cultivation if needed. In cotton, use fluometuron plus cultivation. In soybeans, use alachlor plus metribuzin or vernolate plus metribuzin followed either by post-directed paraquat plus cultivation or linuron plus 2,4-DB plus cultivation. Alfalfa and accompanying management practices included in rotation will do much to reduce population. *Fence Rows and Waste Areas*—Spray young plants with 2,4-D, dicamba, or paraquat.

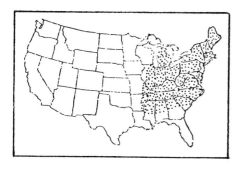

16I

Cassia occidentalis L.
Coffee senna
Pulse family (Leguminosae)

Description

A summer annual herb that has 30–100 cm tall, erect, smooth, branched stems. The 3- to 8-cm long leaves are compound with four to six pairs of ovate-lanceolate shaped leaflets. The yellow flowers are solitary or in groups of two or three in upper leaf axils. The fruit is a straight or slightly curved pod with smooth, flattened sides and about 6–12 cm long. The flat, ovoid, brownish seeds are up to 5 mm long. Reproduction is by seeds. Flowers are present from July to September.

Habitat

Coffee senna may be found in cultivated fields, pastures, roadsides. and waste places. It is a native of the Old World tropics.

Suggested Control

Cropland—Prevent infestation by using clean seed and clean harvesting machinery. Practice good crop rotation complete with tillage and clean cultivation. Herbicides used for control of *Cassia obtusifolia* may be useful. *Fence Rows and Waste Areas*—Spray young plants with 2,4-D, dicamba, or paraquat.

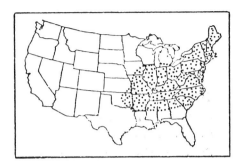

17A
Desmodium canadense
(L.)DC.
Hoary tickclover
Pulse family (Leguminosae)

Description

Perennial herb that has erect, many-branched, hairy, reddish or brown stems up to 2 m tall. The alternate, compound leaves have three lanceolate leaflets. They are hairy on the lower surface, the terminal leaflet is 5–9 cm long and almost half as wide. The other two are shorter. The petioles are hairy and 5–20 mm long. The inflorescence is a dense raceme with conspicuous bracts. The showy flowers are purple and 10–13 mm long. The fruit is a jointed pod, which breaks into sections with one seed. The pods are stiffly hairy enabling the pod segments to adhere to clothing and fur. Reproduction is by seeds. Flowers appear from July to September.

Habitat

This weed may occur in cultivated fields, pastures, and waste places. It is a native of tropical America.

Suggested Control

Cropland—Use a crop rotation that includes spring or fall plowing plus cultivation and a variety of preemergence herbicides to control broadleaf weeds. *Pastures and Waste Areas*—Spray with a mixture of 2,4-D plus dicamba.

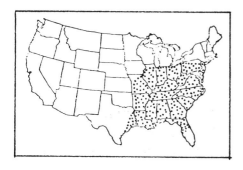

17B
Lespedeza striata (Thunb.)
H. & A.
Common lespedeza
Pulse family (Leguminosae)

Description

A cloverlike summer annual with erect or reclined, diffusely branched, sparsely hairy stems that are 10–40 cm tall. The short-petioled leaves are compound, with brown and persistent stipules that are 4–6 mm long. Each leaf has three oblong-obovate leaflets that are 1–2 cm long and about a third as wide. Two kinds of pink or purple flowers are borne in the upper leaf axils. Some have well-developed petals (6–7 mm long) and some do not and are usually much smaller. The oval-shaped, pointed seed pod is 3–4 mm long, thus slightly exceeding the calyx. Reproduction is by seeds. Flowers occur from July to September.

Habitat

This weed is a very common weed in thin, poorly managed turf, and occurs in pastures, fence rows, and waste places. It is native of Asia.

Suggested Control

Spray with a herbicide mixture containing 2,4-D and dicamba.

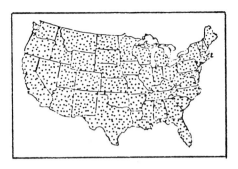

17C
Medicago lupulina L.
Black medic
Pulse family (Leguminosae)

Description

An annual or biennial or perennial herb that has a shallow taproot. The prostrate, or ascending, widely spreading stems are up to 80 cm long. The alternate leaves are compound and have three elliptic leaflets, short petioles, and lance-shaped stipules. The inflorescence is a headlike cluster borne on a slender stalk that is longer than the subtending leaves. The yellow flowers are 2–4 mm long. The nearly black fruit is a 3 mm long kidney-shaped pod that contains a single seed. A number of fruits are clustered together resembling a blackberry. Reproduction is by seeds. Flowering occurs from April to November.

Habitat

Black medic is common in lawns, but also occurs in pastures and hay fields. It is a native of Europe and western Asia.

Suggested Control

Lawns, Pastures and Hay Fields—For selective control, spray while small with dicamba.

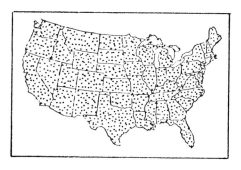

17D
Melilotus alba Desr.
White sweetclover
Pulse family (Leguminosae)

Description

A biennial herb that has erect, many-branched, smooth stems up to 3 m tall. The alternate compound leaves have three lanceolate to narrowly oblong leaflets that are 1–2.5 cm long and have toothed margins. The inflorescence is a long raceme (5–20 cm long including the stalk). The white flowers have a short pedicel. The 3- to 4-mm long fruit is a one- to four-seeded pod. Seed may remain viable in the soil for many years. Reproduction is by seeds. Flowers may be present from June to August.

Habitat

This weed may occur in cultivated fields, pastures, fence rows, roadsides, and waste places. It is a native of Europe and west Asia.

Suggested Control

Cultivated Crops—Use a good crop rotation, coupled with proper land preparation for each crop and recommended herbicides for control of broadleaf weeds. This escaped crop plant will not persist. *Fence Rows, Pastures, Roadsides, and Waste Places*—Spray with dicamba or a mixture of 2,4-D plus dicamba.

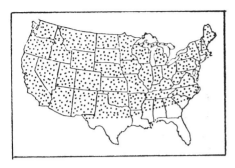

17E
Melilotus officinalis (L.)
Lam.
Yellow sweetclover
Pulse family (Leguminosae)

Description

A biennial herb that has erect or ascending, smooth, many-branched stems that are 0.5–1.5 m tall. The alternate compound leaves have three leaflets. The leaflets are 1–2.5 m and the margins are closely toothed. Inflorescence is a 5- to 15-cm long raceme. The yellow flowers are 5–7 mm long and are borne on a short pedicel. Fruit is a one- to four-seeded pod that is 2.5–3.5 mm long. Reproduction is by seeds. Flowers are present from May to July.

Habitat

This weed may occur in cultivated fields, roadsides, fence rows, pastures, hay fields, and waste places. It is native of Eurasia.

Suggested Control

Cultivated Crops—Use a good crop rotation, coupled with proper land preparation for each crop and recommended herbicides for control of broadleaf weeds. This escaped crop plant will not persist. *Fence Rows, Pastures, Roadsides, and Waste Places*—Spray with dicamba or a mixture of 2,4-D plus dicamba.

17F
Pueraria lobata (Willd.)
 Ohwi
Kudzu
Pulse family (Leguminosae)

Description

High-climbing perennial vine that has edible tuberous roots. The coarse twining stems are densely hairy and herbaceous when young, woody when old and 10–30 m long. They will cover small shrubs and bushes and climb and eventually cover large trees. Mature stems can be 4–5 cm thick. The compound leaves have a long petiole, and three leaflets that have entire or slightly lobed margins and are densely hairy on the lower surface and up to 20 cm long. The inflorescence is a 10–20 cm long raceme borne on long stalk in the leaf axils. The very showy flowers are purple or reddish-purple and 2–2.5 cm long. The flat, several-seeded seed pods are covered with brown hairs and are 4–5 cm long. Reproduction is by seeds and tuberous roots. Flowers are present for a short period in September.

Habitat

Kudzu may be found growing along the borders of fields, roadsides and embankments, often covering shrubs and trees and climbing on buildings. It is native of Japan.

Suggested Control

Noncropland—Kudzu can be controlled by either fencing the infested area and allowing sheep, goats, or cattle to overgraze the area, followed by removal of the livestock and seeding of desirable pasture species, or by persistant mechanical removal with an ax, grubbing hoe, and shovel, making certain to remove all rootstocks, or by repeated applications of glyphosate or 2,4-D plus dicamba in the fall of the year.

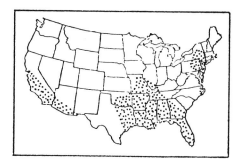

17G
Sesbania exaltata (Raf.)
  Cory
Hemp sesbania
Pulse family (Leguminosae)

Description

A summer annual herb with erect, light green, smooth stems that become woody at maturity and may be up to 3.0 m tall. The alternate leaves are pinnately compound and have numerous narrowly oblong, rounded leaflets. The inflorescence is a raceme of two to six flowers on a long stalk that is shorter than the subtending leaves. The flowers are yellow-dotted with purple and 1.5–2.0 cm long. The fruit is a cylindrical, curved pod about 3 mm wide by 10–20 cm long and is subtended by the persistent calyx. Reproduction is by seeds. Flowering occurs from June to October.

Habitat

This weed may be found in wet, fertile soils in cultivated fields, along roadsides, and waste places. It is native of tropical America.

Suggested Control

Cropland—Use a good crop rotation, which includes crops wherein the following herbicides can be used: acifluorfen, fluometuron, linuron, metribuzin, and methazole. Follow herbicides with cultivation and hand hoeing. Do not allow escaped plants to produce seed. *Noncropland and Waste Areas*—Mow periodically, do not allow to go to seed, spray with acifluorfen or a combination of 2,4-D plus dicamba.

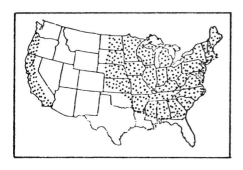

17H
Trifolium procumbens L.
Low hop clover
Pulse family (Leguminosae)

Description

A many-branched, annual herb that has pubescent, erect, or ascending stems up to 40 cm tall. The alternate, compound leaves have three oblong-obovate leaflets, ovate stipules, and slender petioles. The flowers are 3.5–4.5 mm long, individually sessile, but grouped in compact, short, cylindric heads of 20 to 30 yellow flowers. Reproduction is by seeds. Flowering occurs in May and June.

Habitat

Low hop clover is primarily a weed in poor turf stands but may be found in pastures, small grain fields, and waste places. It is native of Europe and western Asia and Africa.

Suggested Control

Home Lawns and Turf—If objectionable, treat with dicamba or a herbicide mixture containing dicamba. Most clovers are not susceptible to 2,4-D. *Cropland*—Use a good crop rotation, involving several crops, spring or fall plowing, cultivation, and common herbicides used to control broadleaf weeds. *Roadsides and Waste Places*—If objectionable, spray with glyphosate, dicamba, or a mixture containing dicamba.

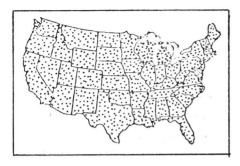

171
Trifolium repens L.
White clover
Pulse family (Leguminosae)

Description

Perennial herb with prostrate creeping stems that sends up long-petioled leaves and long-peduncled heads. Leaves are alternate, compound with three broadly elliptic to obovate, rounded leaflets that are 1–2 cm long. The white flowers are 7–11 mm long and individually stalked in round heads. They are 1.5–3.0 cm in diameter on long, smooth, leafless peduncles. The flower petals are white or tinged with pink. Reproduction is by seeds. Flowering occurs from May to September.

Habitat

White clover is commonly cultivated and is used in lawns and pastures. At times it is considered to be a weed that may be found in lawns, gardens, plant beds, and waste areas. It is a native of Eurasia and possibly of North America.

Suggested Control

Home Lawns and Turf—If objectionable treat with dicamba or a herbicide mixture containing dicamba. Most clovers are not susceptible to 2,4-D. *Cropland*—Use a good crop rotation, involving several crops, spring or fall plowing, cultivation, and common herbicides used to control broadleaf weeds. *Roadsides and Waste Places*—If objectionable, spray with glyphosate, dicamba, or a mixture containing dicamba.

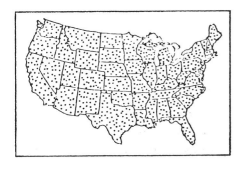

18A
Vicia angustifolia L.
Narrowleaf vetch
Pulse family (Leguminosae)

Description

Annual climbing herb with erect or ascending stems that are up to 1 m long. Leaves are alternate, compound, and end in a tendril. Each leaf has three to five pairs of linear to narrowly elliptic leaflets that are 1.5–3 cm long. Stipules are half-arrowhead and toothed. Flowers are commonly paired in the upper leaf axils. They are generally blue or violet but may be white. The fruit is a dark brown to black pod that is 4–5.5 cm long and 5–7 mm broad. Reproduction is by seeds. It blooms from May to September.

Habitat

Narrowleaf vetch may be found in small grain fields, roadsides, fence rows, and waste areas. It is a native of Europe.

Suggested Control

Small Grains—Destroy all seedlings before planting and apply bromoxynil, 2,4-D, or dicamba according to label restrictions. *Roadsides, Fence Rows, and Waste Places*—Apply 2,4-D or 2,4-D plus dicamba mixture.

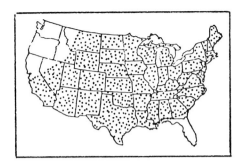

18B
Vicia dasycarpa Tenore
Winter vetch
Pulse family (Leguminosae)

Description

A perennial herb with climbing or trailing, up to 1 m long, stems that are glabrous or sparsely hairy. It has alternate, compound leaves that end in a tendril. Each leaf has 5 to 10 pairs of narrowly oblong to linear-lanceolate leaflets that are rounded or pointed and up to 2.5 cm long. The inflorescences are axillary, long-peduncled, dense racemes, which bear 10 to 30 violet and white flowers. The fruit is an oblong, 2–3 cm long pod. Reproduction is by seeds. It flowers from May to August.

Habitat

Winter vetch may occur in small grain fields, fence rows, roadsides, and waste places. It is a native of Europe.

Suggested Control

Small Grains—Destroy all seedlings before planting and apply bromoxynil, 2,4-D, or dicamba according to label restrictions. *Roadsides, Fence Rows, and Waste Places*—Apply 2,4-D or 2,4-D plus dicamba mixture.

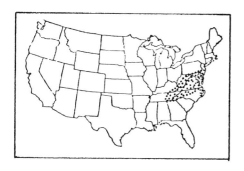

18C
Vicia grandiflora Scop.
Yellow vetch
Pulse family (Leguminosae)

Description

An annual climbing herb with branched stems that are up to 60 cm long. The alternate, compound leaves end in a tendril and have three to six pairs of leaflets, which vary from linear to obovate and are 1–2 cm long. The flowers are usually paired in the upper leaf axils. They are mostly yellow or the upper petal may be marked with violet. Flowers are 2.5–3.0 cm long. The fruit is a black pod that is 3.5–5.5 cm long when mature. Reproduction is by seeds. Flowers occur from June to September.

Habitat

Yellow vetch may occur in small grain fields, fence rows, and waste areas. Native of southwest Europe and west Asia.

Suggested Control

Small Grains—Destroy all seedlings before planting and apply bromoxynil, 2,4-D, or dicamba according to label restrictions. *Fence Rows, and Waste Places*—Apply 2,4-D or a 2,4-D plus dicamba mixture.

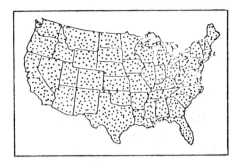

18D
Oxalis stricta L.
Common yellow woodsorrel
Woodsorrel family
(Oxalidaceae)

Description

A perennial herb that has sour watery juice. Its slender, erect or slightly ascending stems are gray-green, branched at base, bushy, slightly hairy, and up to 40 cm tall. It occasionally roots at the nodes that touch the soil. The long-petioled leaves are divided into three heart-shaped leaflets. Flowers are borne in clusters of one to four at end of a long, hairy, slender stalk mostly equaling or over-topping the leaves. Each flower has five yellow petals. The fruit is a cylindric, five-ridged, pointed capsule that is 1–2.5 cm long. The small, flat seeds are brown. Reproduction is by seeds. Flowering occurs from May to October.

Habitat

Woodsorrel may be found in lawns, gardens, cultivated fields, and pastures. It is a native of Europe.

Suggested Control

Home Gardens—Prepare a good seed bed followed by thorough cultivation and hand hoeing. Destroy all plants before flowers are formed to prevent seed formation. *Home Lawns*—If lawn is a cool-season grass, apply 2,4-D or dicamba in the spring; if lawn is warm-season grass, apply DSMA before turf breaks dormancy. *Cropland*—Maintain a good land preparation system with crop rotation and cultivation and this weed will not persist. Herbicides that may be used are acifluorfen, atrazine, dicamba, or 2,4-D. *Pastures*—Apply 2,4-D or dicamba in spring soon after growth is initiated.

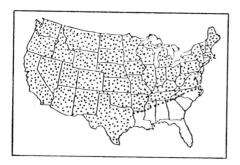

18E
Erodium cicutarium (L.)
  L'Her.
Redstem filaree
Geranium family
(Geraniaceae)

Description

This weed is a winter annual or biennial. It has low, spreading to prostrate stems. At the time flowering is initiated, stems are short and mainly consist of basal leaves but later become diffusely branched and up to 40 cm long. The leaves are pinnately compound and leaflets are deeply and irregularly segmented, each 1–2.5 cm long. Inflorescence is axillary, long-stalked, and has two to eight flowers. Each flower is at the end of a 1- to 2-cm long pedicel and radiates from a central point. Flowers are rose to purple and about 1 cm wide. The fruit is 2–4 cm long and has a long conspicuous "storks-bill" beak. Reproduction is by seeds. Flowers appear from April to September.

Habitat

Redstem filaree may be found in lawns, gardens, and waste places. It is native to the Mediterranean region.

Suggested Control

Home Gardens—Use clean cultivation to prevent establishment and seed production. *Lawns*—Good lawn maintenance programs of proper pH adjustment and adequate fertilization help turf grasses compete with this weed. A mixture of 2,4-D, dicamba, and mecoprop can be applied in late fall or early spring to control this weed. *Waste Areas*—Use 2,4-D plus dicamba for selective control in grass; paraquat or dinoseb for burn down; or atrazine, bromacil, diuron, simazine, or tebuthiuron for residual vegetation control.

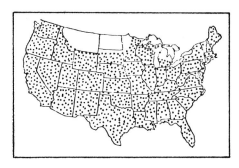

18F
Geranium carolinianum L.
Carolina geranium
Geranium family
(Geraniaceae)

Description

An annual plant with loosely branched stems that eventually elongate to 60 cm long. Stems are softly pubescent with spreading hairs mixed with glandular hairs in the inflorescence. The principal leaves are 3–7 cm wide and are divided into five to nine deeply toothed or lobed segments or leaflets. Flowers are borne at the end of a single peduncle. Peduncles mostly two-flowered, have a conspicuous "storksbill" beak, and small stiff hairs. The seeds are smooth to obscurely pitted. It reproduces by seeds. Flowers appear from May to August.

Habitat

Carolina geranium may be found in lawns, gardens, small grain fields, cultivated fields, and waste places. It is native of North America.

Suggested Control

Home Gardens—Use clean cultivation to prevent establishment and seed production. *Lawns*—Provide good lawn maintenance programs of proper pH adjustment and adequate fertilization to insure strong competition, and if needed apply a mixture of 2,4-D, dicamba, and mecoprop in early spring. *Established Alfalfa*—Apply metribuzin, simazine, or terbacil before alfalfa breaks winter dormancy. *Cropland*—Prepare good seedbed in the spring to destroy seedlings and use a good crop–herbicide rotation. *Waste Areas*—Use paraquat or dinoseb for burn down or bromacil or tebuthiuron for residual vegetation control.

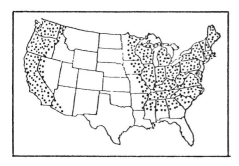

18G
Geranium molle L.
Dovefoot geranium
Geranium family
(Geraniaceae)

Description

An annual or biennial herb with hairy stems that spread on the ground or curve upward. They are branched from the base and are 20–50 cm long. The round basal leaves have a petiole; are 2–5 cm wide, and are divided into five to nine segments each with three lobes. The stem leaves are somewhat reduced and alternate. The inflorescence is scattered in axils of upper leaves with numerous, small, red-violet flowers occurring in pairs. The pedicels are glandular and hairy. The fruit has short beak. Reproduction is by seeds. Flowers occur from May to September.

Habitat

This weed occurs in lawns, gardens, cropland, and waste areas. It is a native of Eurasia.

Suggested Control

Home Gardens—Use clean cultivation to prevent establishment and seed production. *Lawns*—practice a good lawn maintenance program with proper pH adjustment and adequate fertilization. If needed for control of scattered plants, apply a mixture of 2,4-D, dicamba, and mecoprop in early spring. *Cropland*—Prepare a good seedbed in the spring to destroy all seedlings and established plants. Use a good crop–herbicide rotation with herbicides recommended for control of broadleaf weeds. *Waste Areas*—Use paraquat or dinoseb for burn down or bromacil or tebuthiuron for residual vegetation control.

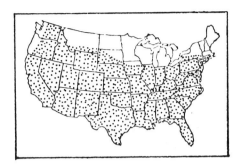

18H
Tribulus terrestris L.
Puncturevine
Caltrop family
(Zygophyllaceae)

Description

A prostrate annual plant with freely branched stems that are covered with short stiff hairs. It will form mats up to 1 m wide and trailing branches may be up to 2 m long. It has a deep taproot. Leaves are compound with six to eight pairs of leaflets. Leaflets are oblong, hairy and 5–15 mm long. The yellow, five-petaled flowers are about 10 mm wide and solitary on a stalk in leaf axils. Fruits are up to 1 cm thick and separated into four or five burs. Each bur has two sharp, coarse, rough, divergent spines. Reproduction is by seeds which have a long period of dormancy before germination. It flowers from June to September.

Habitat

Puncturevine may be found in cultivated fields, pastures, roadsides, and waste places. It is native of Europe.

Suggested Control

Cultivated Fields—Cultivate when plants are small and prevent seed production. Use a crop rotation with crops tolerant to oryzalin, fluometuron, 2,4-D, MCPA, MSMA, norflurazon oryzalin, simazine, or trifluralin, which can be used to control punture vine. *Pastures*—Spray while plants are small with 2,4-D or MCPA. *Roadsides and Waste Places*—Spray with 2,4-D or MCPA for selective control in grass or with atrazine, bromacil, prometon, or sulfometuron for residual vegetation control.

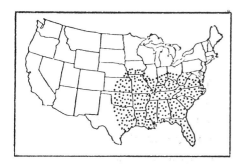

19A
Aclypha ostryaefolia Riddell
Hophornbeam copperleaf
Spurge family
(Euphorbiaceae)

Description

Annual herb with erect, many-branched stems that are densely and finely hairy and 30–60 cm tall. The simple, ovate leaves have heart-shaped bases and long petioles. The lower leaves are opposite and the upper ones are alternate. They are sharp-pointed and have fine, regularly toothed margins. The inflorescence occur in 4- to 8-cm long terminal clusters plus a few short clusters in the leaf axils. The male and female flowers are located in different positions in the inflorescence. The fruit is a few-seeded, three-lobed, bristly capsule surrounded by a leaf bract. It reproduces by seeds. Flowers occur from August to October.

Habitat

This weed may be found in gardens, cultivated fields, roadsides, pastures, and waste places. It is a native of North and Central America.

Suggested Control

Home Gardens—Use clean cultivation to destroy young plants and to prevent seed production. Use of various mulches is helpful in preventing establishment. *Cropland*—Use clean cultivation and crop rotation coupled with one of the following herbicides: acifluorfen, atrazine, cyanazine, alachlor plus dinoseb, oxadiazon, methazole, or simazine. *Noncrop Areas*—Use paraquat or glyphosate for burn down or bromacil or tebuthiuron for residual vegetation control.

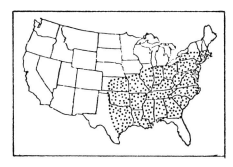

19B
Acalypha virginica L.
Virginia copperleaf
Spurge family
(Euphorbiaceae)

Description

Annual herb with erect, branched stems that have long hairs (occasionally densely) and are 20–50 cm tall. The alternate leaves are simple, ovate, finely hairy, or nearly smooth on the lower surface and 4–9 cm long. The margins are slightly toothed. The inflorescence occurs in axillary clusters. The male and female flowers are separated in the same inflorescence. The fruit is a few-seeded, three-lobed capsule without bristles and surrounded by a leafy bract. Reproduction is by seeds. Flowers appear from July to October.

Habitat

Virginia copperleaf may be found in gardens, cultivated fields, hay fields, and waste places. It is a native of North America.

Suggested Control

Home Gardens—Use clean cultivation to destroy young plants and to prevent seed production. The use of various mulches will help prevent establishment. *Cropland*—Use clean cultivation and crop rotation coupled with one of the following herbicides, which are effective against this weed: acifluorfen, atrazine, cyanazine, alachlor plus dinoseb, oxadiazon, or simazine. *Noncrop Areas*—Use paraquat or glyphosate for burn down or atrazine, bromacil, simazine, or tebuthiuron for residual vegetation control.

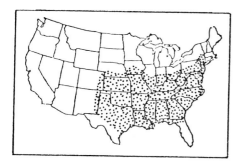

19C
Croton capitatus Michx.
Woolly croton
Spurge family
(Euphorbiaceae)

Description

An annual herb with erect, extensively branched stems that are covered with dense, soft, woolly hairs and are 50–150 cm tall. The simple, narrow, entire, alternate, leaves are ovate to lanceolate-shaped. They have long petioles, are densely woolly with a gray-green color, and are 5–10 cm long. The inflorescence has brown hairs and is in tight spikes at ends of branches with male and female flowers separated. The female flowers are crowded at the base. The fruit is an ovoid, densely hairy, three-lobed capsule with three round, gray seeds. Reproduction is by seeds. It flowers from June to October.

Habitat

Woolly croton may occur in cultivated fields, pastures, stream banks, and waste places. It is native to North America.

Suggested Control

Cropland—Use clean cultivation to destroy young plants and prevent seed production. Practice a crop rotation and use associated herbicides for control of broadleaf weeds. This weed does not appear on any of the herbicide labels; therefore, suggested control on a trial basis would be those herbicides commonly used to control broadleaf weeds such as acifluorfen, atrazine, cyanazine, fluometuron, linuron, metribuzin, simazine, and 2,4-D. A surfactant should be used with foliar applied herbicides such as acifluorfen, 2,4-D, and MCPA. *Pastures*—Apply 2,4-D or MCPA to young plants; repeat as needed. *Noncrop Areas*—Suggested use of paraquat or glyphosate for burn down, or bromacil or tebuthiuron for residual control.

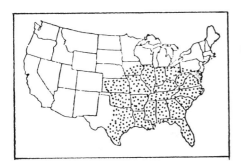

19D
Croton glandulosus L.
Tropic croton
Spurge family
(Euphorbiaceae)

Description

A summer annual herb with erect, extensively branched, brown stems that are 20–50 cm tall, and covered with rough hairs, but not woolly. The simple, oblong to ovate leaves are toothed; have a short petiole and are 3–7 cm long. The inflorescence is in terminal or axillary spikes with male and female flowers separate. The female flowers are clustered at the base. The fruit is a three-lobed capsule about 5 mm wide and has three small, brown seeds. Reproduction is by seeds. Flowering occurs from July to October.

Habitat

Tropic croton may be found in gardens, cultivated fields, pastures, roadsides, and waste places. It is a native of tropical America.

Suggested Control

Home Gardens—Use of various mulches will prevent seed germination and seedling establishment. Existing plants should be hand-hoed or otherwise destroyed to prevent seed formation. *Cropland*—Use clean cultivation to destroy young plants and prevent seed production. Use crop rotation with associated herbicides for control of broadleaf weeds. This weed does not appear on any of the herbicide labels; therefore, suggested control on a trial basis would be those herbicides commonly used to control broadleaf weeds such as acifluorfen, atrazine, cyanazine, fluometuron, linuron, metribuzin, simazine, and 2,4-D. *Pastures*—Apply 2,4-D or MCPA plus a surfactant to young plants and repeat if needed. *Noncrop Areas*—Suggested use of paraquat or glyphosate to kill existing plants, or atrazine, bromacil, or tebuthiuron for lasting residual control.

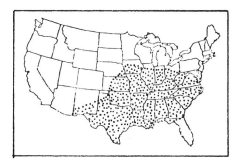

19E
Croton monanthogynus
   Michx.
Prairietea
Spurge family
(Euphorbiaceae)

Description

A summer annual herb that has erect or profusely spreading stems with forking branches, often three to five of the lowest branches may arise from a central point. The plant is 15–50 cm tall. The simple, alternate leaves are silvery green, entire, ovate, rounded at base, and 1–4 cm long. The plant is covered with whitish star-shaped hairs. The inflorescence is axillary in the forks of branches. Male and female flowers are separate. The very few female flowers are on recurved pedicels. The fruit is a two-lobed capsule, with one seed in each valve. Reproduction is by seeds. It flowers from June to September.

Habitat

Prairietea may be found in pastures, roadsides, fence rows, and waste places. It is native of North America.

Suggested Control

Cropland—Use tillage and clean cultivation to destroy young plants and prevent seed production. Use crop rotation and associated herbicides that control broadleaf weeds. This weed does not appear on any of the herbicide labels; therefore, suggested control on a trial basis would be those herbicides commonly used to control broadleaf weeds such as atrazine, cyanazine, fluometuron, linuron, metribuzin, simazine, and 2,4-D. *Pastures*—Apply 2,4-D or MCPA to young plants and repeat as needed. *Noncrop Areas*—Use paraquat or glyphosate to burn down existing plants, or atrazine, bromacil, or tebuthiuron to provide residual control.

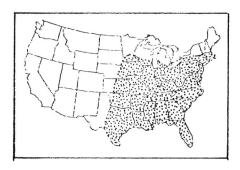

19F
Euphorbia corollata L.
Flowering spurge
Spurge family
(Euphorbiaceae)

Description

A perennial herb that has milky juice and a deep rootstock. Stems are erect, branched near the top, smooth, light green and 30–100 cm tall. The simple, alternate leaves are linear to elliptic or spatulate; either short petioled or sessile; and 3–6 cm long. The uppermost leaves subtending the primary branches are similar but whorled. The inflorescence consists of terminal clusters of small greenish flowers surrounded by white petallike bracts that are up to 1 cm across. They arise from the upper leaf axils. The fruits are three-lobed, smooth, and about 4mm wide. The gray seeds are ovoid and shallowly pitted. Reproduction is by seeds and rootstocks. Flowering occurs from June to September.

Habitat

Flowering spurge may be found along roadsides or in pastures, old fields, and waste areas. It is native to North America.

Suggested Control

Cropland—Tillage and clean cultivation will generally prevent establishment of this weed in cropland areas. *Pastures*—Improve pasture management techniques that specifically use rotational grazing; several times yearly mow after cattle have been removed. Spray with 2,4-D plus dicamba in mid-spring. *Waste Places*—Mow periodically and spray with a combination of 2,4-D plus dicamba.

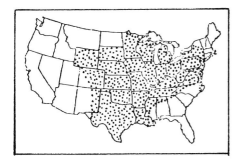

19G
Euphorbia dentata Michx.
Toothed-leaf poinsettia
Spurge family
(Euphorbiaceae)

Description

A summer annual herb that has milky juice. The stem is erect, with ascending branches, sparsely hairy and 20–40 cm tall. The simple, short-petioled leaves are mostly opposite, coarsely toothed, finely hairy, and variable in size and shape. The inflorescence is composed of small clusters of flowers subtended by reduced leaves. The smooth fruits are conspicuously three-lobed. The ovoid, black seeds are rough-surfaced and 2–3 mm long. Reproduction is by seeds. Flowering occurs from July to October.

Habitat

This weed may be found along roadsides, fence rows, waste places, and occasionally in cultivated fields. It is native of tropical America.

Suggested Control

Cropland—Use clean cultivation as needed coupled with crop rotation. This weed does not appear on any herbicide label, but a search of the literature indicates that the following herbicides might be used: atrazine, cyanazine, oxidiazon, linuron, methazole, 2,4-D, 2,4-DB, and paraquat. *Noncrop Areas*—Spray with 2,4-D plus dicamba if selective control in grass is desired, use paraquat or glyphosate for burn down, or bromacil or tebuthiuron for season-long bare ground control.

19H
Euphorbia maculata L.
Spotted spurge
Spurge family
(Euphorbiaceae)

Description

Summer annual herb with milky juice and simple to many-branched stem that is erect or spreading, smooth, reddish, and 0.5–1.0 mm tall. The simple, oblong, opposite, slightly toothed, short-petioled leaves often have a reddish spot or blotch near the base and are 8–30 cm long. The inflorescence is in small clusters at end of branches or in leaf axils. The flowers are small and greenish. The smooth fruits are three-lobed and on a short stalk. The angled, black seeds are 1–1.6 mm long. Reproduction is by seeds. It flowers from June to October.

Habitat

Spotted spurge may be found in gardens, cultivated fields, and non-crop areas. It is a native of North America.

Suggested Control

Home Gardens—Use clean cultivation to prevent establishment and seed production. Various mulches will help prevent seedling establishment. *Cultivated Fields*—Use clean cultivation and crop rotation to include crops where acifluorfen, atrazine, cyanazine, linuron, methazole, metribuzin, norflurazon, and pendimethalin can be used. *Noncropland Areas*—Use paraquat, atrazine, bromacil, diuron, hexazinone, simazine, sulfometuron, or tebuthiuron.

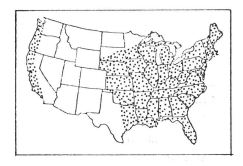

191
Euphorbia supina Raf.
Prostrate spurge
Spurge family
(Euphorbiaceae)

Description

A prostrate summer annual herb that has milky juice. The extensively branched prostrate stems spread over the ground forming flat mats that are 10–60 cm in diameter. The simple, opposite leaves are 4 to 16 mm long, slightly toothed to entire, finely hairy and are usually a mottled purple. The inflorescence is either small terminal clusters or in the leaf axils on the upper side of the branches. The fruits are stiff-haired and sharply angled. The seeds are four-sided, light brown to red. and 1 mm long. Reproduction is by seeds. Flowers appear from July to November.

Habitat

Prostrate spurge may be found in lawns, gardens, sandy fields, and along roadways. It is a native of America.

Suggested Control

Home Lawns—Maintain a vigorous turf through adequate fertilization and proper mowing height plus a spring application of a mixture of 2,4-D plus dicamba. Do not apply within dripline of desirable trees or shrubs. *Home Gardens*—Use clean cultivation to prevent establishment and seed production and various mulches to prevent establishment. *Cultivated Fields*—Use clean cultivation and crop rotation to include crops where acifluorfen, atrazine, cyanazine, linuron, methazole, metribuzin, and norflurazon can be used. *Fence Rows, Waste Areas, Industrial Sites*—Use paraquat, atrazine, bromacil, diuron, simazine, or tebuthiuron.

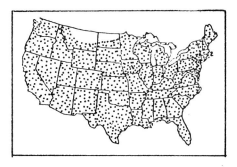

20A
Rhus glabra L.
Smooth sumac
Cashew family
(Anacardiaceae)

Description

A shrub that is up to 5 m tall. The stems are sparsely branched. The younger branches and petioles are smooth and have a whitish bloom that can be rubbed off. Leaves are compound, with 11 to 31 lanceolate shaped leaflets that are 5 to 10 cm long, have sharp points and toothed edges, and are much paler in color on the bottom side. The inflorescence is a panicle and often unisexual. The male is open and very long (up to 45 cm), while the female is dense and smaller. The fruit is bright red, with dense minute, appressed hairs. Reproduction is by seeds and by rootstocks. Flowers appear during July and September.

Habitat

This shrubby weed may be found in abandoned fields, fence rows, pastures, roadsides and waste grounds. It is native to North America.

Suggested Control

Pastures—Use good management practices of rotational grazing and clipping after removal of animals. Spot treatment with 2,4-D plus dicamba. *Fence Rows and Roadsides*—Remove perennial rootstalk with a pickax, sharp spade, or other device. Spray small plants and regrowth with 2,4-D plus dicamba. Repeat treatments as necessary. *Industrial Areas*—Spray with tebuthiuron for total vegetation control, or with 2,4-D plus dicamba for selective control in grasses.

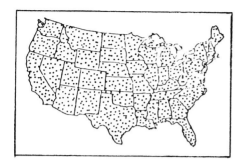

20B
Rhus radicans L.
Poison ivy
Cashew family
(Anacardiaceae)

Description

An upright plant that has several growth habits. It may be a small erect shrub or a trailing, spreading shrub or a high climbing vine. The vine form has aerial clinging rootlets and may be found climbing on other shrubs, trees, buildings, or fence posts. The compound leaves have three leaflets, each has a sharply pointed tip. The terminal leaflet has a longer stalk than the lateral leaflets. The inflorescence is composed of axillary panicles. The flowers are inconspicuous and yellowish-green. The fruit is grayish white, dry and pitted and about 5 mm in diameter. It reproduces mainly vegetatively by creeping rootstocks. It may cause skin irritation. Flowering occurs in May and June.

Habitat

This poisonous plant may be found in fence rows, under trees and shrubs of gardens, and in waste areas. It is native to North America.

Suggested Control

Home Gardens and Landscape Plantings—Hire an individual who is not sensitive to the toxic substances contained in the plants to completely remove all plant parts including creeping rootstocks. The worker should always wear gloves. In areas where it is impossible to remove the rootstocks, the vine or shrub should be cut back and stumps hand-painted with a 1:5 mixture of 2,4-D amine or amitrole and water. *Pastures*—Use good pasture management practices, i.e., good fertilization, rotational grazing, and mowing after removal of animals, followed by an annual application of 2,4-D in the spring or early summer. *Fence Rows, Waste Areas*—Spray with 2,4-D, amitrole, dicamba, glyphosate, or sulfometuron.

20C
Rhus toxicodendron L.
Poison oak
Cashew family
(Anacardiaceae)

Description

A low growing nonclimbing shrub that seldom grows over 1 m tall. The stems are slender, erect, simple, or sparingly branched and the young stems are pubescent. It has no aerial roots, but spreads by subterranean stolons. The leaves are compound with three leaflets, which are obovate to round, pilose above, velvety beneath. The leaf surfaces are covered with fine hair. The leaflets are variously lobed, shaped much like an oak leaf and are 5–8 cm long. The fruit is yellowish-white, dry and pitted, about 5 mm in diameter and temporarily hairy. Reproduction is mainly by vegetative means. It may cause skin irritation. Flowering occurs in May and June.

Habitat

This poisonous plant may be found in fence rows, under trees and shrubs of gardens, and in waste areas. It is native of North America.

Suggested Control

Home Gardens and Landscape Plantings—Hire an individual who is not sensitive to the toxic substances contained in the plants to completely remove all plant parts including creeping rootstocks. The worker should always wear gloves. In areas where it is impossible to remove the rootstocks, the vine or shrub should be cut back and stumps hand-painted with a 1:5 mixture of 2,4-D amine or amitrole and water. *Pastures*—Use good pasture management practices, i.e., good fertilization, rotational grazing, and mowing after removal of animals, followed by an annual application of 2,4-D in the spring or early summer. *Fence Rows and Waste Areas*—Spray with 2,4-D, amitrole, dicamba, or glyphosate.

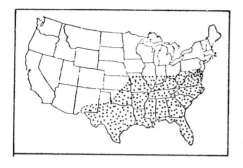

20D
Ampelopsis arborea (L.)
  Koehne
Peppervine
Grape family (Vitaceae)

Description

A perennial plant that can be either a woody high-climbing vine or a bushy nonclimbing shrub. It may or may not have tendrils. The 10- to 20-cm long leaves are compound with three or more ovate, coarsely toothed leaflets, each 2–5 cm long and short-stalked. The inflorescence is a panicle or cyme and is borne in the upper leaf axils. The flowers are greenish. The calyx is five-toothed and adheres to the ovary. The fruit is a two- to four-seeded, egg-shaped, black berry. Reproduction is mainly by seeds. Flowers appear during June and July.

Habitat

The shrubby, viny pest may be found in gardens, shrubs, fence rows, and waste places. It is a native of North America.

Suggested Control

Gardens—Completely remove all plant parts by cutting and digging and then periodically check for regrowth. *Fence Rows and Waste Places*—Same as for gardens. Also, this weed is probably susceptible to glyphosate or a mixture of 2,4-D plus dicamba with a surfactant added.

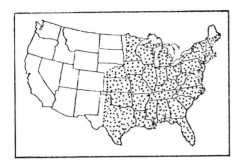

20E
Parthenocissus quinquefolia
(L.) Planch.
Virginia creeper
Grape family (Vitaceae)

Description

A perennial, high-climbing woody vine that is supported by three to eight branched tendrils with disclike clinging structures at their tips. The palmately compound leaves have a long petiole and three to five oblong-ovate leaflets, which are 4–15 cm long and have coarsely toothed margins. The inflorescence is a panicle with 25 to 300 greenish flowers on divergent branches. The fruit is a nearly black berry with one to three seeds and is 5–7 mm in diameter. Reproduction is by seeds and by stem sections. It flowers from June to August.

Habitat

This viny pest can be found climbing on trees, buildings, and fences. It is a native of North America.

Suggested Control

Remove main root below soil level with an ax and sharp shovel and periodically check for regrowth. If the vine is cut above the ground, the fresh stump can be painted with a herbicide–water mixture of 1:5 to prevent regrowth. Use 2,4-D plus dicamba. If virginia creeper is not growing on a desirable plant, it can be treated with 2,4-D plus dicamba.

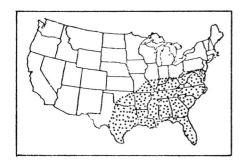

20F
Vitis rotundifolia Michx.
Muscadine grape
Grape family (Vitaceae)

Description

A perennial high-climbing vine that has trailing or twining stems. The young branches are abundantly dotted with small lenticels and simple tendrils. The leaves are simple, rounded to heart-shaped with broadly toothed edges. They are 6–12 cm long, lustrous, nearly smooth, and rarely are slightly lobed. The inflorescence is a short, densely flowered panicle. The fruits are sweet, purple-black, and have a tough skin. They fall promptly at maturity. The seeds are oblong and about 8 mm long. It reproduces by seeds and rooted stems. Flowering occurs in June and fruits mature during September and October.

Habitat

Muscadine grape may be found growing on trees in fence rows and thickets. It is native to North America.

Suggested Control

Remove main root below soil level with an ax and a sharp shovel, or spray the foliage with 2,4-D, or cut the vines near the ground and spray resprouts with 2,4-D.

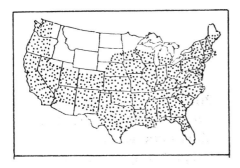

20G
Abutilon theophrasti Medic.
Velvetleaf
Mallow family (Malvaceae)

Description

A coarse, summer annual herb with erect, many-branched stems that are covered with short velvety hairs. It is 60–120 cm tall. The leaves are simple, alternate, large, heart-shaped, pointed, petioled and have a soft, velvety surface. The solitary, showy flowers have five yellow petals and are 1.5–2.5 cm wide. They are borne in the upper leaf axils. The fruit is cup-chaped, about 2.5 cm in diameter, and composed of 10 to 15 seeds in a circle with a ring of beaks pointing upward. The seeds are brown, flattened, notched and about 3 mm long. Reproduction is by seeds. Flowers appear during August and September.

Habitat

Velvetleaf occurs in gardens, cultivated fields, roadsides, barnyards, and waste areas. It is a native of India.

Suggested Control

Home Gardens—Prevent seed production by cultivation and hand hoeing of scattered plants. Various mulches may be used to prevent establishment. *Cropland*—Use mechanical control methods and clean cultivation. This weed is controlled by the following herbicides: ametryn, atrazine, bentazon, bromoxynil, chloroxuron, cyanazine, 2,4-D, dicamba, dinoseb, fluometuron, linuron, metribuzin, glyphosate, oxyfluorfen, propazine, simazine, and terbacil. Use a crop rotation that will utilize these herbicides effectively. *Noncrop Areas*—Use 2,4-D or dicamba for selective control in grass, paraquat for nonselective burn down, or atrazine, bromacil, simazine, or tebuthiuron for nonselective residual control.

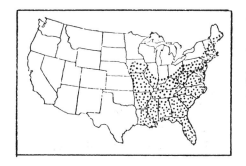

20H
Anoda cristata (L.) Schlecht.
Spurred anoda
Mallow family (Malvaceae)

Description

A summer annual herb that is 50–90 cm tall. The erect or reclined stems are branched and have soft long hairs. The leaves are simple, alternate, ovate, lobed, coarsely toothed, 5–10 cm long, and have the same kind of hairiness as the stems. The pale-blue or violet flowers are 1 cm wide and are borne singly at end of rather long, thin stalks in leaf axils. The fruit is a cup-shaped ring of 8 to 12 seeds, subtended by a persistent saucer-shaped calyx that is about 2 cm wide. Seeds are long-awned and pubescent. Reproduction is by seeds. It flowers from August to October.

Habitat

Spurred anoda may be found in cultivated fields, roadsides, and waste places. It is native of North and South America.

Suggested Control

Cropland—Maintain a good crop rotation. Use clean cultivation; do not allow escaped plants to produce seed. In corn use a triazine herbicide; in cotton use methazole or norflurazon; in soybeans use metribuzin followed by linuron plus 2,4-DB or metribuzin plus 2,4-DB. In each case follow with cultivation if necessary. *Roadsides and Waste Places*—For burndown and desiccation use paraquat, for selective control in grass use a mixture of 2,4-D plus dicamba, for soil sterilization use atrazine, bromacil, prometon, simazine, or tebuthiuron.

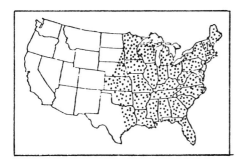

20I
Hibiscus trionum L.
Venice mallow
Mallow family (Malvaceae)

Description

A summer annual herb that is 30–50 cm tall. The stems are erect or spreading, many-branched from the base, and slightly hairy. The leaves are alternate, long-petioled, irregularly shaped, and deeply three-parted. The parts are coarsely toothed or lobed. The flowers are solitary, arise from the leaf axils, and are subtended by numerous linear bracts. The corolla is very showy, with five pale-yellow to whitish petals with a purple base. They are open only for a few hours. The fruit is a ring of hairy capsules surrounded by an inflated calyx. The seeds are kidney-shaped, rough, gray, and about 2 mm long. Reproduction is by seeds. Flowers appear between July and September.

Habitat

Venice mallow may occur in gardens, cultivated fields, roadsides, and waste places. It is a native of Asia.

Suggested Control

Home Gardens—Prevent seed production by cultivation and hand-hoeing. Mulches can be used advantageously to prevent establishment. *Cropland*—Maintain a cropping system where mechanical cultivation can be used if necessary. This weed is controlled by atrazine, bentazon, cyanazine, 2,4-D, dicamba, diuron, fluometuron, linuron, metribuzin, and propazine. Use a crop rotation where these herbicides can be utilized effectively. Cultivate or hand-hoe to control escaped plants. *Noncropland*—Use either 2,4-D or dicamba, for selective control in grass; use paraquat for desiccation of existing vegetation, and atrazine, bromacil, prometon, simazine, or tebuthiuron for residual nonselective control.

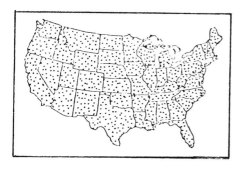

21A
Malva neglecta Wallr.
Common mallow
Mallow family (Malvaceae)

Description

An annual or biennial herb that has a short, straight tap root. Stems are erect and spreading, or trailing on the ground. They are well-branched, 10–30 cm long, and more or less pubescent with star-shaped hairs. The simple leaves are circular to kidney-shaped, long-petioled, hairy and have conspicuously toothed margins. The flowers are clustered in the axils of the leaves and have whitish or pale-lilac petals. The fruit is a flattened disk that breaks up into 10 to 20 hairy, single-seeded sections when ripe. Reproduction is by seeds. Flowers appear from April to October.

Habitat

Common mallow may occur in gardens, yards, lawns, cultivated fields, roadsides, and waste areas. It is a native of Europe.

Suggested Control

Home Gardens and Yards—Prevent seed production and destroy existing plants by cultivation and hand hoeing. Various mulches can be used to prevent establishment. *Lawns*—Spray in spring with a mixture of 2,4-D plus dicamba. *Cropland*—Use a crop and herbicide rotation coupled with cultivation as needed. Herbicides, which can be used for labeled crops, are atrazine, cyanazine, 2,4-D, dicamba, diuron, fluometuron, linuron, metribuzin, or propazine. *Non-cropland*—Use either 2,4-D or dicamba for selective control in grasses, paraquat for desiccation of existing vegetation, or atrazine, bromacil, prometon, or tebuthiuron for residual nonselective control.

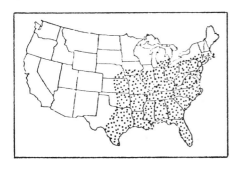

21B
Sida spinosa L.
Prickly sida
Mallow family (Malvaceae)

Description

Summer annual herb that has a tough, 20- to 90-cm tall stem and a slender taproot. The stems are erect, extensively branched, softly hairy, and bear two to three short, spiny projections at the major nodes. The simple, alternate, 2- to 4-cm long leaves are petioled and oblong with toothed edges. The flowers have five pale-yellow petals and are either solitary or in small clusters on short stalks in the leaf axils. The fruit splits at the top into five single-seeded sections, each with two spreading spines at the top. The ovoid, brownish seeds are three-angled. Reproduction is by seeds. Flowering occurs from June to October.

Habitat

Prickly sida can be a pest in gardens, cultivated fields, pastures, and may be found along roadsides and in waste areas. It is native to the tropical world.

Suggested Control

Home Gardens—Prevent seed production by cultivation and hand hoeing. Use of mulches can be advantageous in preventing seedling establishment. *Cropland*—Maintain a good crop rotation and use a herbicide recommended for control of broadleaf weeds. Herbicides that control this weed are atrazine, bentazon, cyanazine, 2,4-D, dicamba, dinoseb, fluometuron plus MSMA, linuron, metribuzin, norflurazon, and prometryn. Cultivate if necessary. *Pastures, Roadsides and Waste Areas*—Use a mixture of 2,4-D plus dicamba.

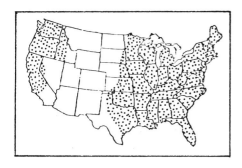

21C
Hypericum perforatum L.
St. Johnswort
St. Johnswort family
(Guttiferae)

Description

A semiwoody perennial herb that arises from a crown with an extensive, deep root system. The erect, smooth stems are branched, somewhat double-edged, woody, and reddish at the base and 30–90 cm tall. The simple, opposite, elliptic leaves are covered with small, clear dotted resinous glands on the surface (observed by holding up to light) and black glands on the edges. The orange-yellow flowers are in showy clusters at ends of branches and occasionally have black dots on the edge of petals. The fruits are elliptic pointed capsules that divide into three parts and contain many tiny, shiny-black seeds. It reproduces by seeds and rootstocks. The plant contains compounds that when ingested by livestock cause the skin of light-colored animals to be photosensitive. A condition similar to severe sunburn may result. Flowering occurs from June to September.

Habitat

St. Johnswort may occur in pastures, meadows, and fence rows. It is native of Europe.

Suggested Control

This weed has been controlled very successfully by a leaf-feeding beetle *Chrysolina quadrigemina* (Suffr.) along the Pacific Coast, where large acreages were infested. In most areas where small infestations are present, plants in a pasture will be reduced by upgrading the level of pasture management through proper fertilization and pH adjustment, rotational grazing, and close clipping after livestock are removed. Occasional plants in pastures, fence rows, and roadsides should be manually removed and/or prevented from producing seed. While not listed on any herbicide label nor in the literature, it would probably be susceptible to spot treatments of picloram, glyphosate, or soil sterilants such as bromacil, sulfometuron, or tebuthiuron.

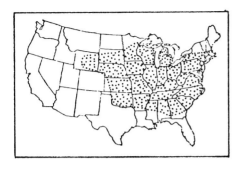

21D
Viola papilionacea Pursh
Meadow violet
Violet family (Violaceae)

Description

A perennial herb that has coarse, branching, horizontal rhizomes. The leaves are simple and arise directly from the nodes of rootstocks on long, slightly hairy petioles. The leaf blades are kidney-shaped or ovate with a heart-shaped base and a sharply pointed tip. They are 6–13 cm wide. The violet or blue flowers are solitary on a long stalk. There is one boat-shaped petal and one bearing a tubular extension (spur). A second kind of flower that never opens is produced on horizontal peduncles. Reproduction is by seeds and rootstocks. It flowers during May and June.

Habitat

Meadow violet may be found in shaded humid areas around lawns, gardens, or dwellings. It is a native of North America.

Suggested Control

Lawns—Improve the level of lawn maintenance through proper pH adjustment, fertilization, and cutting height. Spray in early spring with a combination of 2,4-D, mecoprop, and dicamba. *Under Shrubs, Around Dwellings, etc.*—If undesirable, use hand hoeing or DMSA, MSMA, or paraquat.

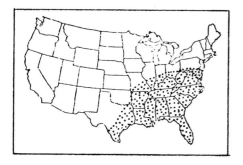

21E
Passiflora incarnata L.
Maypop passionflower
Passionflower family
(Passifloraceae)

Description

A trailing perennial herb that has viny, 5- to 8-m long, hairy stems. The leaves are alternate, deeply three or four-lobed and slightly hairy on the lower surface. The lobes are lanceolate, constricted at the base, and sharply pointed at the tip, with slightly toothed edges. The unique flowers are very showy, variegated purple, 4–6 cm in diameter, and borne at end of an elongated stalk in a leaf axile. They have numerous frilly petals and sepals. The fruit is an edible yellow berry that resembles a small melon. Reproduction is by seeds. It flowers from June to August.

Habitat

Maypop passionflower is found along cultivated fields, fence rows, and in waste lands. It is also cultivated in some gardens. It is native to North America.

Suggested Control

Cropland—Use thorough tillage with spring or fall plowing followed by clean cultivation coupled with crop rotation. The objective is to destroy the root system and deplete underground food reserves. *Fence Rows and Waste Areas*—If the weed is objectionable is should be removed with a hand spade; or since this plant does not appear on herbicide labels, a spray of 2,4-D plus dicamba or glyphosate may be tried.

21F
Opuntia spp.
Pricklypear
Cactus family (Cactaceae)

Description

A succulent perennial that may be prostrate, spreading, or erect depending on species. The stems root freely at the joints. They are flat, fleshy, and covered with sharp spines. The number of spines varies from several per cluster to almost spineless. The roots are fibrous. The large yellow flowers sometimes have a reddish center. They are 5–9 cm across and have 8 to 12 petals. The fruit is pulpy, edible, and green to purplish. These perennials reproduce by seeds and stems. Flowers occur from May to July.

Habitat

Pricklypear may occur in dry pastures, rock outcrops, and roadsides. They are native to the Americas.

Suggested Control

If this weed is a problem it can be removed manually, dried, and burned. If in cropped areas, it can be controlled with consistent cultivation and crop rotation. Also it can be controlled by spot spraying with picloram.

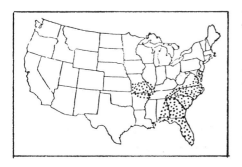

21G
Jussiaea leptocarpa Nutt.
Primrose willow
Eveningprimrose family
(Onagraceae)

Description

A woody, perennial aquatic herb that has erect or reclined stems and adventitious roots on the lower portions. The simple, alternate leaves are sessile on the stem and lanceolate-shaped and gradually narrow at the base. The flowers are borne on a 1.5 cm long stalk in the upper leaf axils and have six yellow petals. The fruits are 2–5 cm long cylindric capsules. The triangular shaped seeds are flat and the surface of the actual seed is exposed through the fruit. Reproduction is by seeds. Flowers appear from July to October.

Habitat

Primrose willow may occur along the edges of lakes and ponds or in areas of wet, marshy sod. It is native to North America.

Suggested Control

Aquatic—Deepen the edges of the pond and fill in depressions along edges to eliminate marshy areas. Apply an ester of 2,4-D in diesel fuel or granular 2,4-D or spray with dicamba. Repeat the treatment as necessary.

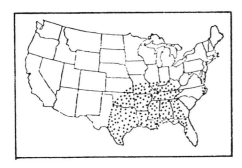

21H
Jusiaea repens L. var.
  glabrescens Kuntze
Creeping waterprimrose
Eveningprimrose family
(Onagraceae)

Description

A perennial aquatic herb that has floating or creeping rooting stems. The weak stems are smooth or sparsely hairy and rooting at the nodes when in contact with mud. The smooth, simple, alternate leaves are lanceolate or spatulate-shaped, 4- to 8-cm long and narrow toward the short, slender petiole. The bright yellow, very showy flowers are borne on long stalks in the upper leaf axils. The petals are 10–15 mm long. The tough, 3- to 5-mm long fruits are nearly cylindric capsules. One series of seed occurs in each locule. The seeds are longer than thick and have a blunt end. Reproduction is by seeds and rooted stem sections. It flowers from June to October.

Habitat

Creeping waterprimrose may be found in muddy areas along drainage ways, streams, ditches, or ponds. It is native of North America.

Suggested Control

Aquatic—Deepen the edges of the pond and fill in depressions along edges to eliminate marshy areas. Apply an ester of 2,4-D in diesel fuel or granular 2,4-D or spray with dicamba. Retreat as necessary.

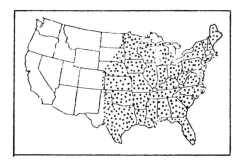

211
Oenothera biennis L.
Common eveningprimrose
Eveningprimrose family
(Onagraceae)

Description

A coarse biennial herb that forms large rosettes of leaves and a fleshy root system the first year. The stems are erect, simple, or branched in the upper portion. The lower section is very leafy, 30–120 cm tall. The sessile leaves are variable, but usually lanceolate. The lower leaves are generally larger and hairy. The showy yellow flowers are 2.5 cm across and are borne singly in the terminal leaf axils. The yellow petals turn purplish with age. The fruits are hairy, woody, four-angled, cylindrical capsules that are 1–3.5 cm long and contain many seeds. The seeds are brown and angular. Reproduction is by seeds. It flowers from July to October.

Habitat

Common eveningprimrose may occur in pastures, roadsides, fence rows, and waste places. It is native of North America.

Suggested Control

Pastures, Fence Rows, and Waste Areas—Do not allow the plant to go to seed. Mow frequently before flowering. If capsules have formed, completely remove plant from area since seed will mature in capsule even after cutting. Primrose can be controlled with an elevated rate of 2,4-D plus dicamba applied while plant is in rosette stage.

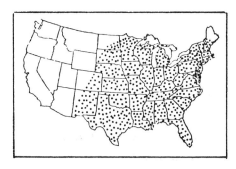

22A
Oenothera laciniata Hill
Cutleaf eveningprimrose
Eveningprimrose family
(Onagraceae)

Description

An annual herb with erect or ascending stems that are simple or branched from the base. The leaves are oblanceolate or lanceolate, 3–8 cm long, tapering to the base, prominently wavy margined, toothed, green and sparsely finely hairy to glabrous. The flowers are sessile in the axils of the upper leaves and have four yellow petals. The linear, 1.5- to 3.5-cm long fruits are straight or curved capsules. The pale brown seeds are thick, ellipsoid, strongly pitted and 1–2 mm long. It reproduces by seeds. It flowers from May to August.

Habitat

Cutleaf eveningprimrose may be found in gardens, crop fields, pastures, roadsides, and waste places. It is a native of North America.

Suggested Control

Gardens—Prevent seed production by cultivation and hand hoeing. A good mulch can be helpful in preventing establishment of new seedlings. *Cropland*—Use a good crop rotation and clean cultivation or the herbicides normally used to control broadleaf weeds such as atrazine, cyanazine, dicamba, 2,4-D, fluometuron, linuron, metribuzin, propazine, and simazine. *Pastures*—Use good pasture management techniques; mow after grazing and spray with a combination of 2,4-D plus dicamba. *Roadsides and Waste Places*—Mow to prevent seed production, cultivate if possible, spray with dicamba, paraquat, or MSMA or glyphosate for burn down, or with bromacil or tebuthiuron for soil sterilization.

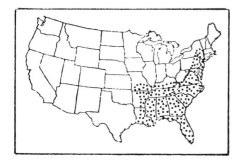

22B
Myriophyllum brasiliensis
  Camb.
Parrotfeather
Watermilfoil family
(Haloragaceae)

Description

A perennial aquatic herb that is rooted to the bottom mud. The coarse, leafy, stems are sparingly branched, with the emersed tip extending 10–30 cm above the water surface. The whorled leaves are generally 2–5 cm long, with 10 to 18 narrow segments on each side of the midrib. The lower segments are much reduced. The leaves above water are green, uniform, and graceful; those underwater are reddish-brown. Flowers are formed in the leaf axils of the submersed leaves. This picture shows only emersed leaves. The fruits are small and 1.5–2 mm long. Reproduction is by seeds and by broken stem sections. Flowering occurs from July to September.

Habitat

Parrotfeather may be found in small fish ponds, lakes, slow-moving streams, and canals. It is a native of South America.

Suggested Control

Aquatic—Mechanically remove from small areas with a hand rake or some type of aquatic harvesting machine. Control chemically with 2,4-D, diquat or endothall; follow label restrictions explicitly.

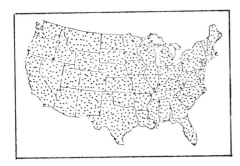

22C
Myriophyllum
    heterophyllum Michx.
Broadleaf watermilfoil
Watermilfoil family
(Haloragaceae)

Description

A perennial submerged aquatic herb with simple or branched stems, which are coarse and up to 10 mm in diameter. It has two leaf forms, submerged and emerged. The submerged leaves are 2–5 cm long, in whorls of four to six and are divided into six to ten pairs of narrow segments. The emerged leaves are simple, 2–5 mm wide and up to 2 cm long. The inflorescence is an emerged 8- to 15-cm long spike. The fruits are subglobose, 1–1.5 mm in diameter, split into two parts. Both are two-ridged on the back and rounded on the sides. Reproduction is by seeds and by vegetative means. Flowering occurs from June to September.

Habitat

This pest has invaded the shallow areas of ponds, lakes, and streams. It is a native of South America.

Suggested Control

Aquatic—Mechanically remove vegetative portions from small areas with a hand rake or some type of aquatic weed harvester. Control chemically with 2,4-D, dichlobenil, diquat, endothall, and simazine. Follow label restrictions explicitly.

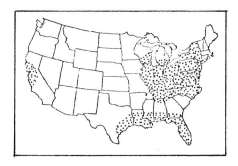

22D
Myriophyllum spicatum L.
Eurasian watermilfoil
Watermilfoil family
(Haloragaceae)

Description

A perennial aquatic submersed herb that is rooted to the bottom mud. The branched stems often rise from a depth of 4 m. Each node will produce roots if it is in contact with the mud. Often large mats will be formed and float free on the water surface. The leaves are in whorls of three or four, with 10 to 14 finely dissected segments on each side. The inflorescence is a spike that is produced 5–10 cm above the water surface. The flowers are light yellow. Eurasian water-milfoil reproduces very rapidly by seeds, rhizomes, stem fragments, and axillary buds (turions). Flowers occur from July to September.

Habitat

This pest has become established in many areas of the country probably as an escape from aquariums. It may be found in fish ponds, lakes, slow-moving streams, and canals. It is a native of Eurasia.

Suggested Control

Aquatic—Mechanically remove from small areas with a hand rake and strainer basket or some type of aquatic harvesting machine. Control chemically with 2,4-D, dichlobenil, endothall, and simazine; follow label restrictions explicitly.

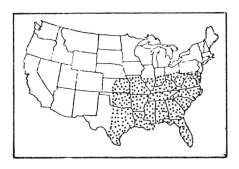

22E
Chaerophyllum tainturieri
   Hooker
Chervil
Parsley family (Umbelliferae)

Description

Summer annual herb that has a pleasant scent. The stem is erect or spreading, densely hairy, especially at base and is usually branched. It is 40 to 80 cm tall. The leaves are three times pinnately compound. The leaf segments or leaflets are elliptic or lance-shaped and hairy on the lower surface. The inflorescence is a compound umbel with one to four primary rows and three to ten pedicels. The flowers are white. The fruit is slender with several ribs up to 8 mm long and has a short beak. Reproduction is by seeds. It flowers from May to July.

Habitat

Chervil may be found in pastures, undisturbed places in gardens, roadsides, and waste places. It is native of North America.

Suggested Control

Home Gardens—Use clean cultivation to prevent establishment and seed production. Various mulches may be used to prevent establishment. *Pastures, Roadsides and Waste Areas*—Mow periodically to prevent seed production. While not specifically mentioned on the label, a mixture of 2,4-D plus dicamba applied before flowering will probably provide effective control.

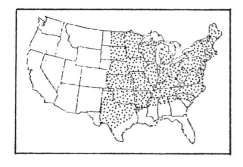

22F
Cicuta maculata L.
Spotted waterhemlock
Parsley family (Umbelliferae)

Description

Perennial herb that has tuberous roots. The erect, stout stems are branched only at the top. They are hollow, smooth, bear purplish stripes and spots, and are up to 2 m tall. The alternate leaves are two or three times compound. The uppermost are reduced to three-parted or even simple leaves. The leaflets are smooth with toothed edges. Sometimes they are spotted. The flowers are small, white, and borne in a broad compound umbel that is 5–12 cm wide. The seeds are flat on one side and rounded on the other. They are ridged lengthwise with light and dark lines. Reproduction is by seeds and by tuberous roots. The roots are deadly poisonous and have a parsnip-like scent. It flowers from June to August.

Habitat

Spotted waterhemlock may be found in swamps and in moist places in pastures, along ditches, and waste places. It is native to North America.

Suggested Control

Pastures, Meadows, and Noncrop Areas—Provide better drainage or level infested areas to eliminate moist areas. If possible rotate infested areas with cultivated crops since tillage operations will control this weed. If rotation is not possible, dig scattered plants and destroy the root system. On larger areas, mow periodically trying to delete food storage and preventing replenishment in the underground tubers. The new regrowth should treated with a mixture of 2,4-D plus dicamba.

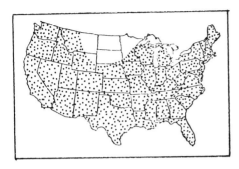

22G
Conium maculatum L.
Poison hemlock
Parsley family (Umbelliferae)

Description

A perennial poisonous herb that has a long white taproot. The stems are erect, widely branched, smooth, green and purple spotted, and from 1 to 3 m tall. The leaves are compound, but variable. The lower ones have a petiole, but the upper ones are without petioles and are borne at the end of the subtending sheath. They are broadly tri-angular-ovate in general outline and three to four times compounded. The leaflets are lance-shaped, with toothed edges and are 5–10 mm long. The inflorescence is a compound umbel, 4–6 cm in diameter and has numerous white flowers. The fruit is pale-brown, egg-shaped, and about 3 mm long with wavy ribs. Reproduction is by seeds. All parts are poisonous. Flowering occurs from June to September.

Habitat

Poison hemlock may occur in pastures, meadows, fence rows, road-sides, and along stream banks. It is a native of Eurasia.

Suggested Control

Pastures, Meadows and Noncrop Areas—Rotate these areas with row crops if possible. Discing and cultivation will control this weed. If rotation is not possible, remove individual plants by digging below the basal leaves. Seed production of second year plants is prevented by mowing prior to flower formation. Poison hemlock can be selectively controlled in grass pastures, meadows, etc., by applying 2,4-D plus dicamba while the plants are young.

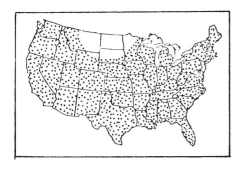

22H
Daucus carota L.
Wild carrot
Parsley family (Umbelliferae)

Description

A winter or summer biennial herb that forms a rosette of leaves and a stout root in the first season. The stem is erect, coarse, widely branched, hollow, hairy, and bristly and 0.3–1.5 m tall. The leaves are alternate or basal and are pinnately compound. The ultimate divisions are lance-shaped, lobed, and sparsely hairy. The stem leaves have sheathing bases. The inflorescence is an erect flat-topped umbel with numerous white flowers, except the central one which is dark purple. The whole inflorescence is subtended by bracts that are divided into narrow segments. The fruits are 3–4 mm long, winged and bristly. Reproduction is by seeds. Flowering occurs from June to August.

Habitat

Wild carrot may be found in pastures, fence rows, roadsides, and waste places. It is a native of Eurasia.

Suggested Control

Cropland—This weed is not a problem if crop rotation and clean cultivation are practiced. *Pastures*—Scattered plants can be controlled by cutting the plant below the basal leaves. Heavily infested areas should be mowed as soon as the flower stalks appear to prevent seed production. Repeated spring applications of 2,4-D will gradually reduce the population. If possible the area should be plowed and rotated to cultivated crop for 2 years. Cultivation will prevent new seedlings from becoming established, will stimulate seed germination and prevent seed production. *Fence Rows and Waste Areas*—Use a soil sterilant such as bromacil, dichlobenil, prometon, sulfometuron, or tebuthiuron.

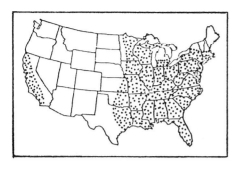

22I
Hydrocotyle umbellata L.
Water pennywort
Parsley family (Umbelliferae)

Description

A perennial, rooted, aquatic herb that has creeping stems. The floating or creeping stems root at nodes and are branched and elongated. The leaves arise singly on long petiole attached to center of the blade from each node on the underwater or underground stems. The smooth blades are rounded or nearly so and have bluntly toothed or slightly lobed edges. They are 4–7 cm in diameter. The inflorescence is a simple many-flowered umbel with spreading pedicels. The flowers are white. The fruit is distinctly notched and 2–3 mm wide. Reproduction is by seeds and by creeping stems. Flowers occur from May to November.

Habitat

Water pennywort may be found rooted in mud along edges of ponds and canals or may be found as a floating mat on the water. It is a native of tropical America.

Suggested Control

Aquatic—Water pennywort can be controlled by physical removal of the plants growing along the water's edge. This can be done by cutting, mowing, raking, pulling, or digging. The edges of the pond or drainageway should be deepened to discourage reestablishment. Also, growing plants can be controlled with 2,4-D or diquat. The herbicide label should be followed carefully.

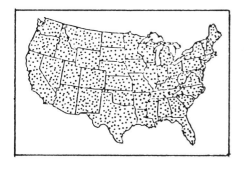

23A
Pastinaca sativa L.
Wild parsnip
Parsley family (Umbelliferae)

Description

A biennial herb that produces a rosette of large upright leaves and a fleshy taproot in the first season. The coarse, erect stem is smooth, branched, and 1–1.5 m tall. The leaves are pinnately compound and 5–10 cm long. Each leaf has 5 to 15 ovate to oblong leaflets that have variably toothed edges. The lower leaves are without petioles and are sheathed while the upper leaves have long petioles. The inflorescence is a compound umbel with 15 to 25 primary rays. The small flowers are yellow. The seeds are flat, rounded in general outline, smooth, low ribbed and 5–7 m long. Reproduction is by seeds. Flowering occurs from May to October.

Habitat

Wild parsnip may occur in pastures, along roadsides, and in waste places. It is a native of Eurasia.

Suggested Control

Cropland—This weed is not a problem if crop rotation and clean cultivation are practiced. *Pastures*—Scattered plants can be controlled by cutting the plant below the basal leaves. Heavily infested areas should be mowed as soon as the flower stalks appear to prevent seed production. Repeated early spring applications of 2,4-D will reduce the infestation. Spraying should be done before the flower stalk starts to elongate. If possible the infested area should be plowed and rotated to a cultivated crop for 2 years. Cultivation will prevent new seedlings from becoming established, will stimulate seed germination and prevent seed production. *Fence Rows and Waste Areas*—Use a soil sterilant such as bromacil, dichlobenil, sulfometuron, or tebuthiuron.

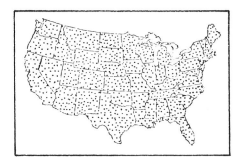

23B
Anagallis arvensis L.
Scarlet pimpernel
Primrose family
(Primulaceae)

Description

An annual herb that has weak, prostrate, ascending or erect stems. They are smooth, well-branched, and 10–30 cm long. The leaves are simple, opposite, sessile, elliptic to ovate, and have black dots on the underside. The flowers are solitary, borne on long stalks in the axils of the leaves, and open only in sunny weather. The petals are scarlet or bluish with fringed margins. The fruit is a many-seeded globular capsule and about 4 mm in diameter. The seeds are brown. Reproduction is by seeds. Flowers appear between May and August.

Habitat

Scarlet pimpernel may be found in gardens, along river banks, and waste places. It is native to Eurasia.

Suggested Control

Cropland—Use a crop and herbicide rotation coupled with cultivation as needed. Herbicides, which can be used on properly labeled crops are atrazine, dichlorprop, dicamba plus 2,4-D, mecoprop, and terbacil. *Noncropland*—Use dicamba plus 2,4-D for selective control in grasses or use bromacil as a soil sterilant.

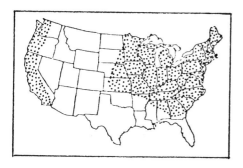

23C
Lysimachia nummularia L.
Moneywort
Primrose family
(Primulaceae)

Description

A perennial herb with smooth, creeping, or trailing stems that are 15 to 30 cm long. They often form mats and root at the nodes. The round leaves are opposite, short-petioled, and 1.5–3 cm long. The solitary flowers are showy and are borne in the leaf axils on a stalk as long as the leaves. The yellow petals are often dotted with dark red and are 2–3 cm wide. The fruit is a many-seeded capsule opening by longitudinal valves. Reproduction is by seeds and rooted stem sections. Flowers appear from May to August.

Habitat

Moneywort may occur in lawns and pastures especially in wet and shaded areas. It is native to Europe.

Suggested Control

Lawns and Pastures—Improved management programs with proper grass selection, proper fertilization, and pH adjustment. Branches of trees and shrubs can be cut and thinned to decrease shading. Maintain vigorous, competitive grass. In lawns rake to raise runners and then mow closely but do not scalp the grass. Spring application of 2,4-D plus dicamba may increase control.

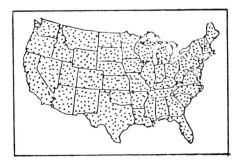

23D
Apocynum cannabinum L.
Hemp dogbane
Dogbane family
(Apocynaceae)

Description

A tough perennial that has fibrous bark and milky sap. The reddish-brown smooth stems are erect or nearly so and multiple branches near the top give it a bushy appearance. It can be up to 1.5 m tall. Leaves are without teeth and 5–15 cm long. The leaves of the primary axil are short-petioled, those of the branches are nearly sessile. The foliage is bright green during the summer and changes to yellow-brown in the fall. Its small, greenish-white, bell-shaped flowers are produced in dense clusters (cymes) generally in the axils of the stem. Each flower produces two brown slender sickle-shaped pods, which are 5–10 cm in length. The pods contain up to 200 small spike-shaped, reddish-brown seeds, which have a tuft of soft silky hairs on one end. Reproduction is by seeds, crown buds, and roots. It flowers from June to August.

Habitat

Hemp dogbane may be found in cropland, pastures, fence rows, and waste areas. It is native to North America.

Suggested Control

Cropland—A crop rotation that includes alfalfa for 3 years will do much to reduce a stand. When in row crops, plow deeply, and follow with clean cultivation. Spot spray dicamba and 2,4-D or glyphosate (will kill existing crop) as needed. Fall application of dicamba and 2,4-D when leaves are still green is better than a spring or summer application. Glyphosate should be applied when hemp dogbane is in the bud to bloom stage. All herbicide treatments may need to be repeated on a yearly basis until infestation has been destroyed. *Fence Rows and Waste Areas*—Use dicamba and 2,4-D or glyphosate. Sulfometuron can be tried as a soil sterilant.

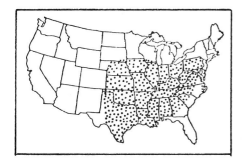

23E
Ampelamus albidus (Nutt.)
  Britt.
Honeyvine milkweed
Milkweed family
(Asclepiadaceae)

Description

A perennial vine with twinning stems that grow up to 2 m long and regenerates from deep rootstocks. The leaves are distinctly opposite, 4–12 cm wide, long-petioled, and triangular-lanceolate to heart-shaped. The leaves are well-separated by long internodes. The fragrant white flowers arise in clusters in the leaf axils. The fruits are slender, smooth, lanceolate pods, 2–2.5 cm in diameter and 10–15 cm long. The seeds have a tuft of silky hair. Reproduction is by seeds and underground stems or rootstocks. It flowers from July to August.

Habitat

Honeyvine milkweed can be found climbing on other plants in gardens, cultivated fields, fence rows, and waste grounds. It is a native of North America.

Suggested Control

Home Gardens and Landscaped Areas—Completely remove all plant parts by cutting and hand hoeing. For a few persistent plants treat with 2,4-D amine or glyphosate. *Cropland*—Use deep plowing followed by clean cultivation and hand hoeing. 2,4-D may be used with care in labeled nonsusceptible crops. 2,4-D should be applied before honeyvine milkweed starts to climb the crop. Glyphosate may be used to spot spray in crops where so labeled. *Noncrop Areas*—2,4-D or glyphosate may be used.

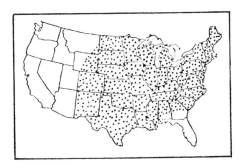

23F
Asclepias incarnata L.
Swamp milkweed
Milkweed family
(Asclepiadaceae)

Description

An erect, perennial herb that has milky juice. The coarse, very leafy stems are 30–150 cm tall and have two downy lines of hairs on the upper branches. The leaves are lanceolate to ovate with fine ascending veins. The inflorescence is composed of one or more clusters of flowers arising from one point. The flowers are pink to rose-purple and 6–8 mm long. The fruits are minutely hairy pods that are 5–9 cm long. Reproduction is by seeds. Flowers appear from June to August.

Habitat

Swamp milkweed may occur in wet areas in pastures and along roadsides. It is a native of North America.

Suggested Control

Pastures and Noncrop Areas—Soils should be drained wherever possible. Scattered plants can be destroyed with a sharp shovel and persistence, or by spot spraying with 2,4-D or glyphosate.

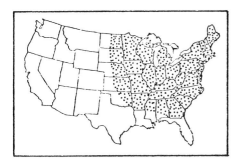

23G
Asclepias syriaca L.
Common milkweed
Milkweed family
(Asclepiadaceae)

Description

A perennial herb that has erect stems and milky juice. The stems are coarse, mostly simple, up to 2 m tall, covered with fine, soft pubescent and arise from creeping rhizomes. The large leaves are thick, 5–18 cm across, and 10–25 cm long and have strong transverse veins. The showy flowers are in terminal and subterminal clusters. They are whitish-green mixed with purple. Seed pods are on downward curved pedicels and are about 10 cm long. The seeds have a tuft of silky hair. Reproduction is by seeds and creeping rhizomes. Flowers occur from June to August.

Habitat

Common milkweed may be found in cultivated fields, especially those under conditions on minimum tillage, pastures, roadsides, and waste places. It is a native of North America.

Suggested Control

Cropland—If possible, use a crop rotation where the land is deep plowed to disrupt the rhizome system, followed by a crop with interrow cultivation. The crop rotation may also include alfalfa. Alfalfa provides strong competition against milkweed and will nearly eliminate a stand in 3 years. Common milkweed can be treated with spot sprays of 2,4-D plus dicamba or glyphosate when milkweed is actively growing and in the bud to early bloom stage of development. *Pastures, Roadsides, and Waste Places*—Spot spray with 2,4-D plus dicamba or glyphosate.

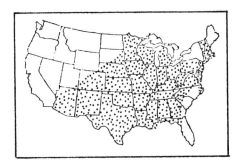

23H
Asclepias tuberosa L.
Butterfly milkweed
Milkweed family
(Asclepiadaceae)

Description

A perennial herb that has bright orange-red flowers and milky juice. The stems are upright, very leafy with branches at the summit. The leaves are oblong and have a short petiole or may be without petioles. They are 5–10 cm long, pubescent, and slightly heart-shaped at base. The orange-red flowers are in numerous clusters, often from the axils of divergent branches. The seed pods are pubescent and at the top of a downward-curved pedicel. Reproduction is by seeds. Flowers are present from June to August.

Habitat

Butterfly milkweed may occur in pastures, roadsides, fence rows, and waste grounds. It is a native of North America.

Suggested Control

Cropland—This showy plant is considered by many to be a wildflower. It will not persist in cropland subjected to deep plowing and cultivation. If scattered plants occur, they can be controlled by a spot spray with 2,4-D plus dicamba or glyphosate when milkweed is actively growing and in the bud to early bloom stage of development. *Pastures, Roadsides, and Waste Places*—If objectionable spot spray with 2,4-D plus dicamba or glyphosate.

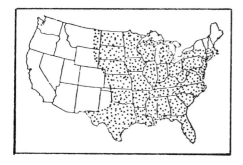

231
Asclepias verticillata L.
Eastern whorled milkweed
Milkweed family
(Asclepiadaceae)

Description

An erect, perennial herb that has milky juice and creeping rootstocks. The very leafy stems are slender, simple, or sparingly branched and 30–90 cm high. Leaves are linear in whorls of three to six and have recurved margins. The small greenish-white flowers are in clusters in the upper nodes. The fruit is a slender 4- to 5-cm long pod on an erect pedicel. Reproduction is by seeds and creeping roots. Flowers may be present from June to August.

Habitat

This plant is poisonous to livestock. It may occur in pastures, meadows, roadsides, and waste grounds. It is a native of North America.

Suggested Control

Cropland—This weed will not persist in fields subjected to deep plowing and cultivation. Therefore, use a crop rotation that includes row crops and mechanical tillage. If scattered plants occur, spot spray with 2,4-D plus dicamba or glyphosate when milkweed is actively growing and in the bud to early bloom stage of development. *Pastures, Roadsides, and Waste Places*—Spot spray with 2,4-D plus dicamba or glyphosate.

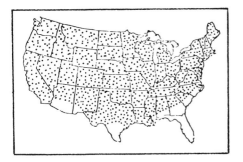

24A
Convolvulus arvensis L.
Field bindweed
Morningglory family
(Convolvulaceae)

Description

A perennial trailing herb that has a deep and extensive root system going beyond 6 m into the soil. The slender trailing or twining stem spreads over other plants and the ground. It is slightly pubescent and up to 3 m long. The simple, alternate leaves are 4–6 cm long, petioled and oblong, with lobed arrowhead-like bases. The funnel-shaped, white or pink flowers are borne in leaf axils on long stalks with two bracts about 15 mm below the flower. The fruit is a capsule with four dark gray, slightly roughened seeds. Reproduction is by seeds and creeping roots. Flowers occur from June to September.

Habitat

Field bindweed may be found in gardens, cultivated fields, roadsides, fence rows, and waste places. It is a native of Eurasia.

Suggested Control

Home Gardens—Hand hoe or cultivate never allowing the plant to obtain 10 inches of new growth for a 2 year period, thus starving the root system or apply a weak solution of 2,4-D using the bottle method. (Mix 1 teaspoon of 2,4-D amine per 1 quart of water in an open-mouth bottle.) Place attached green stems of plant in bottle and allow the herbicide mixture to be translocated into root system. *Cultivated Fields, Pastures, Fence Rows, and Waste Areas*—Spot treatment with 2,4-D or glyphosate in spring and repeat in the fall. If cultivated fields are heavily infested, consult local agricultural extension service for crop–herbicide rotation adapted to local area.

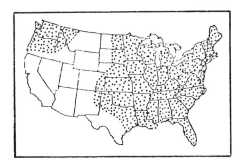

24B
Convolvulus sepium L.
Hedge bindweed
Morningglory family
(Convolvulaceae)

Description

A perennial twining herb that is 2–3 m long and has an extensive and deep root system. The stems are sparsely pubescent, twine on other weeds or crop plants, or spread over the ground. The simple, alternate leaves have a long petiole and are triangular-shaped with a lobed arrowhead-like base. They are up to 10 cm long. The funnel-shaped, pink or white flowers are 4 to 7 cm long and borne on an axillary peducle with paired bracts. The fruit is a capsule with two to four seeds. The dull black seeds are 4–5 cm long. Reproduction is by seeds and by creeping rootstocks. It flowers from June to September.

Habitat

Hedge bindweed may occur in fence rows, cultivated fields, shores, bottomlands, fence rows, and waste areas. It is a native of Eurasia.

Suggested Control

Control measures are the same as for field bindweed, page 236.

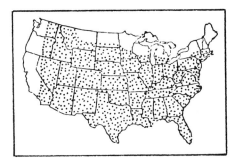

24C
Cuscuta pentagona Engelm.
Field dodder
Morningglory family
(Convolvulaceae)

Description

An annual parasitic herb without chlorophyll that obtains its food by twining around a host plant and sending rootlike projections into its stem. A wide variety of cultivated, weedy, and native plants serve as hosts. The stems are pale brown, stringlike, smooth, branch extensively, and form dense masses. The whitish flowers are somewhat glandular, short-pediceled, and in loose clusters. The fruit is a tiny capsule with four small seeds, each about 1 mm long. Reproduction is by seeds. It flowers from April to October.

Habitat

Field dodder may occur in gardens, cultivated fields parasitizing a variety of crops and weeds. It is a native of North America.

Suggested Control

Legume Crops—Purchase legume seeds that are free of this parasitic pest; maintain a good crop rotation. Chlorpropham and pronamide can be used as a preemergence treatment with some success to prevent dodder establishment in small seeded legumes. Generally, dodder is not a problem in small grains, grain sorghum, or corn. In other crops, vegetation infested should be cut and destroyed on the site before dodder seed can mature or should be desiccated with paraquat or dinoseb in fuel oil.

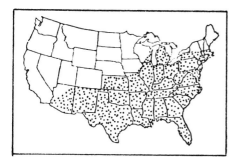

24D
Ipomoea coccinea L.
Scarlet morningglory
Morningglory family
(Convolvulaceae)

Description

An annual herb with smooth, twining, 1- to 3-m long stems that climb on weeds and crop plants. The simple, alternate, entire, long-petioled glabrous leaves are heart-shaped with occasionally toothed or angular margins and 5–10 cm long. The scarlet flowers are funnel-shaped and two to several are borne on a thick, axillary peduncle. The sepals are abruptly long-awned. The fruit is a globose-ovoid capsule with four to six smooth, black seeds. Reproduction is by seeds. Flowers occur from August to October.

Habitat

Scarlet morningglory may occur in gardens, cultivated fields, fence rows, and waste grounds. It is native to tropical America.

Suggested Control

Home Gardens—Do not allow this pest to go to seed regardless of its delightful flowers. It should be controlled by hand weeding and clean cultivation. *Cropland*—Maintain a good crop rotation and use proper herbicides coupled with cultivation as needed. Herbicides to be used are acifluorfen, atrazine, cyanazine, dinoseb, diuron, fluometuron, metribuzin, paraquat, propazine, simazine, and 2,4-D. By use of appropriate herbicides, morningglory can be controlled much easier in corn, grain sorghum, and cotton than in soybeans. *Fence Rows, Waste Areas, etc.*—Apply 2,4-D for selective control in grass or paraquat for desiccation. *Noncropland Areas*—Use residual rates of either atrazine, bromacil, diuron, simazine, or tebuthiuron.

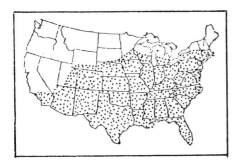

24E
Ipomoea hederacea (L.) Jacq.
Ivyleaf morningglory
Morningglory family
(Convolvulaceae)

Description

Annual herb with slender, hairy, up to 2 m long stems that twine on other plants or spread on the ground. The simple, alternate, hairy leaves are deeply three-lobed with rounded sinuses and sharply pointed lobes. The funnel-shaped flowers are borne in clusters of one to three on a short peduncle. The sepals are lance-shaped, commonly 15–20 mm long and the basal portion is densely hairy. The petals are white to blue. The fruit is a three-celled capsule with four to six dark brown seeds. Reproduction is by seeds. It flowers from July to September.

Habitat

Ivyleaf morningglory may be found in gardens, cultivated fields, fence rows, and waste grounds. It is a native of tropical America.

Suggested Control

Home Gardens—Do not allow this pest to go to seed regardless of its attractive flowers. It should be controlled by hand weeding and clean cultivation. *Cropland*—Maintain a good crop rotation and use proper herbicides coupled with cultivation as needed. Herbicides to be used are acifluorfen, atrazine, cyanazine, dinoseb, diuron, fluometuron, metribuzin, paraquat, propazine, simazine, and 2,4-D. By use of appropriate herbicides, morningglory can be controlled much easier in corn, grain sorghum, and cotton than in soybeans. *Fence Rows, Waste Areas, etc.*—Apply 2,4-D for selective control in grass or paraquat for desiccation. *Industrial Sites*—Use residual rates of atrazine, bromacil, diuron, simazine, or tebuthiuron.

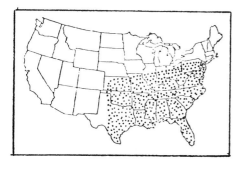

24F
Ipomoea lacunosa L.
Pitted morningglory
Morningglory family
(Convolvulaceae)

Description

Annual, small creeping or twining herb with slender, very slightly pubescent, 1- to 3-m long stems that twine or creep on other weeds or crop plants. The leaves are simple, alternate, hairless, entire, or angulate-three lobed. The lobes are pointed with rounded sinuses. The funnel-shaped flowers are borne on short peduncles, bearing one to four flowers. The sepals have few long hairs, are lance-shaped, and 10–15 mm long. The petals are white, sometimes varying to pink or pale purple. The fruit is a oblong, two-celled capsule with four to six seeds. Reproduction is by seeds. It flowers from August to October.

Habitat

Pitted morningglory may be found in gardens, cultivated fields, roadsides, and fence rows. It is native of tropical America.

Suggested Control

Home Gardens—This pest should not be allowed to go to seed regardless of its attractive flowers. It can be controlled by consistent hand weeding and clean cultivation. *Cropland*—Maintain a good crop rotation and use proper herbicides coupled with cultivation as needed. Herbicides to be used are acifluorfen, atrazine, cyanazine, dinoseb, diuron, fluometuron, metribuzin, paraquat, propazine, simazine, and 2,4-D. By use of appropriate herbicides, morningglory can be controlled much easier in corn, grain, sorghum, and cotton than in soybeans. *Fence Rows, Waste Areas, etc.*—Apply 2,4-D for selective control in grass or paraquat for desiccation. *Industrial Sites*—Use residual rates of atrazine, bromacil, diuron, simazine, or tebuthiuron.

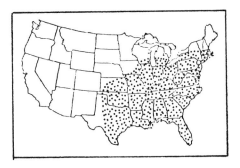

24G
Ipomoea pandurata (L.)
   G.F.W. Meyer
Bigroot morningglory
Morningglory family
(Convolvulaceae)

Description

A perennial herb that arises from a large, deep-seated, tuberlike root. The glabrous (or nearly so) stems climb over bushes and are up to 4.5 m long. The leaves are entire, ovate, and deeply heart-shaped at the base. They are 7–14 cm long and rarely slightly lobed. The funnel-shaped flowers are in groups of one to seven, borne in a terminal cluster. The peduncles are coarse and stiff. The petals are white with red-purple center and 5–8 cm long. The sepals are ovate, 13–20 mm long, glabrous, and broadly rounded. The fruit is a two-celled capsule with four to six dark-brown seeds fringed with soft hairs. Reproduction is by seeds and tubers. Flowers occur from July to September.

Habitat

Bigroot morningglory may occur in cultivated fields, fence rows, roadsides, and waste places. It is native of tropical America.

Suggested Control

Cropland—Because of the large tuberlike roots, this plant can be difficult to control. Deep plowing and cultivation will reduce the root food reserves. This weed is not listed on any of the herbicide labels; but a mixture of 2,4-D plus dicamba applied to actively growing plants in the mid-spring or early fall or glyphosate applied in late summer or early fall may give control. *Fence Rows, Roadsides, and Waste Places*—Try a 2,4-D plus dicamba mixture or glyphosate applied as previously mentioned. Also sulfometuron or tebuthiuron when used as a soil sterilant may control this weed.

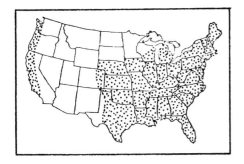

24H
Ipomoea purpurea (L.) Roth.
Tall morningglory
Morningglory family
(Convolvulaceae)

Description

A twining annual vine with pubescent stems that are up to 5 m long. The leaves are simple, alternate, smooth, or sparsely hairy, ovate-heart-shaped, entire, and abruptly short-pointed. The flowers are in groups of one to five with peduncles as long as the subtending leaves. The sepals are lanceolate to oblong, sharp-pointed, and hairy toward the base. The fused petals are blue, purple, white, or variegated and 4–6 cm long. The fruit is a spherical to egg-shaped capsule, three-celled with four to six irregularly shaped black seeds. Reproduction is by seeds. Flowering occurs from July to October.

Habitat

Tall morningglory may occur in cultivated fields, gardens, roadsides, and waste places. It is native of tropical America.

Suggested Control

Home Gardens—Do not allow this pest to go to seed regardless of its beautiful flowers. It should be controlled by hand weeding and clean cultivation. *Cropland*—Maintain a good crop rotation and use proper herbicides coupled with cultivation as needed. Herbicides to be used are acifluorfen, atrazine, cyanazine, dinoseb, diuron, fluometuron, metribuzin, paraquat, propazine, simazine, and 2,4-D. By use of appropriate herbicides, morningglory can be controlled much easier in corn, grain sorghum, and cotton than in soybeans. *Fence Rows, Waste Areas, etc.*—Apply 2,4-D for selective control in grass or paraquat for desiccation. *Industrial Sites*—Use residual rates of atrazine, bromacil, diuron, simazine, or tebuthiuron.

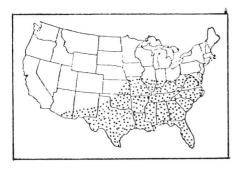

24I
Ipomoea quamoclit L.
Cypressvine morningglory
Morningglory family
(Convolvulaceae)

Description

An annual, twining herb with slender, glabrous to capillary stems that are 1–4 m long and twine on other weeds and crop plants. The leaves are alternate and pinnately dissected into narrow segments, each 1–2 cm long. The petioles are 1–3 cm long. The flowers are on long peduncles, much longer than the subtending leaves and bear one or two flowers. The sepals have a short, slender point, and are flat against the corolla tube. The petals (corolla) are scarlet-red and 3.5–4 cm long. Fruit is a globose-ovoid capsule with four to six seeds. Reproduction is by seeds. Flowering occurs from August to October.

Habitat

Cypressvine morningglory may be found in gardens, crop lands, fence rows, and waste places. It is native of tropical America.

Suggested Control

Home Gardens—Do not allow this pest to produce seed regardless of its unique leaves and delightful flowers. It should be controlled by hand weeding and clean cultivation. *Cropland*—Maintain a good crop rotation and use proper herbicides coupled with cultivation as needed. Herbicides to be used are acifluorfen, atrazine, cyanazine, dinoseb, diuron, fluometuron, metribuzin, paraquat, propazine, simazine, and 2,4-D. By use of appropriate herbicides, morningglory can be controlled in corn, grain sorghum, and cotton much easier than in soybeans. *Fence Rows, Waste Areas, etc.*—Apply 2,4-D for selective control in grass or paraquat for desiccation. *Industrial Sites*—Use residual rates of atrazine, bromacil, diuron, simazine, or tebuthiuron.

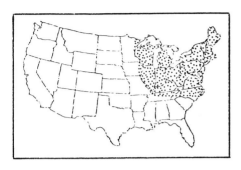

25A
Echium vulgare L.
Blue thistle
Borage family (Boraginaceae)

Description

A biennial herb that has an elongated taproot and produces a rosette of leaves the first year. The erect stem is simple or branched below and up to 80 cm tall. It is coarse and very bristly when young. The bristles become prickles at maturity. The rosette leaves are oblong or elliptic, long-stalked, and bristly hairy. The stem leaves are sessile, alternate, simple, linear-lanceolate, and roughened by stiff hairs. The numerous flowers are borne in the axils of the upper foliage leaves. The blue petals are pink in the bud. The fruit is made up of four obovate nutlets with roughened surface. Reproduction is by seeds. It flowers during June and July.

Habitat

Blue thistle occurs in stony pastures, meadows, cultivated fields, and roadsides. It is a native of Europe.

Suggested Control

Cropland—This weed is not a problem if crop rotation and clean cultivation are practiced, or if paraquat is used in a minimum tillage management system. *Pastures*—Scattered plants can be controlled by cutting the plant below the basal leaves. Heavily infested areas either should be mowed as soon as the flower stalks appear to prevent seed production or should be plowed and rotated to a cultivated crop for several years. Cultivation will prevent establishment of new seedlings, stimulate seed germination, and prevent seed production. This weed will probably succumb to 2,4-D plus dicamba applied before the flower stalk starts to elongate. *Fence Rows, Industrial Areas, and Waste Areas*—Use glyphosate or paraquat for burn down or a soil sterilant such as bromacil, prometon, or tebuthiuron for residual control.

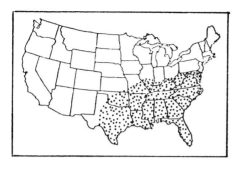

25B
Heliotropium indicum L.
Indian heliotrope
Borage family (Boraginaceae)

Description

A coarse, hairy, annual herb with erect, many branched stems that are up to 80 cm tall. The leaves have a rough surface and are 4–10 cm long. The base gradually narrows into the petiole. The inflorescence is a single elongated axis (8–14 cm long) that is coiled toward apex. The flowers are bluish in color and about 4 mm wide. The fruit is two-lobed, separates into nutlets, each with two seeds. Reproduction is by seeds. It flowers from May to October.

Habitat

Indian heliotrope may be found in pastures, fence rows, roadsides, and waste places. It is a native of Brazil.

Suggested Control

In general, serious populations of this weed do not occur, nor does this weed appear on specific herbicide labels. Therefore, clean cultivation is suggested for row crops and 2,4-D plus dicamba for fence rows and waste areas.

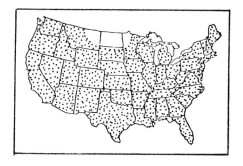

25C
Lithospermum arvense L.
Corn gromwell
Borage family (Boraginaceae)

Description

A winter annual or biennial that has a slender taproot. The erect minutely hairy stems are branched at the base and 30–70 cm tall. The linear or lanceolate leaves are without lateral veins and have stiff, short hairs on both sides. The solitary white flowers are borne in the leaf axils and are scarcely longer than the calyx. The fruit is a gray or pale-brown, one-seeded nutlet that is prominently wrinkled and about 3 mm long. Reproduction is by seeds. Flowers occur from April to June.

Habitat

Corn gromwell may be found in small grain and hay fields, fence rows, and waste areas. It is native of Eurasia.

Suggested Control

Cropland—Corn gromwell can be controlled by crop rotation. It is mainly found in winter wheat. Rotation of wheat with a cultivated row crop will reduce the infestation. Also, only clean crop seed should be sown. Herbicides that may be used to control or suppress this weed are atrazine, bromoxynil, chlorsulfuron, cyanazine, diuron, linuron, methazole, metribuzin, terbutryn, and 2,4-D plus dicamba. These herbicides may be matched with appropriately labeled crops. *Noncropland*—Use paraquat for burn down or a soil sterilant for longer residual control.

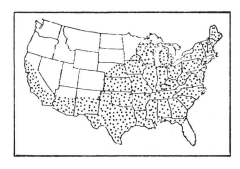

25D
Verbena hastata L.
Blue vervain
Vervain family (Verbenaceae)

Description

A perennial herb that has erect stems and a short rootstock. The stems are branched near the top of the plant, rough with ascending hairs, and 0.4–1.5 m tall. The simple opposite leaves are lanceolate to narrowly ovate, short-petioled, pointed at the apex, 4–18 cm long with coarsely toothed edges, and often three-lobed at the base. The surface may be smooth or slightly hairy. The inflorescence is composed of numerous compact spikes borne on a terminal panicle. The calyx is pubescent with shorter subtending bracts. The small violet-blue flowers have a corolla tube longer than the calyx. The fruits are smooth or linear nutlets, 1.5–2 cm long. Reproduction is by seeds and rootstocks. Flowering occurs from July to September.

Habitat

Blue vervain may be found in pastures, roadsides, fence rows, and waste places, usually in moist soils. It is native of North America.

Suggested Control

Pastures—Use improved pasture management techniques such as correct pH adjustment and fertilization, rotational grazing, and mowing after each grazing to provide increased competition by desirable species and to weaken the weed stand. Further control can be obtained with spring application of 2,4-D plus dicamba. If crop rotation is possible, cultivation will destroy the stand over a two-year period. *Fence Rows, Roadsides, and Waste Places*—Mow periodically to prevent seed production and spray with 2,4-D plus dicamba.

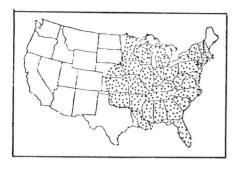

25E
Verbena simplex Lehm.
Narrow-leaved vervain
Vervain family (Verbenaceae)

Description

A perennial herb that has erect stems that are 10–50 cm tall. They are smooth with sparse, stiff, appressed hairs, and may be sparingly branched at the top. The leaves are 3–10 cm long, narrowly lanceolate or linear, taper at base, and have short, stiff hairs on both surfaces. The inflorescence is one or more compact spikes at the ends of branches. The flowers are light blue to purple. The calyx is 4–5 mm long, with pointed lobes, and is usually longer than the subtending bracts. The fruits are linear nutlets that are 2.5–3 mm long. Reproduction is by seeds. Flowers appear from May to September.

Habitat

Narrow-leaved vervain may occur in cultivated fields, rocky places, and roadsides. It is a native of North America.

Suggested Control

Pastures—Use improved pasture management techniques such as correct pH adjustment and fertilization, rotational grazing, mowing after each grazing, and a spring application of 2,4-D plus dicamba. *Fence Rows, Roadsides, and Waste Places*—Mow periodically to prevent seed production; spray with 2,4-D plus dicamba or glyphosate. *Cropland*—This weed will not persist in cropland where a good crop rotation that includes cultivated crops is practiced. Cultivation and tillage destroy the perennial crown and root system.

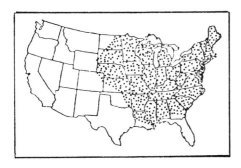

25F
Glechoma hederacea L.
Ground ivy
Mint family (Labiatae)

Description

A perennial herb that has creeping stems and shallow roots. The stems are 40–70 cm long, root at the nodes, and have numerous erect flowering branches. They are four-angled and glabrous or nearly so. The glabrous, bright-green leaves are opposite, palmately veined, petioled, rounded to kidney-shaped with round teeth, 1–3 cm in diameter, and have a minty odor. The small flowers are in axillary clusters. The pubescent, persistant calyx is tubular with five equal teeth. The bluish-purple corolla has two lips. The dark brown nutlets are ovoid and 1.5–2.0 mm long. Reproduction is by seeds and creeping stems. It flowers from April to June.

Habitat

Ground ivy occurs in lawns, gardens, orchards, shaded areas, and waste places. It is a native of Eurasia.

Suggested Control

Home Gardens—Ground ivy does not persist in areas of constant cultivation. Practice clean cultivation and hand weeding or use a mulch plus hand weeding. *Home Lawns*—Treat with a combination of 2,4-D plus dicamba. (Avoid drift to sensitive desirable plants or do not apply within drip line or root area of ornamentals.) *Orchards*— Use simazine, terbacil, or paraquat. *Fence Rows and Waste Areas*— Same as for home lawns. *Industrial Areas*—Use a soil sterilant such as atrazine, bromacil, diuron, prometon, simazine, or tebuthiuron.

25G
Lamium amplexicaule L.
Henbit
Mint family (Labiatae)

Description

An annual aromatic herb that has four-angled stems. The weak ascending stems are branched from the base and are 10–40 cm long. The stems have a few small long-petioled leaves at the base and usually one or two, rarely three, elongated internodes followed by much shorter internodes and sessile, clasping leaves. The leaves are 1–3 cm wide, subrotund with rounded teeth. The flowers are in dense whorls in the axils of the upper leaves. The uppermost clusters are often adjacent. The calyx is 5–7 mm long and densely wavy-haired. The petals (corolla) are pink to purple, bilobed and the upper lip is about one-third as long as the tube. It reproduces by seeds. Flowers occur from March to September.

Habitat

Henbit may occur in gardens, lawns, and small grain fields. It is native of Eurasia and northern Africa.

Suggested Control

Home Lawns—This weed is moderately resistant to 2,4-D, therefore use in mixture with dicamba applied in early spring for good results. *Home Gardens*—Practice clean cultivation plus hand weeding or use a suitable mulch plus hand weeding. *Cropland*—A good crop–herbicide rotation should be practiced. The following herbicides may be used: atrazine, bromoxynil, chlorsulfuron, EPTC, ethalfluralin, metribuzin, napropamide, oxyfluorfen, pebulate, pronamide, terbacil, terbutryn, trifluralin, and 2,4-D plus dicamba.

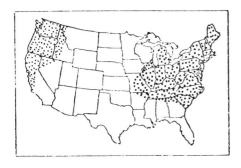

25H
Lamium purpureum L.
Red deadnettle
Mint family (Labiatae)

Description

An annual aromatic herb that has weak, ascending four-angled stems. They are branched from the base, 10–40 cm long, and usually have one or two, rarely three, elongated internodes. All leaves have petioles, are 1 to 3 cm long, and broadly ovate to subrotund with rounded teeth. The flowers are in dense whorls commonly separated by very short internodes thus forming a short, leafy terminal spike. Calyx is 5–7 mm long, and the pink to purple petals (corolla) are 11–15 mm long. Reproduction is by seeds. Flowers appear from March to August.

Habitat

Red deadnettle occurs in lawns, gardens, under shrubbery, and in waste places. It is a native of Eurasia.

Suggested Control

Home Lawns—Remove by hand or spray with a mixture of 2,4-D plus dicamba. *Home Gardens*—Practice clean cultivation plus hand weeding or use a suitable mulch plus hand weeding. *Cropland*— While this weed does not appear on the herbicide labels, it is probably susceptible to the herbicides listed for henbit (page 251). *Waste Areas*—Treat area with 2,4-D plus dicamba for selective control in grass; paraquat for quick burn down; or atrazine, bromacil, diuron, prometon, simazine, or tebuthiuron for residual control.

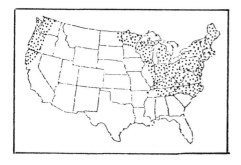

251
Mentha piperita L.
Peppermint
Mint family (Labiatae)

Description

A perennial herb that is found in moist places and is strongly peppermint-scented. The erect, smooth or nearly so, four-sided stems have many branches and are up to 1 m tall. The simple, petioled leaves are oblong or elliptic-shaped, sharp-pointed, and rounded at base. They are essentially smooth with toothed margins and are 4–8 cm long. The inflorescence is a dense spike that is up to 8 cm long and is terminal on the stem and the upper lateral branches. Flowers are purplish, in whorls in the axils of the reduced upper leaves that form the spike. Reproduction is by seeds. Flowers appear from June to October.

Habitat

Peppermint may be found in moist soils of gardens, pastures, and waste places. It is a native of Europe.

Suggested Control

Home Gardens—Remove all plant parts from the soil with a shovel, grubbing hoe, or rake. *Cropland*—Use a good crop rotation and spot-treat scattered plants with 2,4-D plus dicamba. *Pastures*—Remove scattered plants with a grubbing hoe or similar device or spray with 2,4-D plus dicamba. *Fence Rows and Noncrop Areas*—Apply soil sterilant rates of atrazine, bromacil, simazine, or tebuthiuron.

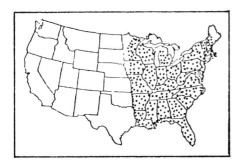

26A
Monarda fistulosa L.
Wild bergamot
Mint family (Labiatae)

Description

A perennial herb that has square stems and minty foliage. The erect simple or branching stems are hairy on the upper internodes and 0.5 to 1.2 m tall. The simple, opposite leaves are 6–10 cm long, gray-green, narrowly triangular-ovate in shape, sharply pointed with toothed edges and have long hairs along the veins on the lower surface. The inflorescence is a compact terminal whorl, subtended by pink-tinged leafy bracts. The flowers are lilac to pink, rarely white. The calyx tube is 7–10 mm long and densely hairy. Reproduction is by seeds. Flowers are present from June to August.

Habitat

Wild bergamot may occur along the borders of woods, roadsides, and fence rows. It is native of North America.

Suggested Control

Cropland—This plant will not persist in areas subjected to tillage. Use a good crop rotation and management that includes tillage and herbicides that are used to control broadleaf. *Noncropland*—Apply 2,4-D plus dicamba for selective control in grasses or a soil sterilant such as bromacil, sulfometuron, or tebuthiuron.

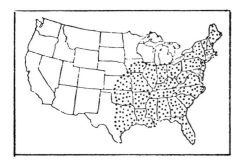

26B
Perilla frutescens (L.) Britt.
Purple mint
Mint family (Labiatae)

Description

An annual aromatic herb that has attractive purplish foliage. The erect, coarse, branching stems are finely hairy and 30–90 cm tall. The simple, opposite leaves are broadly ovate, pointed, wedge-shaped at the summit of the long petiole, with coarsely toothed edges, green-purplish, and 8–15 cm long. The inflorescence is a terminal or axillary spikelike raceme with numerous folded, oval bracts. The flowers are purplish, pink, or white and the corolla tube is shorter than the calyx. Reproduction is by seeds. It flowers from August to October.

Habitat

Purple mint may occur in cultivated fields, pastures, barnyards, and waste places. It is native of India.

Suggested Control

Cropland—In general serious populations of this weed do not occur, nor is this weed mentioned on specific herbicide labels or in specific agricultural extension service recommendations; therefore, clean cultivation is suggested for row crops. *Pastures and Noncropland*—Improved management for pastures including pasture renovation, proper pH and fertility adjustment, rotational grazing, and periodic mowing are suggested. A spring application of 2,4-D plus dicamba mixture is suggested to control the weed in pastures and noncropped areas.

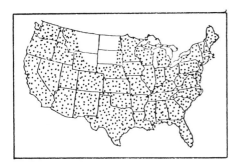

26C
Prunella vulgaris L.
Healall
Mint family (Labiatae)

Description

A perennial herb that is 10–60 cm tall. The tufted erect or reclined four-angled stems are usually branched and root at the lower nodes when in contact with the soil. The simple, opposite, long-petioled leaves are oval with entire or irregularly toothed margins and 3–8 cm long. The inflorescence is a dense terminal or axillary headlike spike that is 2–4 cm long. The flowers are violet or purple. The fruit is flat, pear-shaped, brown, slightly rough, with four seeds. Reproduction is by seeds and short runners. Flowers may be present from May to September.

Habitat

Healall may occur in cultivated fields, lawns, pastures, roadsides, and waste places. It is native of Eurasia.

Suggested Control

Cropland—Use clean cultivation and crop rotation. Weed control practices used in most crops will eliminate this weed. It does not persist under intensive agriculture. *Lawns, Pastures, and Noncropland*—Apply a mixture of 2,4-D plus dicamba in either spring or fall.

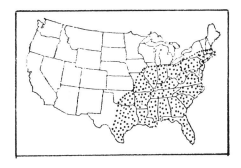

26D
Salvia lyrata L.
Lyre-leaved sage
Mint family (Labiatae)

Description

A perennial herb that forms a basal rosette and has erect, 30- to 60-cm tall, square flowering stems. The principal leaves in a basal rosette are oblong or obovate-oblong, 10–20 cm long, pinnately lobed with rounded segments, and have soft hairs on both sides. The stem leaves are commonly in one pair, rarely in two or three pairs, and resemble the basal ones but are much smaller and have shorter petioles. The inflorescence is a 10- to 30-cm-long raceme with scattered clusters of showy blue or violet flowers. The calyx persists after the corolla drops. Reproduction is by seeds. Flowering occurs in May and June.

Habitat

Lyre-leaved sage may be found in lawns, pastures, and waste places. It is native to North America.

Suggested Control

Home Lawns—Adjust pH and fertility levels to encourage a vigorous turf; maintain a proper mowing height; apply a mixture of 2,4-D plus dicamba in spring if weed infestation is intolerable. Small patches can be dug out by hand. *Pastures*—Rotate badly infested pastures to a clean cultivated crop for two years. If impracticable to rotate, adjust pH and fertilize, use rotational grazing, encourage competitive desirable species, and spray with a mixture of 2,4-D plus dicamba in the spring. *Noncropland*—Mow periodically to prevent seed production. Spray with 2,4-D plus dicamba mixture in spring for selective control in grasses. Apply bromacil, sulfometuron, or tebuthiuron for nonselective residual control.

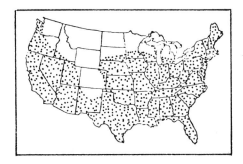

26E
Datura stramonium L.
Jimsonweed
Nightshade family
(Solanaceae)

Description

A summer annual herb that has an unpleasant odor and grows up to 1.5 m tall. The coarse, glabrous, green or purple, hollow stems have spreading branches. The simple, alternate, long-petioled leaves are ovate, pointed, 5- 20 cm long, with a few large triangular teeth. The large, 7- to 10-cm-long, white or pinkish, funnel-shaped flowers are solitary on short stalks borne in the leaf or branch axils. The calyx is about half as long as the corolla. The fruit is an ovoid, 3- to 5-cm long, four-valved capsule that is covered with short stiff spines. The seed is dark brown to black, kidney-shaped, and has a pitted, irregular surface. Reproduction is by seeds. Flowers may be present from July to October. All parts of the plant are poisonous.

Habitat

Jimsonweed may be found in cultivated fields, barnyards, pastures, roadsides, and waste areas. It is of unknown origin.

Suggested Control

Cropland—Prevent seed production by mowing, hand hoeing, and clean cultivation before the first capsules are set. The following herbicides can be used on tolerant crops in accord with label restrictions: acifluorfen, ametryn, atrazine, bentazon, bromoxynil, dicamba, fluometuron, glyphosate, metribuzin, MCPA, oxyfluorfen, paraquat, simazine, terbacil, 2,4-D, and 2,4-DB. *Pastures*—Spray the young plants with 2,4-D, dicamba, or MCPA. Use rotational grazing of pasture followed by mowing after each rotation and improve fertility to stimulate a more vigorous pasture. *Barnyards, Roadsides, and Waste Areas*—To control jimsonweed without injury to grasses, apply 2,4-D, dicamba, or MCPA when plants are young. For total long residual vegetation control, apply atrazine, bromacil, simazine, or tebuthiuron before seedlings germinate.

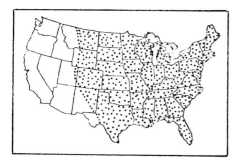

26F
Physalis heterophylla Nees.
Clammy groundcherry
Nightshade family
(Solanaceae)

Description

A perennial herb that has deep underground rootstocks. The erect or slightly spreading stems are extensively branched and bushy later in the season, and 30–80 cm tall. The simple, alternate, petioled leaves are ovate-shaped with rounded bases and round-toothed wavy edges. The solitary, drooping flowers are borne in the upper leaf axils. The bell-shaped, five-lobed corolla (petals) is greenish-yellow with a brown center, and about 2 cm in diameter. The fruit is a round, yellow berry, surrounded by the inflated calyx. The whole entity resembles a hanging lantern. Seeds are flat, 2 mm in diameter, and light orange to straw-colored. Reproduction is by seeds and rootstocks. Flowering occurs from June to August.

Habitat

Clammy groundcherry may be found in gardens, cultivated fields, pastures, roadsides, and waste places. It is native of North America.

Suggested Control

Home Gardens—Use clean cultivation and hand hoeing to prevent replenishment of root reserves and seed production.
Cropland—Destroy perennial plants by spring or fall plowing followed by clean cultivation. Continue cultivation after the crop is harvested to prevent replenishment of carbohydrates in underground rootstalks. In accordance with label restrictions the following herbicides may be used to control this weed: acifluorfen, amitrole, atrazine, cyanazine, fluometuron, 2,4-D plus dicamba, and glyphosate. *Pastures*—Spray with 2,4-D plus dicamba. *Roadsides and Waste Places*—Spray with glyphosate or 2,4-D plus dicamba.

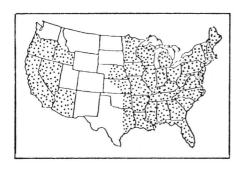

26G
Solanum carolinense L.
Horsenettle
Nightshade family
(Solanaceae)

Description

A perennial prickly herb that has a deep rootstock. The erect or ascending stems are simple or branched, have slender spines, and are 30–120 cm tall. The alternate, simple leaves are oblong, 7–12 cm long, wavy-edged, and coarsely and irregularly lobed. The leaves have yellow spines along the main veins and on the petioles. The violet or white flowers are borne in several-flowered racemes on the upper part of the stem. The corolla is five-lobed and 2 cm wide. The fruit is a round, yellow juicy berry about 1.5 cm in diameter. The seeds are flat, yellow, and 1.5 mm in diameter. Reproduction is by seeds and creeping rootstocks. Flowers may be present from May to October.

Habitat

Horsenettle may occur in gardens, cultivated fields, pastures, and roadsides. It is native of North America.

Suggested Control

Home Gardens—Use clean cultivation and periodic hand hoeing to prevent replenishment of root reserves and to prevent seed production. Apply 2,4-D or glyphosate in the early fall. *Cropland*—Destroy perennial plants by spring or fall plowing followed by clean cultivation. Continue cultivation after the crop is harvested to prevent replenishment of carbohydrates in underground rootstalks. Terbacil may be used in some crops. Spot treatments of amitrole, 2,4-D plus dicamba, or glyphosate may be made. *Pastures and Roadsides*—Spray with a mixture of 2,4-D plus dicamba for selective control. Repeat applications may be necessary. Selective control or spot treatment may be obtained with amitrole or with fall treatments of glyphosate.

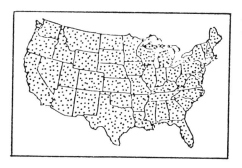

26H
Solanum dulcamara L.
Bitter nightshade
Nightshade family
(Solanaceae)

Description

A weak woody twining or trailing perennial herb that has smooth stems 0.60–2.50 m long. The smooth ovate leaves have a slender petiole and are 7–10 cm long. The leaf usually has several basal segments or lobes. The inflorescence is a 7- to 14-flowered panicle. The flowers are blue or purplish with prominent, upright deep-yellow stamens. The fruit is a scarlet ball-shaped berry about 8–10 mm in diameter. Reproduction is by seeds. It flowers from June to September. It is a poisonous plant if ingested in quantity.

Habitat

Bitter nightshade may occur along roadsides, fence rows, stream-banks, ditches, and in waste areas. It is native of Europe.

Suggested Control

Home Gardens—Destroy seedlings and prevent seed formation by hand hoeing and cultivation. Destroy the perennial root system with a spade. *Cropland*—Use a crop and herbicide rotation coupled with cultivation if needed. The following herbicides may be used on toler-ant crops according to label restrictions: atrazine, EPTC, and sim-azine. Do not include English peas or soybeans in rotation. *Fence Rows and Waste Places*—Use 2,4-D plus dicamba in fuel oil. *Indus-trial Areas*—Use soil sterilant rates of atrazine, simazine, bromacil, or tebuthiuron.

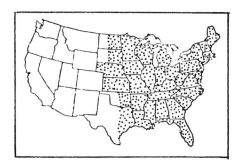

26I
Solanum nigrum L.
Black nightshade
Nightshade family
(Solanaceae)

Description

An annual herb that has pungent foliage when crushed. The stems are erect or spreading, smooth or very sparsely hairy, widely branched, and 30–60 cm tall. The leaves are simple, alternate, 3–7 cm long, and have wavy margins. The inflorescence is composed of axillary clusters of five to ten flowers. The flowers are white with five lobes. The calyx lobes have round tips. The fruit is a smooth, shiny, round berry, which is green while young and turns blue and then black at maturity. It is 5–13 mm in diameter and contains numerous seeds. The seeds are yellow, flat, pitted, and 1–2 mm in diameter. Reproduction is by seeds. Flowers appear from May to October.

Habitat

Black nightshade may occur in gardens, cultivated fields, roadsides, and waste places. It is native of Europe.

Suggested Control

Home Gardens—Because of poisonous berries, care should be taken to eliminate this weed as soon as possible. All plants should be destroyed by cultivation or hand hoeing before flowering. *Cropland*—Use clean cultivation and crop rotation, which includes tolerant crops where acifluorfen, alachlor, atrazine, bromoxynil, chloramben, EPTC, ethalfluralin, glyphosate, oxyfluorfen, paraquat, simazine, or terbacil can be used. *Fence Rows and Waste Areas*—Use brush killer mixtures of 2,4-D plus dicamba in fuel oil. This weed is resistant to 2,4-D applied in water. *Industrial Areas*—Use higher rates of atrazine, simazine, bromacil, or tebuthiuron.

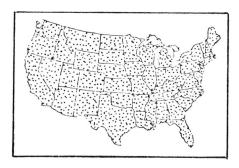

27A
Linaria vulgaris Hill
Yellow toadflax
Figwort family
(Scrophulariaceae)

Description

A perennial herb that has creeping rhizomes. The erect leafy, smooth, sometimes branched stems are frequently in clumps, and up to 1.3 m tall. The linear, smooth, pale green, sessile leaves are generally 2.5 cm long, alternate, and are 2–4 mm wide and about 2.5 cm long. The inflorescence is a dense terminal raceme. The flowers are bright yellow to pale cream with a dull orange center. The petals are 2–3 cm long, including the spur. The fruit is a two-celled, many-seeded capsule, 8–12 mm long. The seeds are disk-shaped, winged, dark brown to black. Reproduction is by seeds and creeping rhizomes. It flowers from May to September.

Habitat

Yellow toadflax may occur in small grain fields, pastures, along railroads and roadsides, and in waste areas. It is native of Eurasia.

Suggested Control

Cropland—Include crops where systematic mechanical cultivation is practiced during most of crop rotation. After cultivation period allow escaped plants to grow until mid-August and spot spray with glyphosate. *Pastures*—Spot spray with glyphosate and reseed desirable species. *Noncrop Areas*–Apply soil sterilant rates of diuron or tebuthiuron.

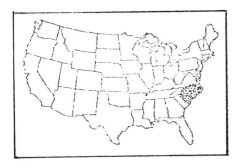

27B
Striga lutea Lour.
Witchweed
Figwort family
(Scrophulariaceae)

Description

An annual herb that parasitizes the roots of 60 species of grass. The bright-green, erect, branched stems are square above the third node and 20–30 cm tall. Soon after germination the seedling penetrates the roots of host plants (grasses). Its linear–lanceolate-shaped leaves are nearly opposite, slightly hairy and bright green. The small, irregular flowers are usually brick-red or scarlet, even yellow or white and borne in the leaf axils. The fruit is a five-sided capsule that terminates in five spurs, containing over a thousand tiny brown seeds. An individual plant can produce half million seeds. Reproduction is by seeds. Flowers appear from June to November.

Habitat

At present witchweed infests cultivated fields in an area on the North Carolina–South Carolina borders. It is a native of India.

Suggested Control

Because of the potential threat that this weed holds for reducing agricultural yields, if this parasitic weed is suspected, immediately contact the U.S. Department of Agriculture's Witchweed Methods Development Laboratory, P.O. Box 279, Whiteville, North Carolina (Phone 919-648-4115) for positive identification and subsequent control measures. An extensive eradication program is in progress. Cooperate fully with state and federal agricultural officials in this eradication program.

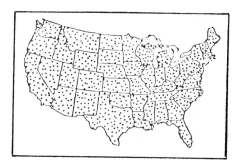

27C
Verbascum blattaria L.
  forma *blattaria* Brug.
Moth mullein
Figwort family
(Scrophulariaceae)

Description

A biennial herb with erect, slender stems that are simple or branched, smooth or with glandular hairs near the top, and 60–100 cm tall. On the lower portion of stem the leaves are in a rosette, are oblanceolate, and taper to the base. The stem leaves are smaller, simple, alternate, narrow-triangular to lanceolate, sessile, coarsely toothed, smooth and sharp-pointed. The yellow flowers are borne in a long loose terminal raceme. The fruit is a round many-seeded capsule and 5–10 mm in diameter. The numerous brown seeds are about 0.8 mm long. Reproduction is by seeds. Flowers occur from June to September.

Habitat

This weed is sometimes found in pastures, meadows, fence rows, and waste areas. It is native of Eurasia.

Suggested Control

Pastures—Remove plant mechanically with a spade before flowering is initiated, or spray with glyphosate or 2,4-D plus surfactant while plants are young. Do not allow seed production. Use improved pasture management to thicken pasture species and reduce space where plant can grow. Reduced cattle numbers, rotational grazing, and mowing after cattle are removed will help pastures species compete with this weed. *Roadsides, Fence Rows, Waste Areas*—Remove mechanically or spray young plants with 2,4-D for selective control, or spray with glyphosate for nonselective control.

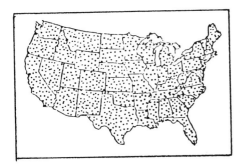

27D
Verbascum blattaria L.
  forma *erubescens* Brug.
Moth mullein
Figwort family
(Scrophulariaceae)

Description

A biennial herb that has white flowers. The erect, slender stems are simple or branched, glandular-hairy at the top, and up to 1 m tall. The smooth leaves are variable, simple, alternate, narrowly triangular to lanceolate and sessile. The basal leaves are larger and taper at the base. The inflorescence is a loose, elongate raceme with a single white flower at each node on a five-lobed 10 mm pedicel. The fruit is a round, many-seeded capsule, 5–10 mm in diameter. The numerous brown seeds are about 0.8 mm long. Reproduction is by seeds. Flowers occur from June to September.

Habitat

This weed is sometimes found in pastures, fence rows, meadows, roadsides, and waste places. It is native of Eurasia.

Suggested Control

Pastures—Remove plant mechanically with a spade before flowering is initiated, or spray with glyphosate or 2,4-D plus surfactant while plants are young. Do not allow seed production. Use improved pasture management to thicken pasture species and reduce space where plant can grow. Reduced cattle numbers, rotational grazing, and mowing after cattle are removed, will help pasture species compete with this weed. *Roadsides, Fence Rows, Waste Areas*—Remove mechanically or spray young plants with 2,4-D for selective control, or spray with glyphosate for nonselective control.

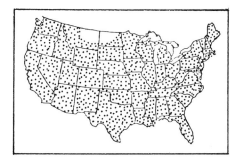

27E
Verbascum thapsus L.
Common mullein
Figwort family
(Scrophulariaceae)

Description

A biennial herb that has dense, softly woolly, gray pubescence throughout. The coarse stem is erect and 1–2 m tall. The petioled lower leaves are simple, alternate, oblong, or oblanceolate and up to 30 cm long whereas the upper leaves are gradually reduced, sessile, and extend downward to the next leaf below. The inflorescence is a spikelike raceme, 20–50 cm long and about 3 cm thick. The petals (corolla) are bright yellow. The fruit is a round, woolly capsule about 6 mm in diameter. The seeds are numerous, brown, 0.8 mm long with wavy ridges alternating with deep grooves. Reproduction is by seeds. Flowers appear from June to September.

Habitat

Common mullein may occur in pastures, fence rows, roadsides, and waste places. It is native of Eurasia.

Suggested Control

Pastures—Remove the plant mechanically with a spade before flowering is initiated, or spray with 2,4-D plus surfactant or glyphosate while plants are young and before the seed stalk has started to elongate. Do not allow seed production. Use improved pasture management to encourage pasture species and increase competition so mullein cannot become established. Fertilization, pH adjustment, reduced stocking rates, rotational grazing, and mowing after cattle are removed will help desirable pasture species to better compete with this weed. *Roadsides, Fence Rows, Waste Areas*—Remove mechanically or spray young plants with 2,4-D plus surfactant or glyphosate.

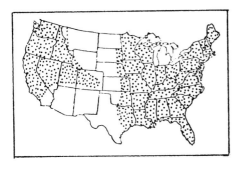

27F
Veronica arvensis L.
Corn speedwell
Figwort family
(Scrophulariaceae)

Description

A winter annual herb that has short, soft hairs throughout. The stems are erect or nearly so, simple or branched, and 10–20 cm tall. The simple, opposite leaves are ovate, 6–12 mm long, rounded at apex, and have two to four blunt teeth on each side. The lower leaves have short petioles while the upper leaves are sessile. The inflorescence is often two-thirds of the plant height and has reduced leaves. The flowers are light blue and are borne on a very short pedicel in the leaf axils. The blunt calyx lobes are oblong-lanceolate in shape. The fruit is a 3–4 mm wide, hairy, deeply-notched capsule. Reproduction is by seeds. Flowering occurs from April to August.

Habitat

Corn speedwell may occur in lawns, gardens, cultivated fields, and pastures. It is a native of Eurasia.

Suggested Control

Home Gardens—A thorough shallow cultivation in late fall or early spring will destroy seedlings and prevent seed formation. *Lawns*— Use improved management practices. Maintain proper pH, follow a good fertilization schedule, overseed thin areas to thicken turf, and use proper mowing height to increase the competiveness of the turf. Control speedwell in bermuda grass turf by applying DSMA before dormancy breaks in the spring. On cool season turf grasses use a mixture of 2,4-D plus dicamba plus mecoprop. *Cropland*—Use a good crop rotation, and till soil in early spring to destroy winter annuals before they produce seed. A shallow cultivation in late fall will kill the seedlings. Chlorsulfuron and terbutryn will give some control in fall-seeded small grains. *Pastures*—Maintain a good stand of desirable pasture species through use of good pasture management plus apply a mixture of 2,4-D plus dicamba in the early spring.

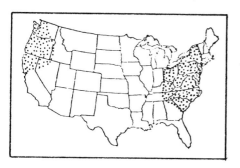

27G
Veronica hederaefolia L.
Ivyleaf speedwell
Figwort family
(Scrophulariaceae)

Description

A winter annual herb with weak, prostrate, or ascending stems that may be well-branched and 20–40 cm long. The leaves are simple, semirotund to nearly kidney-shaped with three to five shallow lobes. They are opposite on the lower stem and alternate on the upper stem. The solitary, small blue flowers are borne on a 8- to 15-mm long pedicel in the leaf axils. The fruit is a smooth, stiff capsule about 6 mm wide and two-thirds as long. Reproduction is by seeds. It flowers from April to August.

Habitat

Ivyleaf speedwell may be found in gardens, lawns, cultivated fields, and pastures. It is a native of Europe.

Suggested Control

For control measures see Corn speedwell (page 268).

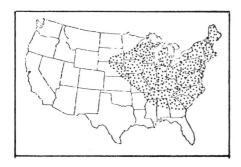

27H
Veronica officinalis L.
Common speedwell
Figwort family
(Scrophulariaceae)

Description

A perennial matted herb with coarse, pubescent, prostrate, or creeping stems that are well-branched and 20–30 cm long. The simple, opposite leaves have a short stalk and are oval or broadly elliptical in shape. They are rather thick, pubescent, with toothed margins. The flowering branches are erect, dense racemes borne in the leaf axils. The bluish flowers have a very short stalk. The fruit is a very hairy, obovate–triangular-shaped capsule and about 4 mm in diameter. The small yellow seeds are flattened and about 1 mm in diameter. Reproduction is by seeds and creeping stems. Flowering occurs from May to July.

Habitat

Common speedwell may be found in gardens, lawns, cultivated fields, pastures, and open woodlands. It is native of Eurasia.

Suggested Control

For control measures see Corn speedwell (page 268).

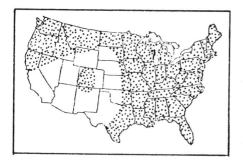

271
Veronica peregrina L.
Purslane speedwell
Figwort family
(Scrophulariaceae)

Description

A winter annual herb that has erect, 10- to 40-cm tall, simple stems or with ascending branches. The simple, opposite leaves are narrowly oblong to oblanceolate in shape, 1.5–3.0 cm long, entire or with a few teeth, and sessile or nearly so. The inflorescence is terminal and has reduced leafy bracts. The flowers are white with pedicels about 1 mm long. The calyx lobes are oblanceolate, rounded at apex and 3–5 mm long. The corolla is approximately the same length as the calyx. The fruit is a flattened, notched capsule about 5 mm wide and 4 mm long. Reproduction is by seeds. It flowers from April to August.

Habitat

Purslane speedwell may occur in gardens, lawns, cultivated fields, pastures, and waste places. It is native of North America.

Suggested Control

For control measures see Corn speedwell (page 268).

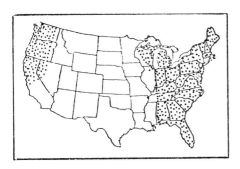

28A
Veronica persica Poir.
Bird's-eye speedwell
Figwort family
(Scrophulariaceae)

Description

An annual herb with hairy, prostrate or ascending, many-branched stems that are 10–30 cm long. The leaves are broadly ovate, 10–20 mm long, rounded at apex, and have three to five coarse teeth on each side. The flowers are solitary on long pedicels (up to 2 cm) arising in the leaf axils. The calyx lobes are pointed, three-veined and up to 8 mm long. The petals (corolla) are blue with deeper blue lines and paler toward the center. The fruit is a broadly notched capsule, 7–10 mm wide, and about two-thirds as long. Reproduction is by seeds. Flowers occur from April to August.

Habitat

Bird's-eye speedwell may occur in gardens, lawns, and cultivated fields. It is native to southwest Asia.

Suggested Control

For control measures see Corn speedwell (page 268).

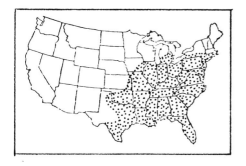

28B
Campsis radicans (L.) Seem.
Trumpetcreeper
Bignonia family
(Bignoniaceae)

Description

A perennial, woody vine with stems up to 10 m long that have aerial rootlets. The leaves are pinnately compound with 9 to 11 leaflets and 2- to 8-cm long petioles. The toothed leaflets are ovate to lanceolate in shape and 4–7 cm long. The showy red-orange flowers are funnel-shaped and 6–8 cm long. The fruit is a 10- to 15-cm long capsule with two longitudinal ridges. The seeds are about 15 mm long and have broad wings. Reproduction is by seeds and roots arising at the stem nodes. It flowers from July to September.

Habitat

Trumpetcreeper may occur as a weed in cultivated fields, pastures, fence rows, and waste grounds. It is native of North America.

Suggested Control

Cultivated Fields—Trumpetcreeper does not persist under a cultivated row-crop culture but may become a problem under minimum or no-tillage farming. Use deep plowing and clean cultivation, followed by spot spraying with 2,4-D or dicamba on label-permissible crops. Repeat applications may be necessary. *Fence Rows or Waste Areas*—Dicamba, 2,4-D, or fosamine can be applied as a spot spray or tebuthiuron can be used as a soil sterilant.

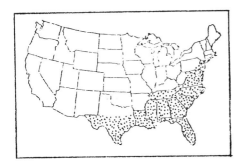

28C
Utricularia inflata Walt.
Floating bladderwort
Bladderwort family
(Lentibulariaceae)

Description

A free-floating aquatic herb that has prolonged, free-floating stems. It has two types of leaves: (1) submersed, alternate, filiform leaves with bladders and (2) floating leaves pinnately divided in filiform segments without bladders but with inflated petioles and in whorls of four to ten. They are attached to the base of the scape. The inflorescence is borne on a scape 4–20 cm tall and has three to 12 yellow flowers that are about 2 cm broad and have a spur 8 mm long. The fruit is a capsule about 3 mm in diameter. Reproduction is by seeds and fragmentation. Flowers appear from May to November.

Habitat

Floating bladderwort may occur in sluggish streams, lakes, ponds, and ditches. It is a native of North America.

Suggested Control

Aquatic—Good to excellent control can be obtained with diquat or endothall.

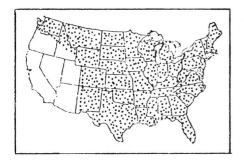

28D
Plantago aristata Michx.
Bracted plantain
Plantain family
(Plantaginaceae)

Description

An annual or short-lived perennial herb that has a long taproot. The erect, simple, hairy, leafless stems are 15–50 cm tall and end in an inflorescence. The basal leaves are 15–40 cm long, entire, linear, dark green, and have soft wavy hairs. The inflorescence is a 2- to 15-cm long spike with dark green, stiffly flexible bracts. The numerous flowers have inconspicuous petals and are borne at the axils of the long bracts. The fruits are ellipsoid, two-seeded capsules that split around the middle. The seeds are oblong, finely netted, light brown and 2 mm long. Reproduction is by seeds. It flowers from June to October.

Habitat

Bracted plantain may occur in lawns, cultivated fields, pastures, and waste places. It is native of North America.

Suggested Control

Lawns—Spray with dicamba, 2,4-D, or MCPA when plants are small and actively growing. *Cultivated Fields*—Use a crop rotation coupled with tillage or one of the following herbicides: atrazine, cyanazine, dicamba, 2,4-D, 2,4-DB, MCPA, mecoprop, metribuzin, simazine, or terbacil. *Waste Places*—Same as for lawns or burn down with glyphosate or paraquat. For complete vegetation control use soil sterilant rates of atrazine, bromacil, simazine, or tebuthiuron.

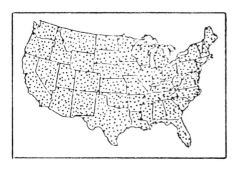

28E
Plantago lanceolata L.
Buckhorn plantain
Plantain family
(Plantaginaceae)

Description

A perennial or rarely an annual herb that has a strong persistent base and tough slender rootlets. The erect, leafless stems are 10–30 cm tall and end in an inflorescence. The hairy basal leaves are ascending to spreading, lanceolate, 6–40 mm wide, 10–30 cm long, and have three to five strong, parallel veins. The inflorescence is a 2- to 10-cm long, densely flowered spike with thin papery bracts. The oblong-ovoid, two-seeded fruits split around the middle. The seeds are shiny brown or black and 2–3 mm long. Reproduction is by seeds. Flowers are present from May to October.

Habitat

Buckhorn plantain may occur in lawns, pastures, and waste grounds. It is native of Europe.

Suggested Control

For control measures see Bracted plantain (page 275).

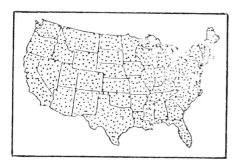

28F
Plantago major L.
Broadleaf plantain
Plantain family
(Plantaginaceae)

Description

A short-lived perennial or annual herb that has fibrous roots. The erect or spreading, leafless stems are 15–30 cm tall and end in an inflorescence. The smooth basal leaves are simple, ovate, 5–20 cm long and have wavy margins and prominent parallel veins. The petioles are broad, usually green and pubescent at the base. The inflorescence is a slender, dense, obtuse spike that is 5–50 cm long and has numerous flowers and small glabrous bracts. The fruit is an ellipsoid capsule that is 2–4 mm long and splits across the upper half. Seeds are net-veined, light to dark brown, and about 1.6 mm long. Reproduction is by seeds. It flowers from July to October.

Habitat

Broadleaf plantain occurs in lawns, cultivated fields, and along roadsides and shores. It is a native of North America.

Suggested Control

For control measures see Bracted plantain (page 275).

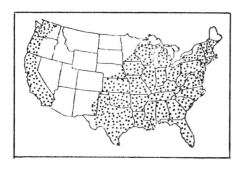

28G
Plantago virginica L.
Paleseed plantain
Plantain family
(Plantaginaceae)

Description

A hairy annual or biennial herb that has a slender taproot. The simple, basal leaves are narrowly obovate, up to 15 cm long, and have soft, long, wavy hairs. The leaf margins are inconspicuously toothed. The inflorescence is a 4- to 15-cm long cylindric spike with numerous flowers and is borne at the end of a long stalk. The flowers are small and subtended by lanceolate bracts. The fruit is an ovoid-oblong, two-seeded capsule. The seeds are less than 2 mm long, finely netted, and dull brown to nearly black. Reproduction is by seeds. Flowering is from April to June.

Habitat

Paleseed plantain may be found in gardens, lawns, cultivated fields, and waste places. It is native of the old world.

Suggested Control

For control measures see Bracted plantain (page 275).

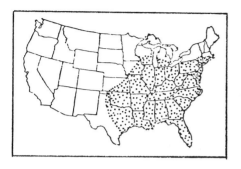

28H
Diodia teres Walt.
Poorjoe
Madder family (Rubiaceae)

Description

A summer annual herb with hairy, erect or spreading, branched, four-angled or nearly circular stems that are 10–70 cm tall. The simple, entire, hairy leaves are narrow and taper to a long point. Two opposite leaves are joined at each node forming a pair, subtended by long bristles or stipules. The small, white, pink or lilac flowers are usually one to three in the leaf axils. The corolla is funnel-shaped with four short lobes. The hairy, nonfurrowed fruits are 3–5 mm long and split into two or three nutlets at maturity. The calyx is persistent with four short, ciliate teeth. Reproduction is by seeds. It flowers from June to October.

Habitat

Poorjoe may be found in cultivated soils, pastures, roadsides, and waste places. It is a native of North America.

Suggested Control

Cropland—Use a good crop rotation system. Use clean cultivation in summer row crops, or select a crop for which a herbicide can be used. Herbicides that control poorjoe are atrazine, cyanazine, isopropalin, pendimethalin, simazine, and trifluralin. *Pastures*—Increase the level of management by proper fertilization and pH adjustment. Maintain a strong, competitive stand of grass and legumes. Do not overgraze. *Roadsides and Waste Places*—Use periodic mowing, spray with dicamba, or sterilize the soil with bromacil or tebuthiuron.

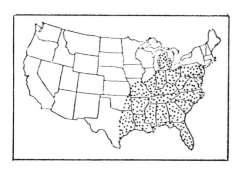

28I
Diodia virginiana L.
Virginia buttonweed
Madder family (Rubiaceae)

Description

An annual herb with weak, ascending or prostrate, diffusely branching stems that are 20–70 cm long and have soft, wavy hairs. The simple, opposite leaves are lanceolate or narrowly elliptic, thin, sessile, and smooth or sparsely hairy. They are 3–8 cm long and gradual narrow at the base. Two leaves are joined at each node forming a pair and are subtended by long bristles or stipules. The white flowers are about 1 cm long and are borne in leaf axils. The corolla is a very slender four-parted tube. The fruit is 7–10 mm long, strongly furrowed, and splits into two or three nutlets at maturity. The calyx is persistent with two teeth. Reproduction is by seeds. Flowers appear from June to August.

Habitat

Virginia buttonweed may be found in wet soils in pastures or meadows. It is a native of North America.

Suggested Control

Pastures—Improve drainage and use good pasture management techniques to maintain strong vigorous pasture species that will aggressively compete and control the weeds. Adequate fertility, proper pH adjustment, and rotational grazing are necessary.

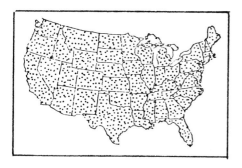

29A
Galium aparine L.
Catchweed bedstraw
Madder family (Rubiaceae)

Description

An annual herb with weak, prostrate, or reclining stems that are 30–100 cm long and covered with hooked, stiff hairs. The simple, 3- to 8-cm long, linear-oblanceolate leaves are in whorls of eight and have hooked hairs on the margins and midveins. The small, white flowers are borne in small clusters on an axillary peduncle. The fruit is two nearly spherical carpels, covered with stiff-hooked bristles. The seed is ball-shaped with a deep pit in one side and short sharp spines on the other side. Reproduction is by seeds. Flowers occur during May and June.

Habitat

Catchweed bedstraw occurs in lawns, small grains, roadsides, and waste places. It is native of Eurasia.

Suggested Control

Lawns—Maintain a strong, vigorous competitive turf through proper fertilization, pH adjustment, watering, drainage, and mowing. If a herbicide is needed use a mixture of 2,4-D, mecoprop, and dicamba. *Small Grains*—Fertilize sufficiently to encourage a vigorous stand of small grain and apply chlorsulfuron or terbutryn if necessary. *Pastures*—If severely infested, the pasture should be rotated to a clean cultivated crop for a year or two and then reseeded to pasture, taking precautions to obtain a good stand. The pasture should be well-managed (proper fertilization, pH adjustment, rotational grazing, etc.). Bedstraw can be controlled with a high rate of dicamba but this should only be used in severely infested areas. *Roadsides and Waste Places*—Mow periodically before seed is set and encourage desirable species.

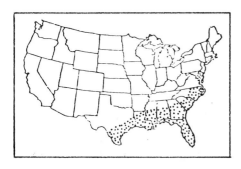

29B
Richardia scabra L.
Florida pusley
Madder family (Rubiaceae)

Description

A summer annual herb with weak, many-branched, prostrate or ascending, diffusely spreading stems that are densely hairy and 15–50 cm long. The simple ovate, elliptic or lanceolate, pointed leaves are opposite, entire, hairy, thick, 2–8 cm long, and the base is narrowed into a short petiole. The numerous white flowers are clustered in a headlike inflorescence at the ends of branches. The corolla is funnel-shaped, six-parted, and 4–6 mm long. The sepals are 1–2 mm long, lanceolate, and have stiff hairs. The fruits break into three or four angled seeds. Reproduction is by seeds. Flowering occurs from May to October.

Habitat

Florida pusley may be found in lawns, cultivated soils, pastures, fence rows, and waste places. It is native to tropical America.

Suggested Control

Lawns—Use good turf management practices and spray 2,4-D if necessary. *Cropland*—Use a crop herbicide rotation coupled with cultivation if needed. Possible herbicides, which can be used if labeled for the specific crop are acifluorfen, ametryn, atrazine, benefin, cyanazine, DCPA, 2,4-D, diphenamid, EPTC, fluchloralin, fluometuron, linuron, metolachlor, metribuzin, norflurazon, oryzalin, pebulate, prometryn, propachlor, simazine, trifluralin, vernolate, and terbacil. *Noncropland*—Use paraquat for no residual control or a soil sterilant rate of atrazine or simazine for residual control.

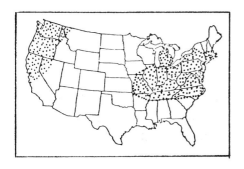

29C
Sherardia arvensis L.
Field madder
Madder family (Rubiaceae)

Description

A diffusely branched, annual herb with square, weakly trailing to erect stems that have rough pubescence and are up to 40 cm tall. The simple hairy sharp-pointed leaves are in whorls of six. They are linear to narrowly elliptic and about 1 cm long. The inflorescence is a terminal head subtended by a whorl of lanceolate bracts fused at the base. The flowers are blue or pink. The corolla is funnel-shaped with a slender tube and about 3 mm long. The fruit is 2 mm long, pubescent, and splits in two. Reproduction is by seeds. Flowering occurs from May to July.

Habitat

Field madder may occur in lawns, gardens, cultivated fields, roadsides and waste areas. It is native to Europe.

Suggested Control

Lawns—Maintain a thick, vigorous turf by periodic fertilization, proper pH adjustment, etc. Do not allow bare or thin areas. A mixture of herbicides containing 2,4-D, mecoprop, and dicamba may be used. Repeated applications may be necessary. *Gardens*—Control in seedling stage through cultivation. Do not allow seed production. Various mulches will prevent seedling establishment. *Cultivated Fields*—Use good crop rotation and clean cultivation. *Roadsides and Waste Places*—Mow periodically, do not allow seed production. Apply a soil sterilant such as bromacil or tebuthiuron.

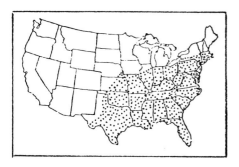

29D
Lonicera japonica Thunb.
Japanese honeysuckle
Honeysuckle family
(Caprifoliaceae)

Description

A woody, trailing perennial vine with tough, wiry stems that root at the nodes. The short-petioled, thick leaves are ovate or oblong and about 4–8 cm long. The very fragrant, white flowers turn yellow with age. They are short-stalked and subtended by leaflike bracts. The tube-shaped corolla is lobed and 3–4 cm long. The stamens and style protrude from the tube. The fruit is a black berry about 5 mm in diameter. Some reproduction is by seeds but most is by vegetative means. Flowers occur from May to August.

Habitat

Japanese honeysuckle can be found climbing on garden shrubbery, fences, and in pastures and waste places. It is a native of eastern Asia.

Suggested Control

Garden shrubbery—Remove all vegetative portions of honeysuckle, including rootstocks; paint any remaining stumps with 2,4-D amine (diluted in a 1:5 ratio with water) being careful not to apply any portion of desirable plants. Repeat as necessary to control new sprouts. *Pastures*—Use good pasture management techniques (rotational grazing, mowing, adequate fertilization, and pH adjustment) followed by spring application of 2,4-D, repeated annually. *Fence Rows and Waste Places*—Use amitrol, 2,4-D, or glyphosate. For soil sterilization use tebuthiuron.

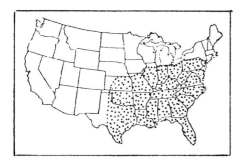

29E
Valerianella radiata (L.)
   Dufr.
Cornsalad
Valerian family
(Valerianaceae)

Description

A winter annual herb with erect, branched, angled stems that are sparingly pubescent and 10–60 cm tall. The simple leaves are smooth or slightly hairy and have entire margins, though they may be toothed at the base. The inflorescence is a cluster of flowers at the end of branches. The fruit is ellipsoid and about 2.5 mm long. Reproduction is by seeds. Flowers appear during April and May.

Habitat

Cornsalad may be found in cultivated fields, meadows, hay fields and waste areas.

Suggested Control

Cultivated Fields—Practice clean cultivation. This weed is not listed on herbicide labels but will probably be controlled by a herbicide normally used for control of broadleaf weeds such as atrazine, cyanazine, 2,4-D, dicamba, diuron, fluometuron, linuron, metribuzin, or simazine. *Meadows and Hay Fields*—Mow before seed is set. *Noncrop Areas*—Use paraquat for burn down, or atrazine, bromacil, simazine, or tebuthiuron for residual control.

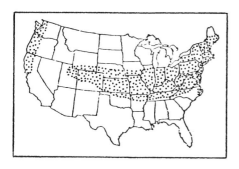

29F
Dipsacus sylvestris Huds.
Teasel
Teasel family (Dipsacaceae)

Description

A biennial prickly herb that overwinters as a rosette. The coarse, second-year stems are erect, 0.5–2 m tall, many-branched, angled and have many short prickles. The first year rosette leaves are often united at their bases (clasping the stem), and are prickly on the midveins and margins. The stem leaves in the second year are simple, entire, sessile, and alternate. The lower leaves have scalloped margins and are 30–60 cm long. The lilac or pink flowers are in 4- to 10-cm long cylindrical heads, and subtended by spiny, awned bracts. The gray-brown seeds are ribbed, hairy and 4–5 mm long. Reproduction is by seeds. Flowering occurs from July to September.

Habitat

Teasel may be found in pastures, roadsides, fence rows, and waste places. It is a native of Europe.

Suggested Control

Pastures—Use improved management practices of proper fertilization and pH adjustment, rotational grazing, and mowing after grazing to prevent seed production. The rosettes can be destroyed in the fall or early spring with a hand spade or by plowing. Rosettes probably be controlled by a mixture of 2,4-D plus dicamba. *Fence Rows and Industrial Sites*—This weed can be burned down with paraquat and can probably be controlled with bromacil or tebuthiuron.

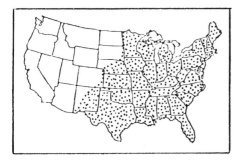

29G
Sicyos angulatus L.
Burcucumber
Gourd family
(Cucurbitaceae)

Description

Annual climbing herb with hairy stems that are up to 3 m long and climb by three-forked tendrils. The leaves are rounded and five-angled or lobed. The lobes are toothed and pointed. The flowers are pale yellow and unisexual. Peduncles of the female flowers are 5–8 cm long while those of the male clusters are slightly longer. Both may arise from a common axil. The dry, ovoid, strongly pubescent spiny fruits occur in clusters. Each fruit is up to 15 mm long and contains one seed. Reproduction is by seeds. Flowers appear from July to October. New seedlings germinate throughout the season following every rain.

Habitat

Burcucumber may be found in gardens, cultivated fields, fence rows, and waste places. It is a native of North America.

Suggested Control

Home Gardens—Hand hoe and destroy all plants before flowering to prevent seed production. Mulches may be used to prevent seedling establishment. *Cropland*—This weed is not susceptible to 2,4-D. Use crop rotation and late planting. Use tillage to destroy as many seedlings as possible before planting. Cultivate during the season to control new seedlings as they germinate after each rain. Atrazine applied at a high rate (2× normal use rate) will give good control in corn. Dicamba will control the weed for a short period of time, i.e., until a new stand germinates. In other crops, till soil several times in spring before planting and plant late allowing for burcucumber to germinate and be destroyed before planting the crop, followed by cultivation and spot hoeing as necessary. *Fence Rows and Waste Areas*—Use glyphosate or paraquat for burn-down. Soil sterilization rates of atrazine will give season long control. Other soil sterilants such as chlorsulfuron and tebuthiuron will probably control this weed.

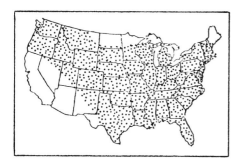

29H
Specularia perfoliata (L.) A.
  DC.
Venus lookingglass
Bluebell family
(Campanulaceae)

Description

An annual herb with erect, pubescent stems that are retrorsely bris-tled on the angles, and 20–80 cm tall. The numerous, round to ovate leaves clasp the stem at the base, are usually toothed, often have stiff hairs, and are 1–3 cm long. The blue flowers are of two kinds: (1) the lowermost are closed, self-pollinated, inconspicuous, whereas (2) the uppermost are open, cross-pollinated, larger, up to 15 mm wide and 1 cm long, with anthers 3–3.5 mm long. The fruit is an obovate to elliptic, 5- to 8-mm long capsule that opens by pores near the middle. The seeds are small, numerous, and often shiny. Reproduc-tion is by seeds. Flowers appear from May to August.

Habitat

Venus lookingglass may occur in gardens, hay fields, pastures, and waste grounds. It is a native of Europe.

Suggested Control

Home Gardens—Scattered plants should be removed mechanically by cultivation and hand hoeing. Various mulches are effective in preventing seedling establishment. *Home Lawns and Turf*—Venus lookingglass is a noncompetitive weed and generally can be con-trolled by good turf management practices, such as proper pH and fertility adjustment, proper mowing height, etc. This weed can also be controlled by applying a mixture of 2,4-D, mecoprop, and dicam-ba in the spring. *Hay Fields and Waste Areas*—Same as turf.

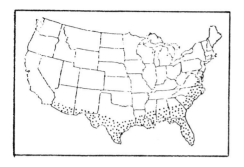

291
Acanthospermum hispidum
   DC.
Bristly starbur
Sunflower family
(Compositae)

Description

A summer annual herb with an erect, coarse, many-branched, spreading yellow-green stem that is covered with long hairs and is 30–100 mm tall. The simple, petioled leaves are opposite and ovate to broadly rhombic-ovate. The leaves have shallowly toothed margins and are very hairy, light green and up to 10 cm long. The yellow flower heads are borne in the leaf axils and form obovate-wedged burs bearing many spines with two long, coarse spines at the top. Reproduction is by seeds. Flowers appear from May to October.

Habitat

Bristly starbur may be found in gardens, cultivated fields, roadsides, and waste places. It is native of tropical America.

Suggested Control

Home Gardens—This weed should be controlled by mechanical cultivation and hand hoeing. Do not allow the weed to produce seed. *Cropland*—Use a crop and herbicide rotation coupled with cultivation as needed. Atrazine, bentazon, dichlobenil, cyanazine, fluometuron, metribuzin, and terbacil will control this weed. Use these herbicides with tolerant crops as recommended on the herbicide label. *Noncropland*—Use a soil sterilant rate of atrazine, bromacil, or terbacil.

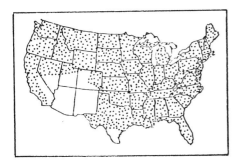

30A
Achillea millefolium L
Common yarrow
Sunflower family
(Compositae)

Description

An aromatic rhizomatous perennial herb with stems that are sparsely to densely covered with long, soft, or woolly hairs and are 20–100 cm tall. The leaves are finely pinnately dissected like a delicate fern. The blade is 3–15 cm long. The leaves in the basal rosette have petioles, however, all but the lowermost stem leaves are without petioles. The numerous flowers are in short, flat, or round-topped inflorescences with subtending bracts. The inflorescence is composed of 10 to 30 central disk flowers about five white or pink ray flowers that are 2–3 mm long. Reproduction is by seeds and rootstocks. Flowers occur from June to September.

Habitat

Common yarrow may be found in lawns, pastures, fence rows, and waste places. Generally it is not found in cultivated fields. It is native to Eurasia.

Suggested Control

Home Gardens—Use clean cultivation and remove all rootstocks. *Turf*—Mechanically remove and reseed. Spray with dicamba or spot spray with glyphosate and reseed. *Industrial*—Use soil sterilant such as atrazine, simazine, or bromacil.

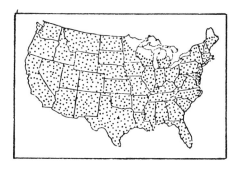

30B
Ambrosia artemisiifolia L.
Common ragweed
Sunflower family
(Compositae)

Description

A summer annual herb with smooth hairy stems that are 20–150 cm tall. The lower leaves on the stem are opposite, whereas the upper leaves are alternate. The leaves have petioles, are once or twice pinnatifed, and are 5–10 cm long. The flower heads are of two kinds: the male flower heads hang down in small clusters at the tips of branches; the female flower heads are fewer and are upright in the axils of leaves. The fruiting bracts are fused into a short-beaked unit that is 3–5 mm long and has several short, sharp spines. Ragweed pollen is a primary cause of hayfever. Reproduction is by seeds. It flowers from July to October.

Habitat

Common ragweed occurs in home gardens, cultivated fields, pastures, hay fields, fence rows, and waste places. It is native of North America.

Suggested Control

Home Gardens—Hoe or pull before bud stage to prevent pollen dissemination and seed production; use herbicides such as 2,4-D, paraquat, or atrazine after careful study of their use and alternatives. *Cropland*—Use mechanical control methods and clean cultivation. This weed is listed on the following herbicide labels: acifluorfen, ametryn, atrazine, chloramben, cyanazine, dinoseb, diuron, EPTC, fluometuron, glyphosate, methazole, metribuzin, monuron, oxyfluorfen, norflurazon, perfluidone, prometryn, propachlor, propazine, pyrazon, simazine, terbacil, MCPA, and 2,4-D. *Waste Areas and Industrial*—Apply 2,4-D or MCPA for selective control in grass or paraquat or glyphosate to desiccate all existing vegetation or atrazine, bromacil, diuron, prometon, simazine, or tebuthiuron for residual nonselective control.

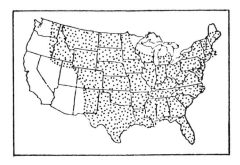

30C
Ambrosia trifida L.
Giant ragweed
Sunflower family
(Compositae)

Description

A summer annual herb that has a rough, sometimes hairy, coarse stem up to 4 m high. The leaves are opposite, petioled, entire to palmately cleft into three to five lobes, and more or less rough on both sides. The flower heads are of two kinds: the male flower heads are in spikelike clusters at the tips of branches; the female flower heads are fewer and in the axils of the upper leaves. The fruiting bracts are fused into a short-beaked unit that is 5–10 mm long, ribbed, and bearing several short, blunt spines. Its pollen causes hayfever. Reproduction is by seeds. Flowers occur from July to October.

Habitat

Giant ragweed occurs in gardens, cultivated fields, pastures, fence rows, roadsides, and waste places. It is a native of Europe.

Suggested Control

Home Gardens—Hoe or pull before bud stage to prevent pollen dissemination, use herbicides such as 2,4-D, glyphosate, and paraquat only after careful study of their use and alternatives. *Cropland*—Use mechanical control methods and clean cultivation; or apply acifluorfen, bentazon, 2,4-D, glyphosate and paraquat in accordance with label. Also most of the herbicides listed for common ragweed (page 291) may give control. *Waste Areas and Industrial*—Apply 2,4-D or MCPA for selective control in grass; paraquat to desiccate all existing vegetation; or atrazine, bromacil, diuron, prometon, simazine, or tebuthiuron for residual nonselective control.

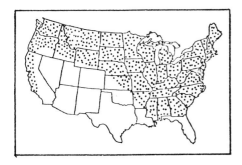

30D
Anthemis arvensis L.
Corn chamomile
Sunflower family
(Compositae)

Description

An annual plant that is 10–50 cm tall and often has several basal stems. The leaves are 2–5 cm long, twice pinnately compound, with narrowly winged axis. Several to numerous, stalked flowerheads are at the end of the branches. Bracts are sparsely silky or woolly. The top of the flower stalk (receptacle) is 6–12 mm wide and becomes egg-shaped with age. It is covered with thin, dry, awn-tipped scales (chaff) that are equal to or shorter than the central disk flowers. The ray flowers are white, about 15 to 20 in number and 6–13 mm long. The seeds are quadrangular and about ten-nerved. Reproduction is by seeds. Flowers appear from May to August.

Habitat

Corn chamomile may occur in gardens, cultivated fields, barnyards, pastures, and idle fields. It is a native of Europe.

Suggested Control

Home Gardens—Hoe or pull existing plants and use various mulches before seed germination. *Cropland*—Use mechanical control and clean cultivation. This weed does not appear on any of the specific herbicide labels but will probably be controlled by some of the preemergence herbicides commonly used to control broadleaf weeds in crops. The following herbicides may be useful if applied properly to labeled tolerant crops: atrazine, diuron, fluometuron, metribuzin, and simazine. Corn chamomile is resistant to 2,4-D. *Waste Areas and Industrial*—Desiccate with paraquat or use bromacil or tebuthiuron for residual control.

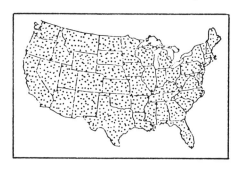

30E
Anthemis cotula L.
Mayweed
Sunflower family
(Compositae)

Description

An annual, branched, nearly glabrous, ill-smelling plant that is 10–60 cm tall. The leaves are 2–6 cm long, two or three times pinnately compound, and have very narrow segments, like a lacy fern. The flower heads are numerous and on short stalks borne at end of the branches. The bracts have a few wavy hairs. The enlarged top of flower stalk is 5–10 mm wide and becomes egg-shaped at maturity and has thin, dry, narrowed, scarcely-awned scales (chaff) near the middle. There are 10 to 20 white 5- to 10-mm long ray flowers. The seeds are nearly round and about ten ribbed with tiny glandular protrusions. Reproduction is by seeds. Flowers occur from June to October.

Habitat

Mayweed may occur in gardens, barnyards, pastures, and idle fields. It is a native of Europe.

Suggested Control

Home Gardens—Hoe or pull plants before early flowering stage. This controls established plants and prevents seed production. Use various mulches to prevent seedling establishment. *Cropland*— Generally not a problem weed in cultivated areas; use cultivation and spot hoeing or include corn in the crop rotation and use atrazine or cyanazine for weed control. *Pastures and Fence Rows*—Use a mixture of 2,4-D plus dicamba to control this weed.

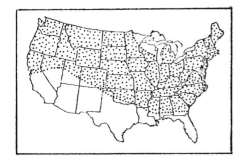

30F
Arctium minus (Hill) Bernh.
Common burdock
Sunflower family
(Compositae)

Description

A biennial plant that can be 1.5 m tall. The stems are erect, branched, ridged, and have small rough hairs. The leaves have a petiole; the lower petioles are mostly hollow. The basal leaves are broadly ovate, about 35 cm wide and up to 50 cm long. They are eventually smooth on the bottom and nearly so on top. The inflorescence is branched and widely spread. The flowerheads are short-stalked, 2.5–3 cm thick, and form a spherical bur of bracts with hooked tips. The flowers are pinkish. Seeds are 5 mm long, three to five angled, smooth and crowned with a row of bristles. Reproduction is by seeds. It flowers from July to October.

Habitat

Common burdock may occur in orchards, around barnyards, in fence rows, pastures, and waste places. It is a native of Eurasia.

Suggested Control

Home Gardens, Orchards, Barnyards, Fence Rows—Cut plant off well below soil surface with sharp spade or spray with a higher rate of 2,4-D plus surfactant when plants are small; repeat if necessary. *Industrial*—Use high rate of atrazine or apply bromacil.

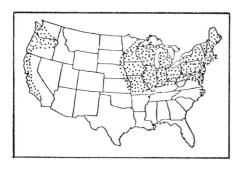

30G
Artemisia vulgaris L.
Mugwort
Sunflower family
(Compositae)

Description

An aromatic perennial herb that has long, stout, horizontal rhizomes. The erect stem is 50–100 cm tall, slightly branched, and smooth or nearly so below the inflorescence. The leaves are dark-green and smooth on the top but covered with dense, white, woolly pubescence underneath. The inflorescence is large and leafy. The bracts are woolly. There are numerous flowerheads. The seeds are ellipsoid, not nerved or angled, and without a crown of bristles. Reproduction is by seeds and rootstocks. Flowers appear from July to October.

Habitat

Mugwort may be found in gardens, cultivated fields, pastures, fence rows, and waste areas. It is a native of the old world.

Suggested Control

Home Gardens and Cultivated Fields—This weed will not survive under continuous tillage and cultivation. In gardens, dig out with a sharp shovel and destroy before flowering. Repeat until all plants have been eliminated. In cultivated fields, deep plow in fall or spring and plant a cultivated row crop. Apply herbicides normally used for broadleaf weed control, followed by cultivation if necessary. Destroy any remaining plants by selective hand hoeing. *Pastures*—Mechanically remove scattered plants or mow closely three times per season and improve pasture management. *Fence Rows and Waste Areas*—Apply amitrole, dichlobenil, or bromacil.

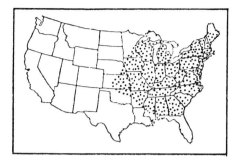

30H
Aster pilosus Willd.
White heath aster
Sunflower family
(Compositae)

Description

A perennial herb that develops from vigorous crown. The erect, irregularly branched stems are tough, smooth to stiffly hairy, and 0.2–1.5 m tall. The numerous simple leaves at the base of the plant are narrowly lance-shaped, while those on the upper stem are smaller and sharp-pointed. The numerous flowerheads are 5–10 mm in diameter and mainly on the upper side of the branches. The light, brown seeds have a tuft of silky hairs attached to the top. Reproduction is mainly by wind-borne seeds. It flowers from August to October.

Habitat

White heath aster may occur in cropland under minimum or no-tillage cropping systems, pastures, roadsides, meadows, and waste areas. It is native to North America.

Suggested Control

It is seldom a problem. If so, rotate crops to a cultivated row crop and use herbicides commonly used for control of broadleaf plants followed by cultivation if necessary. *Pastures and Meadows*—Initiate a good pasture management program with pH adjustment, adequate fertilization, rotational grazing followed by mowing. A spring application of 2,4-D plus dicamba may be helpful. *Noncropland Areas*—For selective control in grass-covered areas, use repeated spring treatments of 2,4-D plus dicamba or for nonselective control use bromacil or tebuthiuron.

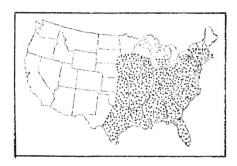

301
Bidens bipinnata L.
Spanishneedles
Sunflower family
(Compositae)

Description

A summer annual herb with glabrous to minutely hairy, erect, square stems that are up to 1.5 m tall and have numerous side branches. The leaves are opposite, mostly twice or thrice pinnately compound, and 5–20 cm long. The petioles are 2–5 cm long. Flower heads have a few orange rays and are borne singly at the ends of long branches. The seven to ten outermost bracts are linear but not leafy and shorter than the innermost ones. The seeds are linear, four-sided, black, often sparsely hairy, 10–18 mm long; some of the outermost are shorter. All have three or four yellowish, barbed awns. Reproduction is by seeds. Flowers appear from August to October.

Habitat

Spanishneedles may occur in gardens, cultivated fields, pastures, fence rows, and roadsides. They are native of North America.

Suggested Control

Home Garden—This weed can be controlled by hand hoeing and cultivation. Border areas should be trimmed and mowed. Various mulches will prevent seedling establishment. Do not allow seed production. *Cropland*—Use a good crop rotation; cultivate and/or use herbicides commonly used to control broadleaf weeds for each specific crop such as atrazine, ametryn, bentazon, cyanazine, dichobenil, diuron, fluometuron, linuron, methazole, metribuzin, simazine, 2,4-D, MCPA. *Fence Rows, Pastures, etc.*—Mow to prevent seed production, spray in juvenile stages with 2,4-D if selective control in grasses is desired. If total vegetation control is desired, use soil sterilization rates of atrazine, bromacil, simazine, sulfometuron, or tebuthiuron.

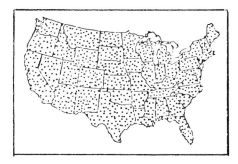

31A
Bidens frondosa L.
Devils beggarticks
Sunflower family
(Compositae)

Description

An annual herb with erect, smooth or nearly smooth stems that branch near the top, and is 0.3–1.2 m tall. The leaves are opposite, borne on petioles about 5 cm long, pinnately compound, and have three to five lance-shaped, long-pointed, toothed leaflets, which may be up to 10 cm long. The flower heads are bell-shaped, with or without a few orange or yellow-orange rays. The outermost bracts, typically eight in number, are more leafy than the innermost bracts, and are longer than the central disk. The seeds are flat, black, wedge-shaped, strongly one-nerved on each face and have marginal hairs and two barbed awns. Reproduction is by seeds. They flower from August to October.

Habitat

Devils beggarticks may be found in gardens, cultivated fields, pastures, and fence rows; often in damper habitats than the preceding species. They are native of North America.

Suggested Control

Follow same control measures as for Spanishneedles (page 298).

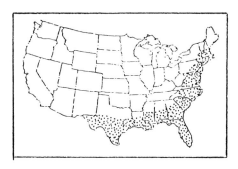

31B
Bidens pilosa L. var. *radiata*
   Sch. Bip.
Hairy beggarticks
Sunflower family
(Compositae)

Description

An annual or summer annual herb with smooth, erect, square stems, which are branched in the upper portion and 40–90 cm tall. The simple leaves are ovate or three- to five-parted, stalked, slightly hairy, and attached in pairs at the stem joints. The flower heads have a yellow center and white to pale-yellow or purplish ray petals that are up to 1.5 cm long. The seeds are linear-tetragonal, pointed, dark brown or black, 5–9 mm long and topped by three or four barbed spines. Reproduction is by seeds. They flower from May to September.

Habitat

Hairy beggarticks may occur in cultivated fields, fence rows, and waste grounds. They are native of tropical America.

Suggested Control

Follow control measures used for Spanishneedles (page 298).

31C
Bidens polylepis Blake
Coreopsis beggarticks
Sunflower family
(Compositae)

Description

An annual or biennial herb with erect, many-branched, smooth to slightly hairy stems that are 30–120 cm tall. The leaves are pinnately or bipinnately compound. The segments are lanceolate, long-pointed, petioled, slightly hairy underneath, and about 10 cm long including the 1- to 3-cm petiole. The flower heads have well-developed yellow ray flowers and two types of bracts. The 12 to 20 outermost bracts have conspicuous, marginal hairs and short stiff hairs on the back. They are 10–25 mm long, often exceeding the length of the innermost bracts. The seeds are flat, often narrowly winged, yellowish black to black and have short marginal hairs with none to two small barbed awns. Reproduction is by seeds. Flowers appear from August to October.

Habitat

Coreopsis beggarticks occur in cultivated fields, pastures, and non-crop areas; usually in damp or seasonally wet habitats. They are native of North America.

Suggested Control

Follow same control measures as used for Spanishneedles (page 298).

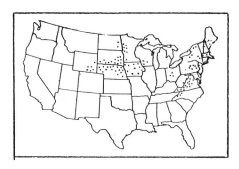

31D
Carduus acanthoides L.
Plumeless thistle
Sunflower family
(Compositae)

Description

A spring biennial herb with erect, tough, branched, very spiny stems that are 30–100 cm tall. The alternate, 15- to 20-cm long leaves are deeply lobed and have long loose hairs on the lower surface, mainly along the midrib and major veins. The flower heads are 1.5–2.5 cm in diameter, erect, single or clustered at the tips of the spiny, winged branches. The bracts are narrow and erect. The middle and outermost are spine-tipped, whereas the innermost are softer and rarely spiny. The seeds have a ring of delicate hairs on the tip. Reproduction is by seeds. Flowering occurs from July to October.

Habitat

Plumeless thistle occurs in pastures and noncropped areas. It is native of Europe.

Suggested Control

Pastures, Roadsides, Waste Areas—A sharp shovel can be used to cut scattered plants well below the crown, or 2,4-D can be sprayed while the plant is still in the rosette stage. Plants become resistant as flower stalk is produced. If plants become too large before 2,4-D is applied, mow to prevent seed production and spray with 2,4-D to inhibit regrowth.

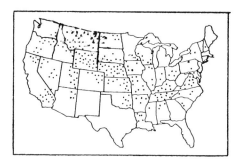

31E
Carduus nutans L.
Musk thistle
Sunflower family
(Compositae)

Description

A large, coarse, biennial herb that is 50–180 cm tall. The erect, spiny stem is winged, and the lower portion is branched. The alternate, very spiny leaves are without pubescence but may have long, loose hairs along the midrib. They are up to 10 cm wide and 25 cm long and are coarse toothed with bases extending down the stem. The purple or lavender flower heads are solitary and nod on the end of the branches. The bracts are spiny-tipped, conspicuously broad and surround the head. The glossy yellow-brown seeds have a ring of delicate hairs at the top. Reproduction is by seeds. Flowers are present from June to October.

Habitat

Musk thistle occurs in pastures and noncropped areas. It is a native of Europe and western Asia.

Suggested Control

Pastures and Noncropped Areas—Scattered plants can be cut off well below the crown with a sharp shovel. Spray with 2,4-D while still in rosette stage; plants become resistant to 2,4-D as the flower stalk is produced. If plants become too large before 2,4-D is applied, mow to prevent seed production and spray with 2,4-D to inhibit growth.

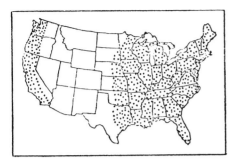

31F
Centaurea cyanus L.
Cornflower
Sunflower family
(Compositae)

Description

An annual or winter annual plant that is 0.2–1.2 m tall. The erect or ascending stems have white woolly hairs when young, which often persist on the lower surface of the leaves. The leaves are linear and entire though the lower ones are toothed or even lobed. They are up to 8 mm wide and 13 cm long. The branches terminate in a flower head. The ray flowers are mostly blue but sometimes purple or white. The bracts are 11–16 mm long, striate, and have a relatively narrow, darkened, lacerated fringe near the tip. The seeds are narrow, 2–3 mm long and have numerous bristles. Reproduction is by seeds. Flowers occur from May to October.

Habitat

Cornflower may occur in cultivated fields, hay fields, roadsides, and waste places. It has escaped from cultivation and is native of the Mediterranean region.

Suggested Control

Cropland—Use good crop rotation; do not follow small grain by small grain. In small grain apply 2,4-D plus dicamba before crop enters the jointing stage. In row crops, use herbicides normally used for broadleaf weeds and cultivate if necessary to control escapes. *Roadsides and Waste Places*—Spray with 2,4-D plus dicamba while in juvenile stages of growth.

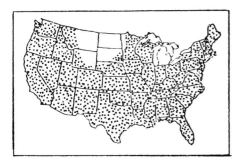

31G
Chrysanthemum
  leucanthemum L.
Oxeye daisy
Sunflower family
(Compositae)

Description

A perennial herb with rhizomes and smooth to sparsely hairy stems that are 20–80 cm tall. The petioled, blunt-toothed, often lobed or cleft basal leaves are oblanceolate or spatulate and 4–15 cm long. The stem leaves are sessile, much smaller and commonly have deep, blunt teeth. The heads have a 1- to 2-cm wide disk and are solitary at the end of naked stalks. The narrow bracts have dark brown bands. The outermost are triangular in shape. The 15 to 30 ray flowers are white and 10–20 mm long. The disk flowers are yellow. The seeds are nearly round and have about 10 ribs. Reproduction is by seeds and creeping rhizomes. Flowers occur from May to October.

Habitat

Oxeye daisy may occur in lawns, cultivated fields, pastures, and waste places. It is native of Eurasia.

Suggested Control

Home Gardens—All plant parts, roots, and rhizomes should be completely removed with a sharp shovel. Periodic inspection to remove escaped plants will prevent reinfestation. *Cropland*—Follow a crop rotation where deep plowing can be used to disrupt the rhizome systems and cultivation can remove subsequent plants. Oxeye daisy is susceptible to atrazine if applied in a tolerant crop. *Pastures*—If possible, rotate with a cultivated crop; if not, spray with mixture of 2,4-D plus dicamba before flower stalks appear. Repeat applications may be needed to completely control the below ground root system.

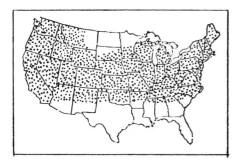

31H
Cichorium intybus L.
Chicory
Sunflower family
(Compositae)

Description

A perennial that has a long deep taproot. The stems are erect and 0.3–1.7 m tall. The lower leaves are oblanceolate, petioled, toothed to pinnatifid, and 8–25 cm long. The upper leaves are reduced, become sessile, and have entire or merely toothed margins. One to three heads are borne together in the axils of the upper leaves. The 4-cm wide flowers are blue or occasionally white. The bracts are 9–15 mm long. The outermost are fewer and shorter than the innermost. They are loose and become thickened at the base. The seeds are 2–3 mm long and have narrow, minute scales at the top. Reproduction is by seeds. Flowers occur from June to October.

Habitat

Chicory may occur in cropland, pastures, and noncropland areas. It is native of Eurasia.

Suggested Control

Urban Areas—The plant should be cut off well below the soil surface with a shovel. *Cropland*—This weed does not persist under a system of intensive mechanical tillage. Use deep plowing and cultivation or spot spraying with a higher rate of 2,4-D plus dicamba. *Pastures*—Apply a mixture of 2,4-D plus dicamba before flower stalk initiation. It may be necessary to repeat the treatment. *Noncropland*—If selective control in grasses is desired, use 2,4-D plus dicamba. If nonselective control is needed use tebuthiuron.

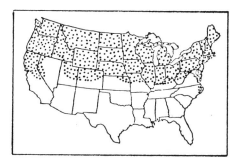

311
Cirsium arvense (L.) Scop.
Canada thistle
Sunflower family
(Compositae)

Description

Perennial herb that has an extensive deep-seated rhizome and root system. The erect stems branch at the top, are slightly hairy when young, and increase in hairiness with maturity. They are 40–120 cm tall. The alternate, lanceolate leaves are white, hairy on the underside and have crinkled edges with spiny margins. They are somewhat lobed and sessile with slightly prolonged bases. The numerous heads have rose purple disk flowers only (no ray flowers) and are surrounded by tight bracts. Male and female flowers are usually in separate heads and borne on different plants. They are 2–2.5 cm in diameter. The seeds are 4 mm long, smooth, dark-brown and have numerous, fine, hairy, delicate bristles. Reproduction is by seeds and horizontal rhizomes. Flowers occur from July to October.

Habitat

Canada thistle may infest cropland, pastures, meadows, roadsides, and waste places. It is a native of Eurasia.

Suggested Control

Cropland—This noxious weed can be extremely difficult to control. Best control is obtained by persistence and a good crop–herbicide rotation. Herbicides that control canada thistle are amitrole, bentazon, chlorsulfuron, dichlobenil, dicamba, 2,4-D, glyphosate, and terbacil. Consult the local agricultural extension service publications and/or personnel for correct combination of crop and herbicides. Mechanical control may be obtained by the bare ground policy of deep plowing and cultivating every 10 days to 2 weeks for a 2-year period thus never allowing any regrowth. *Pastures*—For chemical control apply a mixture of 2,4-D plus dicamba or 2,4-D plus picloram. *Noncropland*—For selective control in grass use suggestions for pastures. For spot treatments use glyphosate. For soil sterilization apply sulfometuron or tebuthiuron.

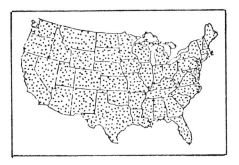

32A
Cirsium vulgare (Savi)
  Tenore
Bull thistle
Sunflower family
(Compositae)

Description

A biennial weed that is 0.5–1.5 cm tall. The stems have conspicuous spines and have winged protrusions. The leaves are pinnatifid. The larger ones have toothed lobes and are rough on top and sparsely white-woolly to green and hairy beneath. There are several purple heads per plant. The bracts are 2.5–4 cm long and spine-tipped. The seeds are less than 4 mm long with fine hairy, delicate bristles. Reproduction is by seeds. It flowers from June to October.

Habitat

Bull thistle may occur in pastures, roadsides, and waste places. It is a native of Eurasia but very widely spread in the United States.

Suggested Control

Home Gardens—Cut rosettes well below the crown with hoe or shovel. *Pastures, Roadsides, Waste Areas*—Spray with 2,4-D while still in rosette stage because the plants become resistant as flower stalk is produced. If plants become too large before 2,4-D is applied, mow to prevent seed production and spray with 2,4-D to inhibit regrowth.

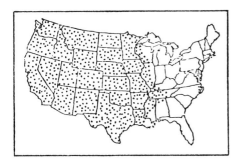

32B
Coreopsis tinctoria Nutt.
Plains coreopsis
Sunflower family
(Compositae)

Description

An annual herb with erect, glabrous, leafy, completely branched stems that is up to 1.2 m tall. The leaves are sessile or with a short-petiole and may be either opposite or alternate. They are 6–10 cm long and once or twice pinnately compound. The ultimate segments or leaflets are linear or lanceolate. The heads are numerous, slender-stalked, and have a brown, 5- to 10-mm wide central disk. The bracts are linear to awnlike. The well-developed flowers are yellow or orange, with or without purplish-brown base. The small narrowly oblong seeds are black with a white scar. Reproduction is by seeds. Flowers occur from July to September.

Habitat

Plains coreopsis may occur in cultivated fields, roadsides, and waste places. It is a plant that has escaped from cultivation. It is a native of North and South America.

Suggested Control

Cropland—Apply herbicides recommended for control of broadleaf weeds in the desired crop such as atrazine, cyanazine, diuron, fluometuron, linuron, metribuzin, propazine, simazine, terbacil, or 2,4-D. *Pastures, Roadsides and Waste Areas*—Apply 2,4-D or dicamba while weed is in the juvenile stages.

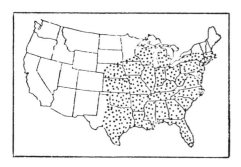

32C
Eclipta alba (L.) Hassk.
Eclipta
Sunflower family
(Compositae)

Description

A summer annual that is up to 50 cm tall and has rough hairs. The weak stems often root at the nodes. The simple leaves are lanceolate to linear in shape and have a few marginal teeth. They are usually 3 to 10 cm long and either sessile or with a short petiole. One to three flower heads in terminal or axillary clusters, each have 10 or more small white or yellow ray flowers. The bracts are usually a little longer than the disk. The seeds are wrinkled or warty and slightly hairy on the flattened summit. Reproduction is by seeds. Flowers occur from August to October.

Habitat

Eclipta may occur in cultivated fields, rather damp sandy soils, and waste areas. It is a native of tropical areas.

Suggested Control

Cropland—Use a crop–herbicide rotation coupled with cultivation if needed. Herbicides that have given good control in some areas are bentazon, butachlor, and oxadiazon.

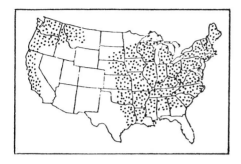

32D
Erigeron annuus (L.) Pers.
Annual fleabane
Sunflower family
(Compositae)

Description

An annual or biennial herb with erect, branched, leafy stems. The stems are smooth with scattered spreading stiff hairs especially at the top. The leaves are alternate, simple, and coarsely and sharply toothed. The lower leaves are elliptic, with a long-petiole and about 7 cm wide and 10 cm long. The stem leaves are lanceolate, entire, mostly sessile, and the upper ones are often linear. The numerous flower heads are about 2 cm in diameter and form a corymbose cluster. The bracts are sparsely hairy, 3–5 mm high. The central disk is yellow, about 8 mm in diameter. The ray flowers are about 6 mm long and white or rarely pink. The achenes are two-veined, obovate, flattened, and about 1 mm long. Reproduction is by seeds. It flowers from June to November.

Habitat

Annual fleabane may occur in cultivated fields, meadows, pastures, and waste places. It is native of North America.

Suggested Control

Cropland—Use a good rotation and normal herbicides recommended for control of broadleaf weeds in the desired crop. *Pastures*—Practice good management techniques, such as proper fertilization, pH adjustment, stand thickening, rotational grazing, and clipping after grazing. Application of 2,4-D in the spring will help reduce the stand. Also, sheep may be used for grazing infested pastures since they apparently prefer this weed over many pasture plants. *Fence Rows and Waste Places*—Apply 2,4-D each spring over a 2- to 4-year period if selective control is desired. Apply sulfometuron or tebuthiuron if soil sterilization is desired.

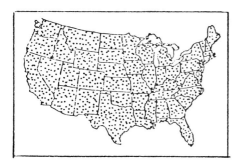

32E
Erigeron canadensis L.
Horseweed
Sunflower family
(Compositae)

Description

A coarse annual herb with an erect stem that is unbranched at the base and covered with bristly hairs. It is 1.5–2 m tall. The simple, alternate leaves are sessile, linear, dark green, and have scattered coarse, white hairs. The leaf margins are entire or slightly toothed. The stem leaves very numerous and almost linear. The flower heads are in elongated axillary panicles. The ray flowers are white and the central disk is yellow. The seeds are 1 mm long with multiple white bristles at the top. Reproduction is by seeds. Flowers appear from July to November.

Habitat

Horseweed may occur in cropland, especially in fields under minimum or no-tillage and in pastures, roadsides, and waste grounds. It is a native of North America.

Suggested Control

Cropland—Use good rotation and normal herbicides recommended for control of broadleaf weeds in desired crop. In low growing crops apply glyphosate using selective wick bar equipment. *Pastures*—Practice good management techniques, such as proper fertilization, pH adjustment, stand thickening, rotational grazing, clipping after grazing, and application of 2,4-D in the spring will help reduce stand. *Fence Rows and Waste Places*—Use 2,4-D in spring of year over a 2- to 4-year period or glyphosate for total burn-down. For soil sterilization use tebuthiuron.

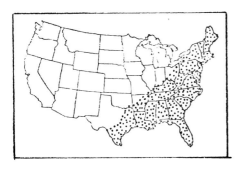

32F
Erigeron philadelphicus L.
Philadelphia fleabane
Sunflower family
(Compositae)

Description

A biennial or short-lived perennial, only rarely an annual, that has a short simple stem. The stems are generally pubescent with long spreading hairs, may be nearly smooth, and are 20–70 cm tall. The basal leaves are narrowly oblanceolate to obovate, blunt toothed or lobed, rounded at the tip, up to 3 cm wide and 15 cm long. The stem leaves are reduced, clasping at the base and mostly oblong. There are one to many heads. The bracts are 4–6 mm long and usually have long hairs. Each head may have 120 or more ray flowers, which are 5–10 mm long, and have long bristles at the top. Reproduction is by seeds and basal offshoots. Flowers appear from May to July.

Habitat

Philadelphia fleabane may occur in cultivated and hay fields, pastures, fence rows, and waste places. It is native to North America.

Suggested Control

Cropland—Use good rotation, tillage, and cultivation and normal herbicides recommended for control of broadleaf weeds in desired crop. *Pastures*—Practice good management techniques, such as proper fertilization, pH adjustment, stand thickening, rotational grazing, and clipping after grazing. An application of 2,4-D in the spring will help reduce the stand. *Fence Rows and Waste Places*—Use 2,4-D each spring over a 2- to 4-year period if selective control is desired. Apply sulfometuron or tebuthiuron if soil sterilization is desired.

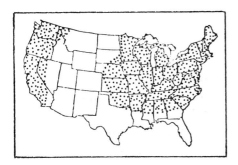

32G
Galinsoga ciliata (Raf.)
   Blake
Hairy galinsoga
Sunflower family
(Compositae)

Description

A hairy many-branched annual with spreading stems that are up to 70 cm tall, though generally much shorter. The simple, opposite, toothed, stiffly hairy leaves are ovate, pointed, 1–4 cm wide, and 2–7 cm long. The open inflorescence is flat-topped and has numerous small, 3- to 4-mm wide, urn-shaped heads that are 3–4 mm wide, and are at the top of glandular pedicels. The few broad bracts are arranged so one is beneath each white ray. The flowers of the yellow central disk are intermixed with papery scales (chaff). The minutely hairy seeds are four-angled and crowned with irregularly awn-tipped, narrow, scales. Reproduction is by seeds. Flowers occur from June to November.

Habitat

Hairy galinsoga may be found in gardens, cultivated lands, and waste places. It is a native of South and Central America.

Suggested Control

Home Gardens—This weed can be controlled by hand hoeing and cultivation. Border areas should be trimmed and mowed. Various mulches can be used to prevent seedling establishment. Do not allow plants to produce seeds. *Cropland*—Use good crop rotation and cultivation or use a herbicide labeled for control of broadleaf weeds, such as acifluorfen, atrazine, cyanazine, diuron, fluometuron, linuron, metolachlor, metribuzin, napropamide, simazine, 2,4-D, or MCPA. *Noncropland*—Keep the area moved to prevent seed production, spray with 2,4-D for selective control in grass, or spray with a high rate of atrazine or simazine if soil sterilization is desirable.

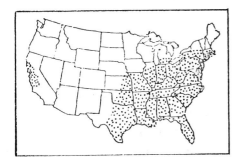

32H
Helenium amarum (Raf.)
H. Rock
Bitter sneezeweed
Sunflower family
(Compositae)

Description

An annual erect herb that is up to 80 cm tall. The stems can be nearly simple to many-branched, glabrous to glandular. The numerous, simple, alternate, linear or linear-filiform shaped leaves are sessile, densely glandular, and 2–8 cm long. The inflorescence is composed of several to numerous heads each on a single naked peduncle. The linear bracts bend downward and are glandular. Each head has five to ten yellow three-lobed ray flowers and a globose yellow central disk that is 6 to 10 mm in diameter. The seeds are four- to five-angled, pubescent on the conspicuous ribs and crowned, but with awns as long as the scales. Flowers appear from June to October.

Habitat

Bitter sneezeweed may occur in pastures, roadsides, fence rows, and waste places. It is a native of North America.

Suggested Control

Pastures—Rotate with cultivated crops if possible, and use herbicide that controls broadleaf weeds. An abundant stand of bitter sneezeweed is indicative of gross mismanagement; therefore, if crop rotation is not possible, use better pasture management techniques such as correct stocking rates, proper fertilization, pH adjustment, stand thickening, rotational grazing, and clipping after grazing. If necessary a mixture of 2,4-D plus dicamba can be applied in mid-spring. Repeat the treatment as needed.

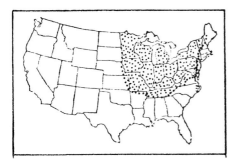

321
Helenium autumnale L.
Common sneezeweed
Sunflower family
(Compositae)

Description

A perennial, fibrous-rooted herb with erect, winged, angled stems that are simple or branched at the summit, smooth to finely pubescent, and 0.5–1.5 m tall. The simple, alternate, pointed, elliptic or oblong-shaped leaves are mostly sessile with extending bases and are 1–4 cm side and 4–15 cm long. The leafy inflorescence is composed of a few to many flower heads, each on a single long stalk. The hairy, narrow bracts curve downward. Each flower head has 10 to 20 yellow three-lobed ray flowers and a globose, yellow central disk that is 8–20 mm in diameter. The seeds are four- to five-angled, pubescent on the conspicuous ribs, and crowned by brown scales with short awns. Reproduction is by seeds. Flowers occur from August to November.

Habitat

Common sneezeweed may be found in pastures, along roadsides and moist shores, and in waste places. It is native of North America.

Suggested Control

Pastures—Rotate with cultivated crops if possible, and use a herbicide to control broadleaf weeds. If crop rotation is not possible, use better pasture management techniques such as proper fertilization, pH adjustment, stand thickening, rotational grazing, and clipping after grazing. Scattered plants can be removed with a sharp spade. A spring application of 2,4-D will reduce the population. Repeat applications may be necessary.

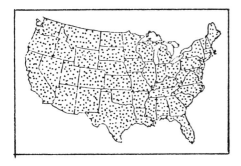

33A
Helianthus annuus L.
Sunflower
Sunflower family
(Compositae)

Description

An annual, coarse herb with erect, coarse, rough, pubescent stems that are 0.5–3 m tall. The simple, toothed, mainly alternate leaves are ovate to heart-shaped, tapered to a point, rough on both surfaces, long petioled and 3–30 cm wide. The flower heads are solitary, terminal, or axillary, 6–12 cm in diameter with large yellow ray flowers. The bracts are ovate and abruptly narrowed above the middle to the tip. The seeds are grayish-white, 4–7 mm wide, and 12 mm long. The tips are sparsely hairy and they may or may not have two small scales. Reproduction is by seeds. It flowers from July to November.

Habitat

Sunflower may occur in cropland especially small grain fields and in pastures, roadsides, fence rows, crop lands, and waste places. It is a native of North America.

Suggested Control

Cropland—Apply herbicides recommended for control of broadleaf weeds in the desired crop such as atrazine, bentazon, bromoxynil, cyanazine, diuron, fluometuron, linuron, metribuzin, propazine, simazine, terbacil, 2,4-D. Cultivate to control any escaped weeds. *Small Grains*—Apply 2,4-D before crop enters jointing stage. *Pastures*—Improve pasture management techniques, and apply 2,4-D while sunflower is in juvenile stages. *Noncropland*—Spray with 2,4-D for selective control in grass; use paraquat for nonselective desiccation of all existing vegetation or use soil sterilant rates of atrazine, simazine, sulfometuron, or tebuthiuron for residual nonselective control.

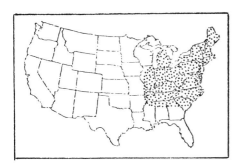

33B
Hieracium pratense Tausch
Yellow hawkweed
Sunflower family
(Compositae)

Description

A perennial herb that has milky juice and with short runners. The stem is erect, unbranched, leafless on the upper portion (scapose), stiffly hairy, and 40–80 cm tall. The simple, nearly sessile, entire or slightly toothed, bristly hairy, narrowly oblanceolate shaped leaves are mostly at the base and are 10–20 cm long. Stem leaves are usually few and reduced in size. The inflorescence is open and flat-topped at the end of the stem, and bears 5 to 40 heads. The ray flowers are yellow. The shiny, black seeds are 1–2 mm long, and topped with white bristles. Reproduction is by seeds and runners. Flowers occur from May to July.

Habitat

Yellow hawkweed may occur in meadows, roadsides, pastures, and waste places. It is native of Europe.

Suggested Control

Cropland—Use a good crop rotation system that includes working the soil between crops and tillage during the cropping system. *Pastures, Fence Rows, Roadsides, and Waste Places*—Mow to prevent seed production. Spray with a combination of 2,4-D plus dicamba.

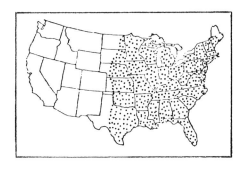

33C
Lactuca canadensis L.
Tall lettuce
Sunflower family
(Compositae)

Description

An annual or biennial herb that has milky juice. The erect, branched, smooth or hairy stems are often waxy, and 0.5–3.0 m tall. The leaves are smooth, or rarely have long soft hairs on the nerves on the underside. They are entire or wavy-pinnatifid with linear to oblong segments. The lowermost leaves are broader, and the uppermost leaves are entire and lanceolate. The leaves are 10–30 cm long. The numerous heads are composed of 12 to 20 yellow flowers that turn blue when dried. The seeds are flat, blackish, long-beaked wrinkled with one to three nerves on each face and topped with deciduous fine hairs. Reproduction is by seeds. It blooms from July to September.

Habitat

Tall lettuce may occur in cultivated fields, pastures, fence rows, and roadsides. It is native of North America.

Suggested Control

Cropland—Use crop rotation so as to include a cultivated row crop or a thick stand of alfalfa. Herbicides that can be used to control this weed in appropriate crops are atrazine, chlorsulfuron, cyanazine, linuron, metribuzin, simazine, terbacil, 2,4-D, and 2,4-DB. *Pastures*—Practice rotational grazing, periodic mowing, and a spring application of 2,4-D. *Waste Places, Fence Rows, Roadsides*—Apply 2,4-D for selective control in grass, or paraquat for nonselective desiccation or atrazine, bromacil, or simazine for nonselective residual control.

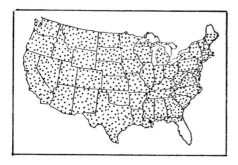

33D
Lactuca serriola L.
Prickly lettuce
Sunflower family
(Compositae)

Description

An annual or biennial herb that has milky juice. The erect stems are often prickly on the lower portion but otherwise are pale-green colored and up to 1.5 m tall. The alternate, bluish-green leaves are variable in size and shape. They are prickly on the underneath side of the midrib and more finely prickly toothed on the margins. The leaves often are twisted into a vertical position and are up to 25 cm long. The long diffuse inflorescence is composed of numerous heads, each with 5 to 12 yellow flowers that may turn blue when dried. The gray or yellow gray seeds have five to seven nerves on each side and a long beak with fine, deciduous hairs. Reproduction is by seeds. Flowers appear from July to September.

Habitat

Prickly lettuce may occur in gardens, cultivated fields, pastures, and noncropland areas. It is a native of Europe.

Suggested Control

Home Gardens—Remove by cutting with a shovel or hoe well below rosette leaves. Various mulches will prevent seedling establishment. Do not allow seed production. *Cropland*—Use crop rotation that includes a cultivated row crop or a thick stand of alfalfa. Herbicides that can be used in appropriate crops are atrazine, chlorsulfuron, cyanazine, linuron, metribuzin, napropamide, simazine, terbacil, terbutryn, 2,4-D, and 2,4-DB. *Pastures*—Practice rotational grazing, periodic mowing, and a spring application of 2,4-D. *Waste Places, Fence Rows, Roadsides*—Apply 2,4-D for selective control in grass, or paraquat for nonselective desiccation, or bromacil, sulfometuron, or tebuthiuron for nonselective residual control.

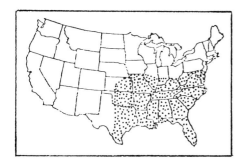

33E
Pyrrhopappus carolinianus
(Walt.) DC.
Carolina falsedandelion
Sunflower family
(Compositae)

Description

An annual or biennial, milky-juiced herb that has smooth stems up to 1 m tall. The leaves are entire to pinnatifid. Stem leaves are very few or none while the basal leaves are largest, up to 25 cm long, but sometimes deciduous. A simple plant may have one or several fairly long stalked heads with lemon-yellow flowers. The seeds are 5 mm long excluding the beak that is often twice as long as the body and topped with a ring of silky white hairs at the base of long reddish, featherlike hairs. Reproduction is by seeds. It flowers from June to October.

Habitat

Carolina falsedandelion may occur in cropland, pastures, fence rows, and noncropped areas. It is native of southern United States and Mexico.

Suggested Control

Cropland—Deep plowing will destroy existing plants; normal cultivation practices and most herbicides for control of broadleaf weeds will control this weed. *Pastures*—Practice good pasture management plus apply 2,4-D in spring. *Fence Rows and Noncropped areas*—If selective control in grass is desired apply 2,4-D in the spring or if nonselective residual control is desired apply bromacil, sulfometuron, or tebuthiuron.

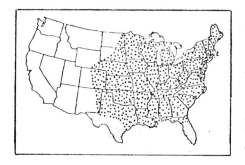

33F
Rudbeckia hirta L.
Hairy coneflower
Sunflower family
(Compositae)

Description

Biennial or short-lived perennial herb that has 0.3–1.0 m tall stems and is more or less coarsely hairy throughout. The simple, alternate leaves are variable in size and shape and are toothed or nearly entire. The basal and lower stem leaves are petioled and oblanceolate to elliptic, while the others are mostly sessile and linera to ovate. The long-stalked flower heads are solitary or several in number with 8 to 20 orange or yellow-orange ray flowers and a dark purple or brown central disk that is 12–20 mm in diameter. The pointed bracts are densely hairy, spreading or reflexed, and equal the ray flowers in length. The seeds are quadrangular and smooth. Reproduction is by seeds. Flowering occurs from June to October.

Habitat

Hairy coneflower may occur in crop fields, hay fields, roadsides, and waste places. It is native of North America.

Suggested Control

Cropland—This plant will not persist in areas where yearly plowing and/or cultivation is practiced. New seedlings are killed by many herbicides commonly used to control broadleaf weeds; therefore, use a good crop–herbicide rotation. *Pastures*—Use good management practices such as proper fertilization, stocking rates, rotational grazing, and mowing to maintain a competitive pasture. If needed apply 2,4-D in mid-spring. *Noncropland*—For nonselective residual control apply bromacil, sulfometuron, or tebuthiuron.

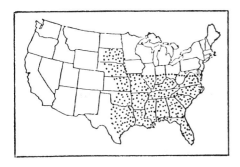

33G
Senecio glabellus Poir.
Cressleaf groundsel
Sunflower family
(Compositae)

Description

Annual or biennial succulent herb with erect simple, mostly solitary stems that are sometimes cobwebby in the leaf axils and 20–100 cm tall. The leaves are alternate, pinnatifid, and rapidly diminish in size toward the apex. The basal leaves are long, up to 20 cm long, with wide, round-toothed terminal lobes. The numerous heads are on thin pedicels. The central disk is 5–10 mm wide and the very showy yellow rays are 5–12 mm long. The seeds are minutely pubescent to smooth. Reproduction is by seeds. It blooms from May to July.

Habitat

Cressleaf groundsel may occur in pastures, fence rows, moist, and shaded waste places. It is native of North America.

Suggested Control

Pastures—Improve drainage if possible. Increase level of pasture management so as to maintain a thick, high-producing sod, and if necessary apply 2,4-D in the spring. *Fence Rows and Waste Areas*—For selective control in grass apply 2,4-D in the spring. For nonselective residual control apply bromacil or tebuthiuron before spring growth occurs.

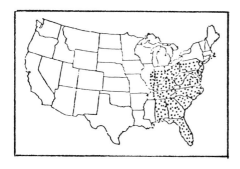

33H
Senecio smallii Britt.
Small's ragwort
Sunflower family
(Compositae)

Description

A fibrous-rooted perennial plant that has many 20- to 80-cm tall stems and is persistently woolly at the base. The entire, firm, basal leaves are narrowly spatulate-oblanceolate to lanceolate, closely toothed and up to 4 cm wide and 10 cm long. The 4 to 12 stem leaves are narrowly pinnatifid; the lower ones are often as large as the basal leaves. The numerous heads are on thin pedicels, 5–8 mm wide central disk and bright yellow, 4–8 mm long rays. The seeds have fine pubescence and are 1.5–2.2 mm long. Reproduction is by seeds. Flowers bloom from May to June.

Habitat

Small's ragwort may occur in pastures, idle fields, roadsides, and waste grounds. It is a native of North America.

Suggested Control

Pastures—Increase the level of pasture management so as to maintain a thick, high-producing sod. If necessary apply 2,4-D in the spring. *Roadsides and Waste Areas*—Mow periodically to reduce seed production. If selected control in grass is desired apply 2,4-D in the spring. If nonselective residual control is wanted apply bromacil or tebuthiuron.

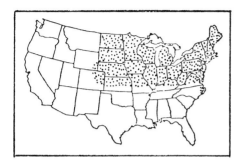

331
Solidago canadensis L.
Canada goldenrod
Sunflower family
(Compositae)

Description

A perennial herb that has creeping rhizome, but has no well-developed, persistent base. The stems may be in groups or solitary, up to 1.5 m tall, and more or less hairy. The numerous, crowded, alternate, simple leaves are sharply serrate to entire and smooth to slightly roughened. The basal leaves are usually lacking or occasionally are similar to the lower stem leaves. The inflorescence is a terminal panicle, 10–40 cm high with conspicuously recurved branches. The bracts are in several series and 2–3 mm long. Each small head has 7 to 17 minute, yellow rays and a few disk flowers. The seeds are small but topped with long, fine white hairs. Reproduction is by seeds and creeping rhizomes. It flowers from August to November.

Habitat

Canada goldenrod may occur in pastures, old fields, fence rows, and waste places. It is a native of North America.

Suggested Control

Pastures—Rotate pasture to a cultivated row crop for 1 or 2 years to destroy the rhizome system and prevent seed production. If impossible to rotate to a cultivated crop, improve pasture management techniques by adjusting pH, adding fertilizer, reducing stocking rate if necessary, rotate grazing, and mow after grazing. Possible herbicides that may be used spot spraying are glyphosate or a mixture of 2,4-D plus dicamba. *Noncrop Areas*—Apply bromacil, prometon, or tebuthiuron for nonselective residual control.

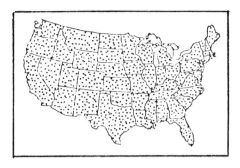

34A
Sonchus asper (L.) Hill
Spiny sowthistle
Sunflower family
(Compositae)

Description

An annual, milky-juiced herb that rarely is a biennial with a short taproot. The stem is erect, often very leafy up to the flowering part and gland-tipped hairs are often found on the upper stems and pedicels. The simple, alternate leaves are crowded on the stem, become gradually smaller and less lobed higher on the stem. They have very long stiff spines on the edges and rounded ear-like projections at the leaf bases. The numerous relatively small heads are 1.2–2.5 cm in diameter. The flowers are pale-yellow. The numerous bracts are 9–13 mm long and somewhat hardened in mature heads. The seeds are 2.5–3 mm long, nonwrinkled, flat, ribbed and crowned with long white hairs. Reproduction is by seeds. Flowers bloom from June to October.

Habitat

Spiny sowthistle may occur in many crops and pastures. It is a native of Eurasia.

Suggested Control

Cropland—Use a good crop rotation with cultivation and/or herbicides recommended for control of annual broadleaf weeds such as atrazine, cyanazine, diuron, fluometuron, linuron, metribuzin, napropamide, propazine, simazine, terbacil, MCPA, or 2,4-D. *Pastures*—If infestation is severe, rotate to cultivated crops and use suggested control measures plus adequate tillage. Prevent seed production. If rotation is not possible, apply 2,4-D in the spring of the year before flower stalk begins to elongate; if flowering has been initiated, mow before spraying to prevent seed production. *Noncropland Areas*—For nonselective residual control use sulfometuron or tebuthiuron.

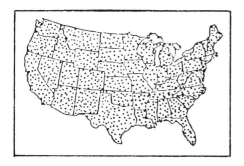

34B
Sonchus oleraceus L.
Annual sowthistle
Sunflower family
(Compositae)

Description

Annual, milky-juiced herb with a short taproot and is commonly 10–100 cm tall. The stem is smooth except for a few spreading gland-tipped hairs on the bracts and pedicels. The leaves are 6–30 cm long, pinnatifid to merely toothed. The leaf margins are weakly prickly. All but the lowermost leaves have prominent, rounded ear-like lobes that are eventually sharply pointed. The leaves become progressively smaller on the upper portion of the stem. The several flower heads are pale yellow and 1.5–2.5 cm wide. The numerous bracts are 9–13 mm long and hardened in mature heads. The seeds are 2.5–3.0 mm long, flat, ribbed, and crowned with long hairs. Reproduction is by seeds. Flowers occur from June to October.

Habitat

Annual sowthistle may occur in cultivated fields, roadsides, and waste places. It is native of Europe.

Suggested Control

Cropland—Use a good crop rotation with cultivation and/or herbicides recommended for control of annual broadleaf weeds such as atrazine, cyanazine, diuron, fluometuron, linuron, metribuzin, napropamide, propazine, simazine, terbacil, MCPA, or 2,4-D. *Pastures*—If infestation is severe rotate to cultivated crops and use suggested control measures plus adequate tillage. Prevent seed production. If rotation is not possible, apply 2,4-D in the spring of the year before flower stalk begins to elongate; if flowering has been initiated, mow before spraying to prevent seed production. *Noncropland Areas*—For nonselective residual control use soil sterilant rates of atrazine, diuron, simazine, sulfometuron, or tebuthiuron.

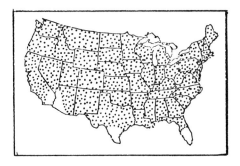

34C
Taraxacum officinale Weber
Dandelion
Sunflower family
(Compositae)

Description

A perennial that has milky juice and a basal rosette. The leaves are sparsely hairy beneath and on the midrib. They are oblanceolate, pinnatifid or lobed, and gradually narrow into a winged petiolar base. The terminal lobe tends to be larger than the others. Leaves are 1–10 cm wide and 6–40 cm long. The flowering stem is leafless, 5–50 cm tall, smooth or with long hairs. The large heads have 1.5- to 2.5-cm long bracts, which are erect at first and then become reflected as the yellow flowers mature. The mature seed head forms a conspicuous fluffy ball that can be blown apart by the wind. The seeds are gray-brown, 3–4 mm long, and have parachutelike appendages. Reproduction is by seeds. Depending on location flowering may occur at any time of the year.

Habitat

Dandelion is well distributed in lawns, pastures, and noncropland. It is a native of Eurasia.

Suggested Control

Home Lawns—Cut the plant off well below the crown using a sharp cutting tool. Repeated treatment may be necessary. Chemical control is obtained by applying 2,4-D in the spring or early summer. *Cropland*—Fall or spring tillage will destroy existing plants and normally cultivation and herbicides used to control broadleaf weeds will control this weed in row crops. Metribuzin and terbacil will control dandelion in alfalfa and 2,4-D gives control in small grains. *Pastures and Noncropland*—Spray with 2,4-D in spring.

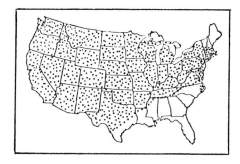

34D
Tragopogon dubius Scop.
Western salsify
Sunflower family
(Compositae)

Description

A biennial herb that has milky juice and a branching taproot. The smooth stem is erect, branched, and 30–80 cm tall. The smooth, simple, alternate, clasping light-green leaves are long and narrow or grasslike, and 10–30 cm long. The solitary heads are 2–4 cm in diameter and composed of bright yellow rays. The top of the flower stalk is enlarged below the head. The rough, narrow, ribbed seeds are 2–4 mm long and long-beaked with long fluffy bristles. Reproduction is by seeds. It blooms from July to September.

Habitat

Western salsify occurs in pastures, roadsides, fence rows, and waste areas. It is native of Europe.

Suggested Control

Cropland—Fall or spring tillage will destroy existing plants. Normally weed control practices of cultivation and herbicides used to control broadleaf weeds will control this weed. *Pastures and Noncrop Areas*—Mechanically remove with a sharp shovel by cutting well below the soil or in the spring apply 2,4-D.

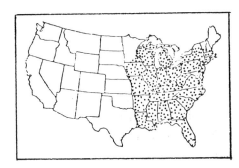

34E
Verbesina alternifolia (L.)
  Britt.
Wingstem
Sunflower family
(Compositae)

Description

A coarse perennial herb that is 1–2 m tall and arises from a large woody rootstock. The stems often have spreading hairs and are usually, but not always, winged. The simple, alternate, lanceolate leaves are 10–25 cm long and rough-hairy on both surfaces. They are sharply toothed to subentire. The open inflorescence may be comprized of 10 to many yellow flower heads. Each has two to eight ray flowers that are 1–3 cm long. The few, smooth bracts are curved downward. The flat seeds are often winged and topped with minute scales. They are loosely arranged in a globose head. It reproduces by seeds and rootstocks. Flowers appear from August to October.

Habitat

Wingstem may occur in pastures, fence rows, borders of woods, and waste places. It is a native of the new world.

Suggested Control

Pasture—Use improved management techniques (such as proper fertilization, pH adjustments, correct stocking rates, rotational grazing, and mowing after grazing) to create a productive, well-managed pasture that will provide strong competition against weed invasion. This plant does not appear on any specific herbicide label or in any agricultural extension publication; therefore, the authors suggest that for pastures a mixture of 2,4-D plus dicamba be tried on a trial basis, remembering that all restrictions on the herbicide labels be strictly observed. *Waste Areas*—The preceding mixture or glyphosate may be tried. For residual control, bromacil, sulfometuron, or tebuthiuron may be tried.

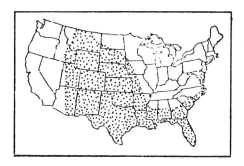

34F
Verbesina encelioides (Gray)
Crownbeard
Sunflower family
(Compositae)

Description

An annual herb with an erect, well-branched stem that has gray pubescence and is usually 30–70 cm tall. The leaves are alternate, opposite on the lower part of the stem, ovate or heart-shaped, coarsely toothed, pale and have gray pubescence on the lower surface. They are commonly 3–5 cm wide and 4–9 cm long. The petioles are winged at the base. The heads are borne on a long peduncle in an open inflorescence. They have 10 to 15 yellow rays that are evidently trilobed and about 1–2 cm long. The hairy, blackish brown seeds are broadly winged, awned at apex and 4–6 mm long. Reproduction is by seeds. Flowers occur from May to August.

Habitat

Crownbeard may occur in cultivated fields, roadsides, and waste places. It is a native of the tropical world.

Suggested Control

Cropland—Maintain a good crop rotation coupled with cultivation and the herbicides normally used to control annual broadleaf weeds. *Pastures, Waste Areas and Industrial Sites*—Use methods suggested for *Verbesina alternifolia* (page 330).

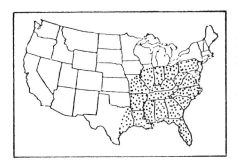

34G
Verbesina occidentalis (L.)
  Walt.
Western crownbeard
Sunflower family
(Compositae)

Description

A coarse perennial herb that is 40–100 cm tall and has a large woody root. The four-winged stem is smooth on the lower portion and commonly finely hairy on the upper portion, at least in the inflorescence. The simple, opposite, ovate, acuminate, three-veined leaves are often pubescent underneath, 7–17 cm long, and have winged petioles. The inflorescence is open with 20 to 100 flower heads. The bracts are erect or loose and sparsely hairy. Each head has two to five yellow rays and is 0.5–2 cm long. The flat, wingless seeds are topped with minute scales. Reproduction is by seeds and rootstocks. Flowers bloom from August to October.

Habitat

Western crownbeard may occur in pastures, idle fields, open woodlands, and fence rows. It is a native of the new world.

Suggested Control

Pasture—Use improved management techniques (such as proper fertilization, pH adjustments, correct stocking rates, rotational grazing, and mowing after grazing) to create a productive, well-managed pasture that will provide strong competition against weed invasion. This plant does not appear on any specific herbicide label or in any agricultural extension publication; therefore, the authors suggest that for pastures a mixture of 2,4-D plus dicamba be tried on a trial basis, remembering that all restrictions on the herbicide labels be strictly observed. *Waste Areas*—The preceding mixture or glyphosate may be tried. For residual control, bromacil, sulfometuron, or tebuthiuron may be tried.

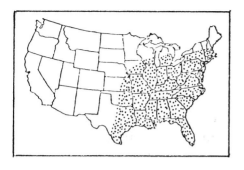

34H
Vernonia altissima Nutt.
Tall ironweed
Sunflower family
(Compositae)

Description

A perennial herb that has strong rootstocks. The stems are smooth to velvety, branched, and up to 2 m tall. The leaves are simple, alternate, thin, lanceolate, and about 5 cm wide and 20 cm long. They are smooth on top and thinly pubescent underneath with finely toothed to entire edges. The inflorescence is loose and flat-topped. The numerous principle bracts of the abundant heads are overlapping and often have marginal hairs. The upper stem, pedicels, and heads are purple. Ray flowers are absent but each head has 10 to 30 purple flowers in the central disk. The seeds are oblong, sparsely hairy on the ribs, and crowned with several deep purple bristles. Reproduction is by seeds and by rootstocks. Flowers bloom from August to October.

Habitat

Tall ironweed may occur in pastures, fence rows, barnyards, roadsides and waste places. It is native of North America.

Suggested Control

Pastures—Use improved management techniques (such as proper fertilization, pH adjustments, correct stocking rates, rotational grazing, and mowing after grazing) to create a productive, well-managed pasture that will provide strong competition against weed invasion. This plant does not appear on any specific herbicide label or in any agricultural extension publication; therefore, the authors suggest that for pastures a mixture of 2,4-D plus dicamba be tried on a trial basis, remembering that all restrictions on the herbicide labels be strictly observed. *Waste Areas*—The preceding mixture or glyphosate may be tried. For residual control, bromacil, sulfometuron or tebuthiuron may be tried.

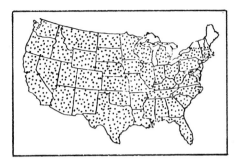

341
Xanthium pensylvanicum
Wallr.
Common cocklebur
Sunflower family
(Compositae)

Description

A summer annual herb that has coarse, rough, well-branched stems up to 1.5 m tall. The rough, simple, alternate leaves have petioles as long as the blades. The flowers are small, with sexes being separated in groups. The male flowers are in terminal spikes; the female flowers are in axillary clusters. The female clusters have tough, spiny, hairy bracts that surround two female flowers. This oval-shaped structure becomes a hard, woody, dull-brown bur, with numerous, hooked spines, 1–2 cm long. Each mature bur or fruit contains two seeds with different germination times. Reproduction is by seeds. Flowering occurs from August to October.

Habitat

Common cocklebur is a pest occurring in gardens, cultivated fields, roadsides, bottomlands, pastures, and waste places. It is native of Eurasia and Central and North America.

Suggested Control

Home Gardens—Do not allow this pest to produce seed. Remove established plants by pulling or hoeing. Various mulches will prevent seedling establishment. *Cropland*—Use a good crop–herbicide rotation. Periodic cultivation before planting will reduce the seed reservoir. Plant crops in rows to allow cultivation if needed. Do not allow seed production. Herbicides that can be used in tolerant crops are acifluorfen, ametryn, atrazine, bentazon, cyanzine, dicamba, 2,4-D, 2,4-DB, fluometuron, glyphosate, MCPA, methazole, metribuzin, naptalam, oxyfluorfen, prometryn, simazine, and terbacil. *Pastures*—Use rotational grazing followed by mowing to prevent seed production. If necessary apply 2,4-D to young plants or if legumes are present use 2,4-DB. Small cockleburs are poisonous to cattle; do not graze heavy infestations. *Noncrop Areas*—For residual control use atrazine, bromacil, diuron, simazine, sulfometuron, or tebuthiuron at recommended rates.

GLOSSARY OF BOTANICAL TERMS

A

Achene   A small, dry, one-celled, one-seeded indehiscent fruit; the seed attached to the pericarp at one place
Acuminate   Tapering gradually to the apex or tip
Acute   Sharp pointed
Alternate   Not opposite to each other on the stem, but born at regular intervals at different levels
Annual   Living one growing season
Anthesis   The opening of the flower bud
Aristate   Having awns or stiff bristles, usually at the apex
Attenuate   Gradually narrowing to a tip or base, this usually slender
Awn   A slender bristlelike organ usually at the apex of a structure
Axil   The angle between the leaf or branch and the main axis

B

Beak   A hard or firm point or projection
Bearded   Furnished with long or stiff hairs
Berry   A fleshy pulpy fruit with imersed seeds
Biennial   Requiring two growing seasons to complete the life cycle
Bipinnate   Doubly or twice pinnate
Blade   The expanded part of a leaf or floral part
Bract   A more or less modified leaf situated near a flower or inflorescence
Bristle   A short, stiff hairlike structure.
Bulb   A subterranean bud with fleshy scales
Bur   A seed or fruit bearing spines or prickles

C

Calyx   The outer set of steril floral parts
Campanulate   Bell-shaped
Capillary   Very slender and hairlike
Capitate   In a globular or head-shaped cluster
Capsule   A dry fruit made up of more than one carpel
Carpel   A portion of the ovary or female portion of the flower
Cauline   Of or pertaining to the stem
Ciliate   Having fine hairs or projections, usually as marginal hairs

Clasping Describing a sessile leaf with the lower edges of the blade partly surrounding the stem
Cleistogamous Pollination and fertilization before the flower has opened
Compound Composed of several parts or divisions
Cordate Heart-shaped
Corolla In broadleaved plants, the inner covering of the stems and pistils, usually showy
Corymb A flat-topped or convex open inflorescence
Culm The hollow stem of grass and sedges
Cuspidate Tipped with a sharp and firm point

D

Decumbent Reclining, but with the summit ascending
Deltoide Triangular
Dentate Toothed
Diffuse Loosely spreading
Digitate Diverging like the fingers of the hand
Dioecious Having male and female flowers on totally different plants
Disk flower The tubular flowers in the center of the head of many members of the composite family in contrast to the ray flowers around them
Dissected Divided into many segments

E

Elliptic Oval
Emersed Amphibious; protruding upward out of the water
Entire Without teeth, lobes, or serrations

F

Fibrous A mass of adventitious fine roots
Filiform Thread-shaped; long, slender, and terate
Flocose Cottony
Forked Divided into nearly equal branches
Frond The leaf of a fern
Fusiform Spindle-shaped-elongated and tapering toward the end

G

Glabrous Smooth or hairless
Glaucus Covered with bluish or white bloom (wax)
Glume One of the scaly bracts found at the base of and enclosing the spikelet of grasses

H

Hastate Like a arrow-head, but with the basal lobes pointing outward at wide angles
Head A dense cluster of sessile flowers as in Compositae
Hirsute With rather coarse, stiff hairs
Hoary Covered with white or gray short hairs
Hypanthium An enlargement of the floral axis below the calyx

I

Imbricate Overlapping
Imperfect flowers Lacking either male or female organs
Incised Cut into sharp lobes
Indehiscent Not opening; remaining persistently closed
Inflated Bladderlike
Inflorescence The arrangement of the several flowers on the flowering shoot, as a spike, panicle, etc.
Internode The portion of stem between two successive nodes

K

Keel A projecting ridge like the keel of a boat, as in the flowers of Leguminosae

L

Lanceolate Lance-shaped
Leaflet One of the divisions of a compound leaf
Legume Seed pod of leguminosae
Lenticular Lens-shaped
Linear A long and narrow organ with the sides parallel, as a grass leaf blade
Lobed Divided to about the middle or less
Locule A compartment divided by a septa of an ovary or anther

M

Membranaceous Thin, more or less translucent and rather soft
Mericarp A portion of a fruit that splits up at maturity
Midrib The midvein; the center rib of a leaf
Monoecious Flowers unisexual but the male and female are borne on the same plant

N

Neddlelike Long, slender, rather stiff, and more or less sharp at apex
Nerved Veined
Netted Reticulated
Node The part of a stem where the leaves originate

O

Obcordate Inverted heart-shaped, attached at the tip
Oblanceolate Inversely lanceolate, attached at the tip
Oblong Two to four times longer than wide and the sides nearly parallel
Obovate Inversely ovate, attached at the narrow end
Orbicular Nearly circular
Ovate Egg-shaped

P

Palmate The divisions diverging like the fingers of a hand
Panicle An inflorescence, a branched raceme, with each branch bearing a raceme of flowers
Parasite An organism growing upon and obtaining nourishment from another
Pedicel The stalk of a single flower of an inflorescence

Peduncle   The stalk to a solitary flower or to an inflorescence
Perfect   A flower with both functional male and female organs
Petal   One of the individual parts of the corolla, usually colored
Petiole   The stalk of a leaf blade
Pilose   With long soft straight hairs
Pinnate   Leaves divided into leaflets along a common axis
Pistil   The seed producing organ, or female organ of a flower
Pitted   Marked with small depressions
Prickle   A stiff, sharp-pointed outgrowth of the young bark
Procumbent   Lying or trailing on the ground
Prostrate   Lying flat on the ground
Puberulent   With very short hairs
Pubescent   Covered with hairs

R

Raceme   An inflorescence with pedicelled flowers borne along a more or less elongated axis
Rachis   The axis of an inflorescence or of a pinnately compound leaf
Ray   The marginal flower in the Compositae, or the branch of an umbel
Receptacle   The enlarged end of a flowering stalk
Reclining   Lying upon something
Reniforme   Kidney shaped
Reticulate   Netted
Retrorse   Directed backward or downward
Rhizome   An elongated and prostrate underground stem
Rootstock   A rootlike stem or branch under or sometimes on the ground
Rosette   A dense basal cluster of leaves arranged in circular fashion
Rugose   With wrinkled surface

S

Sagittate   Arrowhead-shaped
Scape   A naked flowering stem rising from the ground without proper leaves
Sepal   One of the parts of the outer whorl of the flower envelope or calyx
Septum   Any kind of a partition
Serrate   With a sharp teeth directed forward
Sessile   Lacking a stalk or petiole
Setaceous   Bristlelike
Spathe   A large bract sheathing or enclosing an inflorescence
Spatulate   Broad and round at the top like a spatula
Spike   An inflorescence with sessile flowers on a more or less elongate axis
Spine   A short, thornlike organ
Spore   The small reproductive body in Pteridophytes (ex. ferns)
Spreading   Diverging from the root and nearly prostrate
Spur   A hollow, saclike extension of a floral organ
Stamen   A male organ of a flower, which produces pollen grains
Standard   Same as banner; the large petal that stands up at the back of the flower in Leguminosae
Stipule   An appendage borne at the base of the petiole or leaf
Stolons   A trailing shoot above ground stems and root at the nodes
Strigose   With appressed, stiff, or ascending hairs

Submersed   Growing under water
Subtending   Situated closely beneath something, usually enclosing it
Subulate   Awl-shaped
Succulent   Fleshy and full of juice

T

Taproot   A root system with an elongated and prominent main root
Tendril   A slender, coiling outgrowth of the stem of the leaf
Terate   Circular in cross section
Throat   The orifice of a tubular corolla or calyx
Tomentose   Covered with dense woollike hairs
Trailing   Prostrate but not rooting
Toothed   Dentate
Trifoliate   A compound leaf with three leaflets
Trigonous   Three-angled
Truncate   Terminating bluntly
Tuber   A thickened modified branch, usually underground
Tufted   Having a cluster of hairs; stems in a very close cluster
Twining   Ascending by coiling around a support

U

Umbel   A flat-topped or convex inflorescence in which the flower stalks arise at the same point
Unisexual   With either stamens or pistils, not both

V

Valve   One of the parts into which a dehiscent fruit splits
Vein   The vascular portion of leaves
Villous   With long, soft, wavy hairs
Vine   A plant climbing on some support

W

Whorled   With three or more leaves or other structures arranged in a circle round a stem or axis
Woolly   With long, soft, interwoven hairs

BIBLIOGRAPHY

Anon. 1960. Weeds of the North Central States, Circular 718. North Central Regional Publ. No. 36, University of Illinois, 262 pp.

Anon. 1980. Suggested Guidelines for Weed Control. Agriculture Handbook No. 565. U.S. Department of Agriculture, 330 pp.

Bailey, L. H. 1961. Manual of Cultivated Plants. Macmillan Co., New York, 1116 pp.

Baldwin, F. L., and Smith, E. B. 1981. Weeds of Arkansas. University of Arkansas Printing Services, Fayetteville, Arkansas, 71pp.

Beal, E. O. 1977. A Manual of Marsh and Aquatic Vascular Plants of North Carolina, Technical Bulletin No. 247. Agricultural Experiment Station, North Carolina State University, Raleigh, North Carolina, 300 pp.

Crockett, L. J. 1977. Wildly Successful Plants, A Handbook of North American Weeds. Macmillan Co., New York, 268 pp.

Fernald, M. L. 1950. Gray's Manual of Botany, 8th edition. American Book Co., New York, 1632 pp.

Fryer, J. D., and Makepeace, R. J. 1972. Weed Control Handbook, 7th edition. Blackwell Scientific Publications, Boston, Massachusetts, 424 pp.

Georgia, A. E. 1914. A Manual of Weeds. Macmillan Co., New York, 593 pp.

Gilkey, H. M. 1957. Weeds of the Pacific Northwest. Agricultural Experimental Station, Oregon State College, Corvallis, Oregon, 441 pp.

Gleason, H. A. 1975. The New Britton and Brown Illustrated Flora of the Northeastern United States and Adjacent Canada, Rev. edition. Hafner Press, New York, 3 Volumes.

Gould, F. W. and Shaw, R. B. 1968. Grass Systematics, 2nd edition. Texas A & M University Press, College Station, Texas, 416 pp.

Harrington, H. D., and Durrell, L. W. 1975. How to Identify Plants. The Swallow Press, Chicago, Illinois.

Hitchcock, A. S. 1950. Manual of the Grasses of the United States. (Revised by Agnes Chase). United States Department of Agriculture, U.S. Government Printing Office, Washington, D.C., 1051 pp.

Holm, L. G., Plucknett, D. L., Paucho, J. V., and Herberger, J. P. 1977. The World's Worse Weeds—Distribution and Biology. East-West Center Book. The University Press of Hawaii, Honolulu, Hawaii, 609 pp.

Isely, D. 1962. Weed Identification and Control in the North Central States. Iowa State University Press, Ames, Iowa, 400 pp.

Klingman, G. C. 1966. Weed Control as a Science. John Wiley & Sons, Inc., New York, 421 pp.

Lewis, G. W., and Miller, J. F. 1980. Identification and Control of Weeds in Southern

Ponds. Cooperative Extension Service, University of Georgia, Athens, Georgia, 27 pp.

Meunscher, W. C. 1980. Weeds, 2nd edition. Macmillan Co., New York, 560 pp.

Montgomery, F. H. 1964. Weeds of the Northern United States and Canada. Frederick Warne and Co., New York, 226 pp.

Nuss, J. Methods of Weed Control for the Homeowner. Cooperative Extension Service, Pennsylvania State University, University Park, Pennsylvania, 18 pp.

Radford, A. E., Adhles, H. E., and Bell, C. R. 1968. Manual of the Vascular Flora of the Carolinas. The University of North Carolina Press, Chapel Hill, North Carolina, 1183 pp.

Smith, J. P. 1977. Vascular Plant Families. Mad River Press, Eureka, California, 320 pp.

Tarver, D., Rodgers, J., Mahler, M., and Lazor, R. 1978. Aquatic and Wetland Plants of Florida. Bureau of Aquatic Plant Research and Control, Florida Department of Natural Resources, Tallahassee, Florida, 127 pp.

Thompson, W. T. 1984. Agricultural Chemicals: Book II, Herbicides. Thompson Publications, Fresno, California, 285 pp.

Underwood, J. K. 1965. Tennessee Weeds, Bulletin 393. Agricultural Experiment Station, The University of Tennessee, Knoxville, Tennessee 113 pp.

USDA. 1970. Common Weeds of the United States. Dover Publications, New York, 463 pp. (Published also as "Selected Weeds of the United States," U.S. Department of Agriculture, U.S. Government Printing Office, Washington, D.C.).

Whitlett, J. N. 1968. Weeds. Department of Agriculture, Australia, 487 pp.

Wilkinson, R. E., and Jaques, H. E. 1972. How to Know the Weeds. Wm. C. Brown Co., Dubuque, Iowa, 232 pp.

INDEX

Numbers in **boldface** refer to plate numbers